LUTHER'S WORKS

LUTHER'S
WORKS

VOLUME 30

THE CATHOLIC EPISTLES

JAROSLAV PELIKAN

Editor

WALTER A. HANSEN

Associate Editor

CONCORDIA PUBLISHING HOUSE · SAINT LOUIS

ISBN   978-0-5700-6430-5

Biblical Studies / Commentaries
15-1772

Copyright 1967 by
CONCORDIA PUBLISHING HOUSE
Saint Louis, Missouri

Library of Congress Catalog Card No. 55-9893

Contents

General Introduction

The first editions of Luther's collected works appeared in the sixteenth century, and so did the first efforts to make him "speak English." In America serious attempts in these directions were made for the first time in the nineteenth century. The Saint Louis edition of Luther was the first endeavor on American soil to publish a collected edition of his works, and the Henkel Press in Newmarket, Virginia, was the first to publish some of Luther's writings in an English translation. During the first decade of the twentieth century, J. N. Lenker produced translations of Luther's sermons and commentaries in thirteen volumes. A few years later the first of the six volumes in the Philadelphia (or Holman) edition of the *Works of Martin Luther* appeared. Miscellaneous other works were published at one time or another. But a growing recognition of the need for more of Luther's works in English has resulted in this American edition of Luther's works.

The edition is intended primarily for the reader whose knowledge of late medieval Latin and sixteenth-century German is too small to permit him to work with Luther in the original languages. Those who can, will continue to read Luther in his original words as these have been assembled in the monumental Weimar edition (*D. Martin Luthers Werke*. Kritische Gesamtausgabe; Weimar, 1883 ff.). Its texts and helps have formed a basis for this edition, though in certain places we have felt constrained to depart from its readings and findings. We have tried throughout to translate Luther as he thought translating should be done. That is, we have striven for faithfulness on the basis of the best lexicographical materials available. But where literal accuracy and clarity have conflicted, it is clarity that we have preferred, so that sometimes paraphrase seemed more faithful than literal fidelity. We have proceeded in a similar way in the matter of Bible versions, translating Luther's translations. Where this could be done by the use of an existing English version—King James, Douay, or Revised Standard—we

have done so. Where it could not, we have supplied our own. To
indicate this in each specific instance would have been pedantic;
to adopt a uniform procedure would have been artificial — especially in view of Luther's own inconsistency in this regard. In each
volume the translator will be responsible primarily for matters of
text and language, while the responsibility of the editor will extend principally to the historical and theological matters reflected
in the introductions and notes.

Although the edition as planned will include fifty-five volumes,
Luther's writings are not being translated in their entirety. Nor
should they be. As he was the first to insist, much of what he wrote
and said was not that important. Thus the edition is a selection
of works that have proved their importance for the faith, life, and
history of the Christian Church. The first thirty volumes contain
Luther's expositions of various Biblical books, while the remaining
volumes include what are usually called his "Reformation writings"
and other occasional pieces. The final volume of the set will be an
index volume; in addition to an index of quotations, proper names,
and topics, and a list of corrections and changes, it will contain
a glossary of many of the technical terms that recur in Luther's
works and that cannot be defined each time they appear. Obviously
Luther cannot be forced into any neat set of rubrics. He can provide
his reader with bits of autobiography or with political observations
as he expounds a psalm, and he can speak tenderly about the meaning of the faith in the midst of polemics against his opponents. It
is the hope of publishers, editors, and translators that through this
edition the message of Luther's faith will speak more clearly to the
modern church.

J. P.
H. L.

Introduction to Volume 30

The three commentaries of Luther presented in this volume are the only extant ones on epistles of the New Testament that were not attributed to Paul. As the introduction to Volume 29 points out, Luther was never consistent in either accepting or rejecting the Pauline authorship of the Epistle to the Hebrews but spoke of Paul as its author even when he had set forth the bold and brilliant suggestion that it was written by Apollos. Neither on the Epistle of James nor on the Book of Revelation did he deliver a connected series of sermons or lectures, at least partly, it would seem, because of his misgivings about their status in the canon; in 1528 he did publish an older commentary on the Book of Revelation with his own preface (Weimar, XXVI, 123−124). But the two epistles of Peter, the Epistle of Jude in conjunction with the Second Epistle of Peter, and the First Epistle of John all claimed his attention during the 1520s.

The dating of Luther's sermonic commentary on 1 Peter (Weimar, XII, 259−399; St. Louis, IX, 958−1111) has been a problem for Luther's editors. Thus the Weimar editor, Paul Pietsch, surmised in 1891 that the sermons should be attributed to the year 1523, even though the Wittenberg edition of Luther's works had given the date as 1522. But only two years or so after the appearance of the twelfth volume of the Weimar edition, a collection of manuscripts of George Rörer was discovered in the library of the University of Jena. Among them was a manuscript which made it possible to date Luther's sermons on 2 Peter and Jude (see below) with some precision as having been delivered in the first two months of 1523. Since they presuppose the sermonic commentary on 1 Peter and refer to it (see p. x), it follows that this commentary belongs in 1522, not in 1523. Any further attempt to fix the dates of the sermons must be speculative. George Buchwald has suggested that there were perhaps 23 sermons on 1 Peter, that they probably could not have been begun before Jubilate Sunday, May 11, 1522, and that

they may well have occupied Luther until the end of the year.
In the absence of other information to corroborate or refute such
a conjecture, it seems plausible, and the date 1522 seems quite
definite. The printed version appeared in Wittenberg in 1523.

Shortly after he had completed his sermons on 1 Peter, Luther
moved on to an exposition of 2 Peter and of Jude (Weimar, XIV,
14–91; St. Louis, IX, 1342–1397, 1742–1755). Thanks to the dis-
covery of the Rörer manuscripts and to the scholarship of Buchwald, it seems possible to assign dates to most of these sermons,
all delivered in 1523:

2 Peter 2:4-12, January 25   Jude 1-13, February 22
2 Peter 2:13-16, February 2   Jude 14-25, March 1
2 Peter 3 (the entire chapter),
   February 8

Extrapolating from the length of these sermons, Buchwald has
suggested that the first chapter was expounded in three sermons,
for which he proposes the dates January 3, 6, and 11; and that the
opening verses of the second chapter were Luther's text on January 18. Although it seems, therefore, that the sermons were
delivered during the winter of 1523, they do not appear to have
been published until the spring of the following year; one copy
bears the date April 26, 1524.

The lectures on 1 John (Weimar, XX, 599–801; St. Louis, IX,
1398–1523) contain no chronological problems to match those
connected with the sermons on 1 Peter. Instead, they present
textual difficulties of a very subtle and complex sort. The following
seems to have been the schedule of the 28 or 29 lectures, from
August 19 to November 7, 1527:

1:1, August 19   2:20-23, September 17
1:2-4, August 20   2:24-27, September 18
1:5-7, August 21   2:27–3:2, September 23
1:8-9, August 26   3:3-8, September 24
1:10–2-1, September 2   3:8-17, September 30
2:1-2, September 3   3:18-24, October 1
2:3-6, September 4   4:1-3, October 2
2:7-11, September 9   4:3-6, October 7 (conjecture)
2:12-14, September 10   4:7-10, October 8
2:15-17, September 11   4:10-12, October 9
2:18-19, September 16   4:13-16, October 14

4:17-21, October 16   5:9-12, November 5
5:1-3, October 28   5:13-15, November 6
5:4-5, October 29   5:16-21, November 7
5:6-8, October 30

The source of this unusually detailed information about Luther's lectures is a manuscript of Rörer. Luther had been lecturing on Isaiah (see Volumes 16—17) but had to interrupt his lectures after an outbreak of the plague, because of which many students and faculty members had fled from Wittenberg to Jena. To those who remained behind in Wittenberg with him Luther delivered a series of lectures on 1 John. Among his hearers was Rörer, who was also ministering to the victims of the plague and living through domestic tragedy: his own wife died of the pestilence. Another of Luther's hearers seems to have been responsible for the version of the lectures underlying our translation. It was first published in 1708 and has been attributed to Luther's associate, Jacob Propst in Bremen. Although its connection with Propst and the circumstances of its preparation can no longer be ascertained, it does seem to contain some authentic material from Luther's lectures that is not in Rörer; some of the material preserved by Rörer, on the other hand, is missing here. It seems obvious that the eighteenth-century editor was responsible for the Biblical references by chapter and verse and for the completeness of the quotations. A good case could be made for the adoption either of the Rörer or of the "Propst" version. In keeping with our general principle of following the printed form of Luther's lectures whenever this is editorially defensible, we have opted for "Propst."

J. P.

SERMONS ON THE FIRST EPISTLE OF ST. PETER

Translated by
MARTIN H. BERTRAM

FOREWORD

B efore we take up St. Peter's epistle, it is necessary for us to say a few words by way of instruction. One must know how this epistle is to be regarded, and one must get a proper understanding of it.

First of all, we must realize that all the apostles teach one and the same doctrine, and that it is incorrect to speak of four evangelists and four gospels; for everything the apostles wrote is one Gospel. And the word "Gospel" signifies nothing else than a sermon or report concerning the grace and mercy of God merited and acquired through the Lord Jesus Christ with His death. Actually, the Gospel is not what one finds in books and what is written in letters of the alphabet; it is rather an oral sermon and a living Word, a voice that resounds throughout the world and is proclaimed publicly, so that one hears it everywhere. Therefore it is not a book of laws that contains many good teachings, as it has been regarded in the past. It does not tell us to do good works to make us pious, but it announces to us the grace of God bestowed gratis and without our merit, and tells us how Christ took our place, rendered satisfaction for our sins, and destroyed them, and that He makes us pious and saves us through His work.

Now he who preaches these facts and writes about them teaches the true Gospel, just as all the apostles, particularly St. Paul and St. Peter, do in their epistles. Therefore what is preached about Christ is all one Gospel, although every writer has his own distinctive literary style. The discussion may be short or long and may be presented briefly or at some length. But whenever it deals with Christ as our Savior and states that we are justified and saved through faith in Him without our works, then there is one Word and one Gospel, just as there is but one faith and one Baptism (Eph. 4:5) in all Christendom.

Thus one apostle has recorded the same things that are found in the writings of the other. But those who stress most frequently

and above all how nothing but faith in Christ justifies are the best
evangelists. Therefore St. Paul's epistles are gospel to a greater
degree than the writings of Matthew, Mark, and Luke. For the latter
do little more than relate the history of the deeds and miracles of
Christ. But no one stresses the grace we have through Christ so
valiantly as St. Paul does, especially in his Epistle to the Romans.
Now since greater value attaches to the words of Christ than to
His works and deeds—and if we had to dispense with one or the
other, it would be better for us to do without the deeds and the history than to be without the words and the doctrine—those books
that treat mainly of Christ's teaching and words should in all conscience be esteemed most highly. For even if Christ's miracles
were nonexistent, and if we knew nothing about them, His words
would be enough for us. Without them we could not have life.

Accordingly, this Epistle of St. Peter is also one of the noblest
books in the New Testament; it is the genuine and pure Gospel.
For St. Peter does the same thing that St. Paul and all the evangelists do; he teaches the true faith and tells us that Christ was
given to us to take away our sin and to save us, as we shall hear.

On this basis you can now determine concerning all books and
doctrines what is and what is not gospel. For with regard to what
is not preached or written in this way you may freely judge that it
is false, no matter how good it seems to be. All Christians have
this power to judge, not the pope or the councils, who boast that
they alone have the power to judge doctrine. Let this suffice as
introduction and foreword. Now we want to hear the epistle.

CHAPTER ONE

1. *Peter, an apostle of Jesus Christ, To the exiles of the dispersion in Pontus, Galatia, Cappadocia, Asia, and Bithynia,*

2. *chosen and destined by God the Father and sanctified by the Spirit for obedience to Jesus Christ and for sprinkling with His blood.*

This is the superscription and the signature. Here you see at once that this is the Gospel. St. Peter states that he is an apostle, that is, a messenger. Therefore the word has been correctly translated into German with *Eyn bott* or *zwolffbott*, because of the Twelve. Since it is now understood what the Greek word ἀπόστολος means, I have not translated it into German. But it really denotes a messenger—not one who bears letters, but an emissary who puts forth and takes care of a matter by word of mouth. In Latin such men are called *oratores*. Thus St. Peter wants to say: I am an apostle of Jesus Christ; that is, Jesus Christ has commanded me to preach about Christ. Take note that all who preach human doctrines are immediately excluded. For he who carries out what Christ has commanded is a messenger of Jesus Christ. If he preaches anything else, he is not a messenger of Christ. Therefore we should not listen to him. But if he preaches what Christ has commanded, this is no different from hearing Christ Himself in person.

To the exiles of the dispersion in Pontus, Galatia, Cappadocia, Asia, and Bithynia.

St. Peter addressed his epistle to the countries named here. In times past Christians dwelt there. Today, however, the Turk rules. But perhaps one still finds Christians there. Pontus is a large and wide land situated on the sea. Cappadocia is hard by and almost contiguous. Galatia lies behind it. Asia and Bithynia border on the sea. All are large countries, and all lie toward the east. Paul, too, preached in Asia and in Galatia. I do not know whether he also preached in Bithynia. He did not preach in the two countries named last. The exiles are people whom we call foreigners. Saint Peter calls them exiles because they were heathen. It is surprising that while St. Peter was an apostle to the Jews, he is nevertheless writing here to the heathen. The Jews called them proselytes, that is, converts to Judaism and its law but not of the Jewish house and blood of Abraham. Accordingly, he is writing to those who had formerly been heathen but had now been converted to the faith and had joined the believing Jews. He calls them chosen foreigners who surely are Christians. He writes only to these. This is an important point, as we shall hear.

Chosen and destined by God the Father.

St. Peter declares that they are chosen. How? Not by themselves but according to God's arrangement. For we shall not be able to bring ourselves to heaven or to create faith in ourselves. God will not admit all men to heaven; He will count His own very exactly. Now the human doctrine of free will and of our own powers no longer amounts to anything. Our will is unimportant; God's will and choosing are decisive.

And sanctified by the Spirit.

God has predestined us to be holy, and in such a way that we become spiritually holy. The belly-preachers have also perverted the precious words "holy" and "spiritual" for us; they have called their priestly and monastic estate holy and spiritual. So shamefully have they abused this dear and noble name. They have done the same thing with the name "church" by asserting that the pope and the bishops are the church. When they wilfully do what they please, they say that the church has commanded it. Holiness does not consist in being a monk, priest, or nun, in wearing tonsures and cowls. It is a spiritual word which states that inwardly we are sincerely holy in the spirit before God. And his real reason for making this statement was to point out that nothing is holy but the holiness that God works in us. For at that time the Jews had much external holiness, but this was not a true holiness. Therefore St. Peter means: God has chosen you to be truly holy. Thus in Eph. 4:24 St. Paul also speaks of being "in true righteousness and holiness," that is, in a genuine and completely good holiness; for the external holiness of the Jews has no validity before God.

Thus Scripture calls us holy while we are still living here on earth, if we believe. The papists have taken this name away from us and say: "We should not be holy; only the saints in heaven are holy." Therefore we must get the noble name back. You must be holy. But you must be prepared not to think that you are holy of yourself or on the strength of your merit. No, you must be holy because you have the Word of God, because heaven is yours, and because you have become truly pious and holy through Christ. This you must avow if you want to be a Christian. For it would be the greatest slander and blasphemy of the name of Christ if we refused to honor Christ's blood for washing away our sin or refused to believe that this blood makes us holy. Hence you must believe and confess that you are holy, but by this blood and not by reason of your own piety. Therefore you must be willing to surrender life and all possessions for this and to face whatever may be your lot on this account.

For obedience to Jesus Christ and for sprinkling with His blood.

With these words St. Peter says that we become holy if we obey and believe the Word of Christ and are sprinkled with His blood. He expresses himself differently from St. Paul. But the purport is identical with Paul's declaration that we are saved through faith in Christ. For faith makes us obedient and subject to Christ and His Word. Therefore to be submissive to the Word of God and Christ and to be sprinkled with His blood is the same as believing. For it is difficult for nature to submit completely to Christ and to desist from all its doings, despise them, and regard them as sin; it struggles against this and tortures itself in the process. Yet it must surrender itself.

The psalm *Miserere,* also speaks of this sprinkling. "Purge me with hyssop," it says, "and I shall be clean" (Ps. 51:7). This alludes to the Law of Moses, from which St. Peter took this expression. He wants to uncover Moses for us (2 Cor. 3:14) and lead us into Scripture. When Moses built the tabernacle, he took the blood of goats and sprinkled the tabernacle and all the people, as Ex. 24:6, 8 says (cf. Heb. 9:19). But the sprinkling does not sanctify in the spirit; this is only an external sanctification. Consequently, there must be a spiritual purification (Heb. 9:13-14). The former was a fleshly and external holiness that does not avail before God. Therefore with this sprinkling God typified the spiritual sprinkling. Accordingly, Peter says: The Jews are outwardly holy; in the eyes of the people they are pious and lead a respectable life, while you are regarded as wicked. But you have a better sprinkling; you are sprinkled in the spirit, in order that you may be pure inwardly. The Jews sprinkled themselves externally with the blood of goats. We, however, are sprinkled inwardly in our conscience, so that the heart becomes clean and glad.

Thus the heathen are no longer heathen. The pious Jews, with their sprinkling, are no longer pious. Now the situation is reversed. There must be a sprinkling which converts us and makes us spiritual. But to sprinkle means to preach that Christ shed His blood, intercedes for us before His Father, and says: "Dear Father, here Thou seest My blood, which I shed for this sinner." If you believe this, you are sprinkled. Then you know the right way to preach. If all the popes, monks, and priests were to melt what they do and say into one big pile, they could not teach and accomplish as much as St. Peter does here with a few words.

This is the signature St. Peter appends to this chapter, in which he tells what his office is and what he preaches, as we have heard. Therefore only this is the Gospel. Everything not in agreement with this must be trodden underfoot, and you must forswear all other books where you find beautiful titles dealing with works, prayers, and indulgences—books that do not teach the Gospel and are not obviously founded on it. All the papistic books do not contain one letter about this obedience, about this blood and sprinkling. Now comes the greeting to those to whom Peter is writing.

May grace and peace be multiplied to you.

Here St. Peter's greeting is almost like the one used by the apostle Paul. He means: You now have peace and grace, but not yet in perfect measure. Therefore you must grow constantly until the old Adam dies completely. Grace is God's goodwill. It begins in us now, but it must continue to be active and grow until we die. And he who realizes and believes that he has a gracious God, he has Him. Then his heart gains peace, and he fears neither the world nor the devil. For he knows that God, who is omnipotent, is his friend and will rescue him from death, hell, and all adversity. Therefore his conscience has peace and joy. This is what St. Peter wishes for the believers, and this is a true Christian greeting. All Christians should greet one another in this way.

Thus we have the superscription and the greeting. Now Saint Peter introduces the epistle and says:

3. *Blessed be the God and Father of our Lord Jesus Christ! By His great mercy we have been born anew to a living hope through the resurrection of Jesus Christ from the dead,*

4. *and to an inheritance which is imperishable, undefiled, and unfading, kept in heaven for you,*

5. *who by God's power are guarded through faith for a salvation ready to be revealed in the last time.*

6. *In this you rejoice, though now for a little while you may have to suffer various trials,*

7. *so that the genuineness of your faith, more precious than gold which though perishable is tested by fire, may redound to praise and glory and honor at the revelation of Jesus Christ.*

8. *Without having seen Him, you love Him; though you do not now see Him, you believe in Him and rejoice with unutterable and exalted joy.*

9. *As the outcome of your faith you obtain the salvation of your souls.*

In this foreword you see a truly apostolic speech and an introduction to the theme. It bears out what I said earlier,[1] namely, that this epistle is a paragon of excellence. For here St. Peter begins without further ado to tell us what Christ is and what we have acquired through Him. He says that by God's mercy "we have been born anew to a living hope through the resurrection of Jesus Christ from the dead." He also says that everything has been given to us by the Father out of pure mercy and without any merit on our part.

---

[1] Cf. p. 4 .

[W, XII, 265, 266]

These are geniunely evangelical words. They must be proclaimed.
God help us, how little preaching of this kind one finds in all the
books, even in those that are said to be the best, as, for example,
the writings of St. Jerome and St. Augustine! How little they have
in common with these words! Therefore one must preach about
Jesus Christ that He died and rose from the dead, and why He died
and rose again, in order that people may come to faith through such
preaching and be saved through faith. This is what it means to
preach the genuine Gospel. Preaching of another kind is not the
Gospel, no matter who does it.

These words can be summarized by saying that through His
resurrection Christ has led us to the Father. Here St. Peter wants
to lead us to the Father through the Lord Christ and sets Him up
as the Mediator between God and us. Up to now preachers have
told us to call upon the saints in order that they may be our interces-
sors before God. Then we hied ourselves to Our Dear Lady, made
her our mediatrix, and let Christ remain an angry judge.[2] Scripture
does not do this; it insists on going to the truth of the matter and
praises the Lord Christ as our Mediator through whom we must
come to the Father. O what an inestimable blessing has been given
to us through Christ! It enables us to step before the Father and to
demand the inheritance of which St. Peter speaks here.

These words point out what the apostle had in mind by beginning to praise the Father with such great devotion and asking us
to laud and bless Him because of the inestimable riches He conferred on us by bringing about our rebirth, and by doing so before
we thought of or expected such a thing. Here there is nothing to
praise but sheer mercy. Therefore we can boast of no works, but
we must confess that everything we have is ours because of pure
mercy. No longer does the Law or God's wrath frighten us as the
Jews were terrified when they had to flee and did not dare approach
the mountain (Ex. 19:16; 20:19). No longer does God drive and
smite us. No, He deals with us in the friendliest manner possible
and renews us. He does not give us the ability to do one work or
two but brings about a completely new birth and a new existence
in us, so that we become something different from what we were
before, when we were the children of Adam. This means that He
has transplanted us from the inheritance of Adam into the in-

2 Cf. *Luther's Works*, 13, p. 326.

heritance of God, so that God is our Father and we are His children and thus also heirs of all His blessings. Note how thoroughly Scripture deals with this. Everything is alive. We are not dealing with unnecessary words here. Since we are now born anew and are God's children and heirs, we become equal in honor and glory with St. Paul, St. Peter, Our Dear Lady, and all the saints; for we possess the treasure and all the blessings from God as richly as they do. For they had to be born anew, just as we did. Therefore they have no more than all Christians have.

To a living hope through the resurrection of Jesus Christ from the dead.

We have no other reason for living on earth than to be of help to others. If this were not the case, it would be best for God to kill us and let us die as soon as we are baptized and have begun to believe. But He permits us to live here in order that we may bring others to faith, just as He brought us. But as long as we are on earth, we must live in hope. For although we are sure that we have all the blessings of God through faith — for faith is surely accompanied for you by the new birth, the filial relationship, and the inheritance — we do not yet see this. It is still something to be hoped for and still somewhat remote. We cannot see it with our eyes. St. Peter calls this the hope of life. This is a Hebrew way of speaking, as if one said in Latin *homo peccati*, "a man of sin." We speak of a living hope, that is, a hope in which we may hope with certainty and be sure of eternal life. But this is still concealed. It is still covered with a cloth. One does not see it. At present it can be grasped only with the heart and through faith, as St. John says in 1 John 3:2:[3] "Beloved, we are God's children; it does not yet appear what we shall be, but we know that when He appears, we shall be like Him; for we shall see Him as He is." For this life and the life to come are mutually exclusive and cannot exist together in such a way that we eat, drink, sleep, wake, and do other natural things of this life and are in heaven at the same time. We cannot enter into eternal life unless we have died and this life passes away. Therefore we must be in hope while we are here and until God wants us to see the blessings we have.

But how do we attain the living hope? Peter says that we do so

[3] The original has "1 John 5."

"through the resurrection of Jesus Christ from the dead." I have
often said that no one should believe in God without employing
means.[4] Therefore we cannot deal with God on our own initiative,
for we are all children of wrath (Eph. 2:3). We must have someone
else through whom we can come before God—someone to repre-
sent us and to reconcile us with God. And there is no other Mediator than the Lord Christ, who is the Son of God. Therefore the faith
of the Jews and the Turks is false. They say: "I believe that God
created heaven and earth." The devil believes the same thing
(cf. James 2:19), but it does not help him. For the Jews and the
Turks have the audacity to come before God without Christ the
Mediator.

St. Paul states in Rom. 5:2: "We have obtained access to God
in faith"—not through ourselves but "through Christ." Therefore
we must bring Christ, come with Him, pay God with Him, and carry
out all our dealings with God through Him and with Him. This
is what St. Peter means here. He wants to say: We are looking forward with certainty to life, even though we are still on earth. But
we owe all this to Christ's resurrection from the dead, to His ascension into heaven, and to the fact that He sits at the right hand of
God. For He ascended into heaven to bestow His Spirit on us, to
give us a new birth, and to give us the courage to come to the Father
and say: "Behold, I come before you and pray, not in reliance
on my petition, but my Lord Christ represents me and is my
Intercessor." These are all words of fire where there is a heart
that believes. Otherwise everything is cold and does not go to the
heart.

But from this one can judge what true Christian doctrine or
preaching is. For when one wants to preach the Gospel, one must
treat only of the resurrection of Christ. He who does not preach
this is no apostle. For this is the chief article of our faith. And those
books that teach and stress this most are indeed the noblest books,
as has been stated above.[5] This enables one to observe that the
Epistle of James is no truly apostolic epistle, for it does not contain
a single word about these things.[6] The greatest power of faith is
bound up in this article of faith. For if there were no resurrection,

[4] For example, in his commentary on Ps. 68, *Luther's Works*, 13, p. 12.

[5] Cf. p. 4

[6] Luther had recently formulated his views about the origins of the Epistle of
James; cf. *Luther's Works*, 35, pp. 395–397.

we would have no consolation or hope, and everything else Christ did and suffered would be futile (1 Cor. 15:17).

Therefore one must teach as follows: "Behold, Christ died for you! He took sin, death, and hell upon Himself and submitted Himself. But nothing could subdue Him, for He was too strong; He rose from the dead, was completely victorious, and subjected everything to Himself. And He did all this in order that you might be free from it and lord over it. If you believe this, you have it. For we are not able to do all this with our own power. Consequently, Christ had to do it. Otherwise there would have been no need for Him to come down from heaven." When we preach about our works, it is impossible for this message to be accepted and understood. O how well we Christians should be aware of this! How clear this epistle should be to us!

And to an inheritance which is imperishable, undefiled, and unfading.

That is, we do not hope for a blessing or inheritance that does not exist. On the contrary, we live in the hope of an inheritance that does exist and is imperishable and also undefiled and unfading. This blessing is ours forever and ever, even though we do not see it now. These are powerful and extraordinary words. He who knows what they mean will, I think, not be greatly concerned about a temporal blessing and pleasure. How can anyone cling to a perishable blessing and to pleasure if he really believes this?

For if one compares the worldly blessing with this, one sees that the former passes away completely and lasts only for a time. Only the latter remains forever and is not consumed. Furthermore, the former is totally unclean and defiles us; for no one is so pious that the temporal blessing does not make him unclean. But this inheritance alone is pure. He who has it is forever undefiled. Nor does it fade, wither, and rot. Everything on earth is changeable, even if it is as hard as iron and stone; it lacks permanency. A human being is ugly as soon as he becomes old. But this inheritance does not change; it remains fresh and green forever. On earth no pleasure is so great that it does not become unpleasant as time goes on. We see that one becomes weary of everything. But this blessing is different. All this is ours in Christ, by God's mercy, if we believe. It is given to us gratis. For how could we poor people merit such a great blessing with our works? No human reason and intelligence can grasp it.

Kept in heaven for you.

This imperishable, undefiled, and unfading inheritance is surely ours. Only now it is hidden for a short time until we close our eyes and are buried. Then we shall certainly find and see it, if we believe.

Who by God's power are guarded through faith for a salvation.

St. Peter declares that we await the precious inheritance in the hope into which we have entered through faith. For this is the sequence: Faith follows from the Word, the new birth follows from faith, and from this birth we enter into the hope of looking forward to the blessing with certainty. Therefore Peter has stated here in a truly Christian manner that this must come to pass through faith and not through one's own works.

But in reality St. Peter says here: "You are guarded for salvation by the power of God." For there are many people who — when they hear the Gospel that faith alone, without any works, makes pious — plump in and say: "Yes, I, too, believe." They regard their own self-invented notions as faith. Now we have taught on the basis of Scripture that we are unable to perform even the slightest works without the Spirit of God. How, then, could we by our own strength perform the greatest work, namely, to believe? Therefore such notions are nothing else than a dream and fiction. God's power must be present and work faith in us, as Paul says in Eph. 1:17-19: "That God . . . may give you a spirit of wisdom . . . that you may know . . . what is the immeasurable greatness of His power in us who believe, according to the working of His great might." It is not only God's will but also His power to spend a great deal. For when God creates faith in man, this is as great a work as if He were to create heaven and earth again.

Therefore those fools do not know what they are saying when they declare: "Ah, how can faith alone do it? After all, many a person who does not perform a single good work believes." For they suppose that their own dream is faith and that faith can exist without good works. We, however, declare with Peter that faith is a power of God. Where God works faith, man must be born again and become a new creature. Then good works must follow from faith as a matter of course. Therefore one should not say to a believing Christian: "Do this or that work!" For he does good works automatically and unbidden. But he must be told not to be deluded by a false and imaginary faith. Therefore pay no attention to the windbags who can speak volubly about this yet talk nothing but nonsense and balderdash. Of these Paul says in 1 Cor. 4:19-20: "But I will come to you . . . and I will find out not the talk of these arrogant people but their power. For the kingdom of God does not consist in talk but in power." Now where this power of God is lacking, there can be no true faith and no good works. Therefore those people who boast of the Christian name and faith and yet lead an evil life are liars. If this were the power of God, they would be different.

But what does St. Peter mean when he says that you are guarded for salvation by the power of God? This is his meaning: The faith which works in us the power of God—which dwells in us and with which we are filled—is such a tender and precious thing that it gives us a true and clear understanding of everything that pertains to salvation, so that we are able to judge everything on earth and say: "This doctrine is right. That one is false. This life is right. That one is not. This work is good and well done. That one is evil." What such a person concludes is right and true; for he cannot be misled but is preserved and protected, and he remains a judge of all doctrine.

On the other hand, where faith and this power of God are lacking, there one finds nothing but error and blindness. There reason lets itself be led hither and thither from one work to another; for it would like to go to heaven by means of its works and always thinks: "Ah, this work will bring you to heaven! Do it, and you will be saved." This is why so many foundations, cloisters, altars, priests, monks, and nuns have arisen in the world. God lets unbelievers come into such blindness. But He keeps us believers in a proper understanding in order to save us and preserve us from damnation.

For a salvation ready to be revealed in the last time.

That is, the inheritance for which you are destined was acquired and prepared a long time ago, ever since the beginning of the world. But it is still hidden, is still covered, locked and sealed up. Yet in a short time it will be revealed and exposed to our view.

In this you rejoice, though now for a little while you may have to suffer various trials.

If you are a Christian and look forward to the inheritance or salvation, you must cling only to this goal, despise everything on earth, and acknowledge that all worldly reason, wisdom, and holiness are nothing. The world will not be able to tolerate this. Therefore you must be prepared to be condemned and persecuted. In this way St. Peter sums up faith, hope, and the holy cross; for one follows from the other.

And he also gives us consolation when we suffer and are persecuted. Your mourning will last for a short time. Then you will rejoice, for salvation is already prepared for you. Therefore be patient in your suffering. This is true Christian consolation. It does not comfort as the teachings of men do. They seek no more than how to find help for external misfortune. St. Peter says: I am not speaking of physical comfort. The fact that you must have outward misfortune does no harm. Go ahead boldly, and stand firm. Do not think that you will be rid of misfortune, but think as follows: "My inheritance is already prepared and at hand. My suffering will last but a short while. Then it will cease." Thus one must lay the temporal consolation aside and oppose to it the eternal comfort which we have in God.

Furthermore, one must note that the apostle says: "You may have to suffer." Later, in the third chapter, he will say: "If that should be God's will" (v. 17). Many want to take heaven by storm and would like to enter at once. Therefore they impose a cross on themselves at their own discretion. After all, reason always wants to extol only its own works. God does not want this. We should not choose our own works, but we should wait to see what God imposes on us and sends for us, in order that we may go and follow as He leads us. Therefore you need not run after it yourself. If it is to be, that is, if God disposes that you must suffer, accept it, and console yourself with bliss that is eternal, not temporal.

So that the genuineness of your faith, more precious than gold which though perishable is tested by fire, may redound to

*praise and glory and honor at the revelation of Jesus Christ.
Without having seen Him, you love Him; though you do not
now see Him, you believe in Him.*

It is the purpose of the cross and adversities of all kinds to
enable one to differentiate between the false and the true faith.
God afflicts us in this way in order that our faith may be proved
and made manifest before the world, with the result that others
are attracted to the faith and we are praised and extolled. For God
will praise, extol, and honor us as we praise Him. Then the false
hypocrites, who do not approach the cross and adversities in the
proper way, will necessarily be put to shame.

All Scripture compares temptation to fire.[7] Thus here St. Peter
also likens the gold that is tested by fire to the testing of faith by
temptation and suffering. Fire does not impair the quality of gold,
but it purifies it, so that all alloy is removed. Thus God has imposed
the cross on all Christians to cleanse and to purge them well, in
order that faith may remain pure, just as the Word is, so that one
adheres to the Word alone and relies on nothing else. For we really
need such purging and affliction every day because of the coarse
old Adam.

It is characteristic of a Christian life to improve constantly and
to become purer. When we come to faith through the preaching of
the Gospel, we become pious and begin to be pure. But as long as
we are still in the flesh, we can never become completely pure.
For this reason God throws us right into the fire, that is, into suffering, disgrace, and misfortune. In this way we are purged more
and more until we die. No works can do this for us. For how can an
external work cleanse the heart inwardly? But when faith is tested
in this way, all alloy and everything false must disappear. Then,
when Christ is revealed, splendid honor, praise, and glory will
follow. Therefore Peter continues:

*You believe in Him and rejoice with unutterable and exalted joy.
As the outcome of your faith you obtain the salvation of your
souls.*

St. Peter says that unutterable and exalted joy will redound to
honor and glory. The world has the kind of joy which results in

[7] Luther is thinking especially of passages such as Zech. 13:9, Mal. 3:2, and
1 Cor. 3:13-15.

nothing but dishonor and of which one must be ashamed. Here
St. Peter has spoken clearly of the joy that is to come, and in
Scripture there is hardly another verse like this one about the
future joy. Yet St. Peter cannot express it.

This is a part of the foreword, in which the apostle has pointed
out what faith in Christ is and how this faith must be proved and
become pure through the adversities and the sufferings which God
sends us. And now we hear how this faith is recorded and promised in Scripture.

10. *The prophets who prophesied of the grace that was to be yours
searched and inquired about this salvation;*

11. *they inquired what person or time was indicated by the Spirit
of Christ within them when predicting the sufferings of Christ
and the subsequent glory.*

12. *It was revealed to them that they were serving not themselves
but you, in the things which have now been announced to you
by those who preached the good news to you through the Holy
Spirit sent from heaven, things into which angels long to look.*

Here St. Peter refers us to Holy Scripture in order that we may
see there how God keeps His promise not because of any merit on
our part but out of pure grace. For it is the purpose of all Scripture
to tear us away from our works and to bring us to faith. And it is
necessary for us to study Scripture well in order to become certain
of faith. Thus St. Paul also leads us into Scripture when he says in
Rom. 1:2 that God promised the Gospel "beforehand through His
prophets in the Holy Scriptures." And in Rom. 3:21 he says that the
Law and the prophets bear witness to the faith through which one
is justified.

In Acts 17:2 ff. we read that Paul preached the faith to the
Thessalonians, led them into Scripture, and expounded it to them,
and that they returned to Scripture every day and searched to see
whether his teachings were in agreement with it (v. 11). Therefore
we must do the same thing. We must go back to the Old Testament
and learn to prove the New Testament from the Old. There we
shall see the promise concerning Christ, as Christ Himself declares in John 5:39: "You search the Scriptures . . . and it is they

that bear witness to Me." Likewise (v. 46): "If you believed Moses,
you would believe Me; for he wrote of Me."

Therefore we must ignore the good-for-nothing babblers who
despise the Old Testament and say that it is no longer necessary;[8]
for we must derive from it alone the basis of our faith. For God sent
the prophets to the Jews to bear witness to the Christ who was to
come. Consequently, the apostles also convicted the Jews everywhere from their own Scriptures and proved that this was the
Christ.

Thus the books of Moses and the prophets are also Gospel,
since they proclaimed and described in advance what the apostles
preached or wrote later about Christ. But there is a difference. For
although both have been put on paper word for word, the Gospel,
or the New Testament, should really not be written but should be
expressed with the living voice which resounds and is heard
throughout the world. The fact that it is also written is superfluous. But the Old Testament is only put in writing. Therefore it
is called "a letter." Thus the apostles call it Scripture; for it only
pointed to the Christ who was to come. But the Gospel is a living
sermon on the Christ who has come.[9]

Furthermore, there is also a difference among the books of the
Old Testament. First, the five books of Moses are the chief part of
Scripture. They are actually what is meant by the Old Testament.
Then come histories and historical books. They contain all kinds
of examples of those who either kept or did not keep the Law of
Moses. In the third place, we have the prophets. They are based on
Moses and have enlarged on and explained the writings of Moses
more clearly. But Moses and all the prophets have one purpose.

The statement that the Old Testament has been abolished and
cast aside must be understood in the following way: In the first
place, the difference between the Old and the New Testament,
as we have just stated, is this, that the former pointed to Christ,
while the New Testament now gives us what was promised and
prefigured in the Old Testament. Therefore the figures are now

---

[8] Luther may be referring to Marcion and other heretics from the early church,
who rejected the authority of the Old Testament; but only two or three years later
he speaks explicitly of "many . . . who consider Moses and the whole Old Testament
of very small value and claim to be content with the Gospel" (*Luther's Works*, 9,
p. 6), and he may have them in mind here also.

[9] Cf. *Luther the Expositor*, p. 85, note 54.

done away with, for they have served their purpose and have accomplished and fulfilled all that they promised. Henceforth no distinction is to be made of food, clothing, place, and time. Everything is the same in Christ, to whom all was directed. The Jews were not saved through the Old Testament, for it was not given to them to make them pious; it was given to foreshadow for them the Christ who was to come.

Furthermore, in the Old Testament God carried on a twofold government: external and internal.[10] He determined to rule the people Himself, both inwardly and outwardly—inwardly in their hearts and outwardly in their bodies and their property. This explains why He gave them so many kinds of laws mingled together. Thus it was an instance of physical government when a husband could give his wife a bill of divorce and send her out of his house if he did not want her (Deut. 24:1). But the commandment which says: "You shall love your neighbor as yourself" (Lev. 19:18) is part of the spiritual government. Now, however, God reigns only spiritually in us through Christ. He executes the physical and external rule through the civil government. Therefore the external rule was abrogated when Christ came. Now God no longer assigns external persons, times, and places; but He governs us spiritually by means of the Word, so that we are lords over everything external and are not bound to anything physical. What belongs to the spiritual government, however, has not been repealed but always continues to be in force, as, for instance, the laws in Moses concerning the love for God and one's neighbor. God still wants these laws observed, and with this Law He will condemn all unbelievers.

In addition, the figures remained spiritual; that is, the spiritual meaning set forth by means of the external figures remained, although it was externally abolished. Thus the fact that a husband divorces his wife because of adultery is a figure and has a meaning which has now also been fulfilled spiritually. For in this way God also cast off the Jews and chose the heathen, because the Jews refused to believe in Christ. God does the same thing today. If a person refuses to walk in faith, He has him put out of the Christian congregation in order that he may change for the better.

The same thing is true of the law that after her husband's death a wife must take her husband's brother and bear him children, and

[10] Luther's word is *regiment;* cf. *Luther's Works,* 13, p. 147, note 4, also p. 76 of this commentary.

that he must succeed to the name of his brother and come into his property (Deut. 25:5-6). Although this is no longer in force, or has really become a matter of choice, so that one may do or not do it without sinning, yet it is a figure that points to Christ. For Christ is our Brother. He died for us, ascended into heaven, and commanded us to make souls pregnant and fruitful through the Gospel. In this way we retain His name, succeed to His name, and also come into His property. Therefore I dare not boast of converting people, but I must ascribe all this to the Lord Christ. This is true of all other figures of the Old Testament. It would take too long to enumerate them.[11]

Thus all that is not external in the Old Testament still stands. I mean everything the prophets say about faith and love. Therefore Christ also confirms this in Matt. 7:12: "Whatever you wish that men would do to you, do so to them; for this is the law and the prophets." In addition, Moses and the prophets bear witness to the Christ who is to come. If I, for instance, want to preach about Christ that He is the only Savior and that everyone must be saved through Him, I can choose the statement in Gen. 22:18: "In your Seed shall all the nations of the earth be blessed." I transform this into a living voice and say: "Through Christ, who is Abraham's Seed, all men must be blessed." From this it follows that we are all cursed and condemned in Adam. Therefore we must believe in the Seed if we want to escape condemnation. On such statements we must base our faith. We must let them stand in order that we may see in them how they testify of Christ for the strengthening of faith. This is what St. Peter means when he says:

The prophets who prophesied of the grace that was to be yours searched and inquired about this salvation.

This is the way Paul also speaks in Rom. 16:25-26. "According to the revelation of the mystery which was kept secret for long ages," he says, "but is now disclosed and through the prophetic writings is made known." Thus in the New Testament you find many statements taken from the prophets with which the apostles show that everything has happened as the prophets foretold. Thus Christ Himself shows this from the prophet Isaiah when He says

[11] See Luther's allegorical interpretation of these laws, published in 1525, *Luther's Works*, 9, pp. 244–245, 250–251.

in Matt. 11:5: "The blind receive their sight, and the lame walk, etc." It is as if He were saying: "Just as it is written there (cf. Isaiah 35:5-6), so it is happening." We also read in Acts 9:22 about Paul and in Acts 18:28 about Apollos how they drove the Jews into a corner and proved from Scripture that this was the Christ. For what the prophets had proclaimed, all this now took place in the case of Christ. And in Acts 15:14 ff. the apostles show how the Gospel had to be preached to the heathen in order that they might believe. All this proceeded and was accomplished in such a way that the Jews were convinced and had to admit that it was happening as Scripture had predicted.

They inquired what person or time was indicated by the Spirit of Christ within them.

St. Peter wants to say: Although the prophets had no knowledge of a fixed and definite time, they nevertheless indicated in general all the circumstances of time and place, as, for example, how Christ would suffer, how He would die, and how the heathen would believe in Him. Thus one could know for certain from the signs when the time had come. The prophet Daniel came close, yet he spoke vaguely about when Christ would suffer and die, when this or that would take place (Dan. 9:25-27). The Jews also had a definite prophecy that their kingdom would cease before the coming of Christ. But the day and the definite time when this would occur were not specified. For it was sufficient for them to have the certain knowledge that when this time came, Christ was not far away. Thus the prophet Joel also prophesied concerning the time of the coming of the Holy Spirit when he said: "And it shall come to pass afterward, that I will pour out My Spirit on all flesh" (2:28). St. Peter quotes this verse in Acts 2:17 and shows that Joel was speaking about that time and about definite persons.

From all this you see how painstakingly the apostles always pointed out the basis and the proof of their preaching and teaching. Today the councils and the pope come along and want to deal with us only without Scripture. They command us to believe them because we owe obedience to the church, and they threaten us with excommunication if we refuse to believe. The apostles were filled with the Holy Spirit and were certain that they had been sent by Christ and that they preached the true Gospel. Yet they humbled themselves and did not want to be believed unless they proved completely from Scripture that what they said was true. It was also their purpose to stop the mouths of the unbelievers, to prevent them from being able to bring up anything against what they preached. And we are expected to believe the stupid, uneducated persons who never preach one word of God and can do nothing else than cry out incessantly: "Indeed, the fathers could not err. This was settled long ago. Therefore one need not account for it." To be sure, we can prove from Scripture that no one is saved unless he believes in Christ. They cannot say anything against this. But they will not be able to adduce Scripture passages to prove their nonsense that he who does not fast on this or that day will be damned. Therefore we will not believe them, and we are not obligated to do so. Now St. Peter continues:

The Spirit of Christ within them when predicting the sufferings of Christ and the subsequent glory.

This can be taken to mean both Christ's and our sufferings. St. Paul also calls the sufferings of all Christians the sufferings of Christ (Col. 1:24). For just as faith, the name, the Word, and the work of Christ are mine by reason of my belief in Him, so His sufferings are also mine; for I suffer for His sake. Thus Christ's sufferings are fulfilled in the Christians every day until the end of the world.

In all our sufferings we take comfort in the knowledge that we have all these sufferings in common with Christ and that He regards all our sufferings as His own, as well as in the certainty that glory will immediately follow the suffering. But we must also know that just as Christ did not enter into His glory before His suffering, so we must also first bear the cross with Him. Then we shall also have joy with Him.

St. Peter declares that everything we preach today was clearly proclaimed and foretold in times past by the prophets because the Holy Spirit revealed it to them. The fact that we have so little understanding of the prophets today is the result of our inability to understand the language. In any case, they spoke clearly enough. Therefore those who are familiar with the language and have the Spirit of God, as all believers do, understand without any difficulty, since they know the purport of all Scripture. But if one does not understand their language and does not have the Spirit or Christian discernment, the prophets seem to be drunk and full of wine. Yet if one of these is lacking, the Spirit without the language is better than the language without Spirit. The prophets have a special way of speaking, but they mean exactly what the apostles preach; for both have said much about the suffering and the glory of Christ and of those who believe in Him. Thus David says of Christ in Ps. 22:6: "I am a worm, and no man." With these words He shows the depth of His abject humiliation in His suffering. David also writes of the afflictions of his people and the Christians in Ps. 44:22: [12] "We are accounted as sheep for the slaughter."

It was revealed to them that they were serving not themselves but you, in the things which have now been announced to you by those who preached the good news to you through the Holy Spirit sent from heaven.

That is, it was sufficient for the prophets to know this. But for our sakes they handed it down to us, became our servants, and served us with it, in order that we might go to their school and learn it from them. Now we have a foundation, so that our faith becomes all the stronger and we can arm and defend ourselves against all false doctrine.

Things into which angels long to look.

Through the Holy Spirit, who descended on them from heaven, the apostles proclaimed to us great things of the kind the angels like to see. St. Peter orders us to close our eyes and see what the Gospel is. This will give us joy and delight. As yet we cannot see this with our physical eyes; but we must believe that we partake of and share in the righteousness, truth, blessedness, and all the good things God has. For since He gave us Christ, His only Son, the highest Good, He, through Him, also gives us all His good things, riches, and treasures, from which the angels in heaven derive all pleasure and joy. All this is offered to us in the Gospel; and if we believe, we necessarily take such joy in it. But while we are living

[12] As in other early works and in some later works (cf. *Luther's Works*, 14, p. 116, note 11, and the references there), Luther tends to follow the Vulgate's numeration of the psalms in the commentaries presented here; but in this case "Ps. 45" does not refer to either Ps. 45 or Ps. 46 but to Ps. 44.

on earth, our joy cannot be perfect like that of the angels. Through faith we are now beginning to feel some of it. In heaven, however, it is so great that no human heart can grasp it. But when we get there, we, too, shall feel it.

Thus you see how St. Peter teaches us to outfit and equip ourselves with Scripture. Up to this point he has been describing what it means to preach the Gospel, and how the prophets proclaimed beforehand that it was to happen and was to be preached this way. Now in this chapter he proceeds to admonish us to cling to this proclamation of the Gospel by faith and to follow up on it with our love. He says:

13. *Therefore gird up your minds, be sober, set your hope fully upon the grace that is coming to you at the revelation of Jesus Christ.*

14. *As obedient children, do not be conformed to the passions of your former ignorance,*

15. *but as He who called you is holy, be holy yourselves in all your conduct,*

16. *since it is written: You shall be holy, for I am holy.*

This is an exhortation to faith. It means: Since things in which even the angels rejoice and which they are delighted to see have been proclaimed and given to you through the Gospel, cling to them and place full confidence in them, so that it is a genuine faith and not a colored or fictitious delusion and dream.

Gird up your minds.

Here Peter is speaking about a spiritual girding of the mind, just as one girds a sword physically to one's loins. Christ also touched on girding when He said: "Let your loins be girded" (Luke 12:35). In several places in Scripture the loins denote physical unchastity.[13] But here St. Peter is speaking of spiritual loins. In a physical sense Scripture calls the loins the source of the natural descent from the father. Thus we read in Gen. 49:10 that

---

[13] Luther may be thinking of passages such as Ps. 38:7.

Christ is to come from the loins of Judah.[14] Thus the physical girding of the loins is nothing else than chastity, as Is. 11:5 states: "Righteousness shall be the girdle of His waist, and faithfulness the girdle of His loins." That is, one suppresses and overcomes evil lust only through faith.

But the spiritual girding—of which the apostle is speaking here—takes place as follows: Just as a virgin is physically pure and blameless, so the soul is spiritually blameless because of faith, through which it becomes the bride of Christ. But if it falls from faith into false doctrine, it must go to ruin. For this reason Scripture consistently calls idolatry and unbelief adultery and whoring, that is, if the soul clings to the teachings of men and thus surrenders faith and Christ.[15] St. Peter forbids this here when he tells us to gird the loins of the mind. It is as if he were saying: You have now heard the Gospel and have come to faith. Therefore see to it that you remain in faith and not be moved by false doctrine, that you do not waver and run hither and thither with works.

Here St. Peter adopts a peculiar expression—different from that of St. Paul—when he speaks of "the loins of your mind." He uses the word "mind" for what we mean when we speak of being minded, as if I said: "I regard this as right," or, as St. Paul expresses himself (Rom. 3:28), "We hold that"; that is, "So we are minded." With this he actually means faith and wants to say: "You have come to the proper understanding, namely, that one is justified by faith alone. Now cling to this understanding. Gird it well. Hold fast to it, and do not let anyone wrest it from you. Then all is well with you. For many false teachers will appear and will set up human doctrines, to take away your understanding and loosen the girdle of faith. Therefore be warned, and give careful thought to this." The hypocrites, who rely on their works and lead a fine moral life, think that God must take them to heaven because of their works. They become puffed up and arrogant. Like the Pharisee in Luke 18:11-12, they insist on their understanding and opinion. Mary speaks about them in the *Magnificat,* where she uses the same little word Peter employs here. She says: "He has

[14] The thought of Christ's descent from Judah was, for Luther and the exegetical tradition, the meaning of Gen. 49:10 (cf. *Luther's Works,* 8, pp. 238—245); but the term "loins" does not actually appear there.

[15] Luther is thinking of passages such as Jer. 3:8-9, Hos. 2:1-5, and Col. 3:5.

scattered the proud in the imagination of their hearts" (Luke 1:51),
that is, in their understanding.

Be sober.

Sobriety serves the body externally and is the chief work of
faith. For even though man has become righteous, he is not yet
completely rid of evil lusts. To be sure, faith has begun to subdue
the flesh; but the flesh continues to bestir itself and rages nevertheless in all sorts of lusts that would like to assert themselves
again and do what they want. Therefore the spirit must busy itself
daily to tame the flesh and to bring it into subjection, must wrestle
with it incessantly, and must take care that it does not repel faith.
Therefore those who say that they have faith, think that this is
enough, and, in addition, live as they please, are deceiving themselves. Where faith is genuine, it must attack the body and hold it
in check, lest the body do what it pleases. For this reason, St. Peter
says that we must be sober.

But he does not want the body to be destroyed or to be weak-
ened too much. Thus one finds many who have fasted themselves
mad and have tortured themselves to death. Even though Saint
Bernard was a saintly man, he, too, was afflicted for a time with
such folly. He denied his body so much that his breath stank and
he could not associate with people.[16] Later, however, he came to
his senses and also told his brothers not to hurt the body too much.
For he realized that he had made himself unable to serve his
brothers. Therefore St. Peter demands no more than that we be
sober, that is, that we stint the body as long as we feel that it is still
too lascivious. He does not prescribe any definite length of time for
fasting, as the pope has done; but he leaves it to everyone's discretion to fast in such a way that he always remains sober and does
not burden the body with gluttony. He must remain reasonable and
sensible, and he must see to what extent it is necessary for him to
mortify the body. It does no good at all to impose a command about
this on a whole crowd or community, since we are so different from
one another. One has a strong body, another has a body that is
weak. Therefore one person must deny it much, and another

[16] Cf. the *Vita prima* of Bernard, *S. Bernardi vita et res gestae*, 22, *Patrologia,
Series Latina,* CLXXXV-1, 239, 240; Luther refers to this repeatedly in his writings,
as, for example, in *Luther's Works,* 4, p. 273; 22, p. 360.

person must deny it little, in such a way that when this is done, the body remains healthy and able to do good.

But it is also wrong for the other crowd to come along and say that they are getting on well by not fasting and by feeling free to eat meat.[17] For these people, like the others, do not understand the Gospel either and are of no importance. They do no more than disdain the pope's command. Yet they do not want to gird the mind and the understanding, as Peter says. They let the body have its way, with the result that it remains indolent and lascivious. It is good to fast. But one fasts in the right way by not giving the body more food than is needed to keep it healthy, and by letting it work and wake, in order that the old ass may not become too reckless, go dancing on the ice, and break a leg but may be bridled and follow the spirit. It should not imitate those who, when they fast, fill themselves so full of fish and the best wine at one time that their bellies are bloated.

This is what St. Peter means by being sober. Now he continues:

Set your hope fully upon the grace that is coming to you.

Christian faith is ready to rest completely on God's Word with all confidence and courage, and then to go joyfully on its way. Therefore Peter says: Then the loins of your mind are girded, and your faith is genuine, if you have such courage, no matter whether property, honor, body, or life are involved. With these words he has surely given an excellent description of a genuine and true faith. It must not be an indolent and sleepy faith and only a dream. No, it must be a living and active thing, so that one devotes oneself to it with all confidence and clings to the Word, no matter what happens, in order that we may press forward through fortune and misfortune. Thus when I must die, I must rely boldly on Christ, readily put forth my neck, and trust in the Word of God, which cannot lie to me. Then faith must go straight ahead, let nothing lead it astray, and ignore everything it sees, hears, and feels. This is the kind of faith St. Peter demands — a faith that consists in such power, not in thoughts or words.

In the second place, St. Peter says: Set your hope upon the grace that is offered you. This means that you did not earn this great

[17] Apparently a reference to Andreas Carlstadt's declaration of freedom from rules of fasting and the like; cf., for example, *Luther's Works*, 45, pp. 72-73.

grace, but that it is offered to you completely without cost. For the Gospel, which proclaims this grace, is not our invention or fabrication. No, the Holy Spirit let it come down into the world from heaven. But what is being offered to us? That which we heard above,[18] namely, that he who believes in Christ and clings to the Word has Him with all His blessings, so that he becomes lord over sin, death, devil, and hell, and is sure of eternal life. This treasure is brought to our door and laid into our laps without our cooperation or merit, yes, unexpectedly and without our knowledge or thoughts. Therefore the apostle wants us to set our hope cheerfully on this grace, for the God who offers it to us will surely not lie to us.

At the revelation of Jesus Christ.

God does not let His grace be offered to anyone in any other way than through Christ. Hence no man should presume to approach Him without this Mediator, as we have heard sufficiently above.[19] For God will listen to no one who does not bring Christ, His dear Son, with him. God has regard for Him alone, and for His sake He also has regard for those who cling to Him. He wants us to acknowledge that we are reconciled to the Father through the blood of the Son and for this reason need not be afraid to come before Him. For the Lord Christ came, assumed flesh and blood, and attached Himself to us for the purpose of acquiring such grace for us before the Father. Thus all the patriarchs and prophets were preserved and saved through such faith in Christ; for they all had to believe in the words which God spoke to Abraham: "In your Seed shall all the nations of the earth be blessed" (Gen. 22:18). Therefore, as we have said, [20] the faith of the Jews, the Turks, and of those who rely on their own works and want to go to heaven because of them is invalid. Peter says: "Grace is offered to you," but at the revelation of Jesus Christ, or, to translate it more clearly, because Jesus Christ is revealed to you.

Through the Gospel we are told who Christ is, in order that we may learn to know that He is our Savior, that He delivers us from sin and death, helps us out of all misfortune, reconciles us to the Father, and makes us pious and saves us without our works. He who

[18] Cf. pp. 9–14.
[19] Cf. p. 12
[20] Cf. p.12.

does not learn to know Christ in this way must go wrong. For even though you know that He is God's Son, that He died and rose again, and that He sits at the right hand of the Father, you have not yet learned to know Christ aright, and this knowledge still does not help you. You must also know and believe that He did all this for your sake, in order to help you. Consequently, all that has hitherto been preached and taught at the schools of higher learning is sheer rubbish. They had no understanding of this, and they never went beyond the thought that Christ suffered intensely and that He is now sitting in heaven above with nothing to do and is enjoying Himself. Thus their hearts remain barren, and faith cannot come to life in them. The Lord Christ should not be isolated as existing for Himself but should be preached as belonging to us. Otherwise why would it have been necessary for Him to come down to earth and shed His blood? But since, as He says in John 3:17, He was sent into the world that the world might be saved through Him, He must have accomplished what the Father sent Him to do. The fact that He was sent by and came from the Father should not be understood as having taken place only according to the divine nature. No, this must also be understood of the human nature and of His office. As soon as He was baptized, He began to carry out what He had been sent and had come into the world to accomplish, namely, to proclaim the truth and to announce to us that all who believe in Him should be saved. Thus He revealed and manifested Himself, and He offered us grace.

As obedient children.

That is, conduct yourselves as obedient children. In Scripture faith is called obedience.[21] The pope, with his schools of higher learning and his cloisters, has also mangled this little word for us and has applied to their silly lies what Scripture says about obedience, as, for example, the statement in 1 Sam. 15:22, where we read: "To obey is better than sacrifice."[22] For since they see clearly

---

[21] Luther is thinking of passages such as Rom. 1:5 and Rom. 16:19.

[22] Luther had had occasion to reflect at some length on the meaning of obedience; cf. *On Monastic Vows* (W, VIII, 645–651). On the application of 1 Sam 15: 22-23 to this issue cf. Johann Cochlaeus, *Ein nötig und christlich bedencken auff des Luthers artickeln, die man gemeynsamen concilio fürtragen soll* (1538), ed. Hans Volz, *Corpus Catholicorum*, XVIII (Münster i. W., 1932), 57.

that obedience is greatly praised in Scripture, they have appropriated this in order to blind the people and to give the impression that the obedience of which Scripture speaks is their affair. In that way they bring us away from God's Word to their lies and to the obedience of the devil. He who hears the Gospel and God's Word, and believes in it, is an obedient child of God. Therefore tread underfoot and care nothing about what is not God's Word.

Do not be conformed to the passions of your former ignorance.

That is, do not deport yourselves as you did before. One should not regard you as what you formerly were. Formerly you were idolatrous; and you lived in unchastity, gluttony, drunkenness, greed, vanity, anger, envy, and hatred. This was an evil, heathenish way of life. It was unbelief. You went along in such a way of life like the blind. You did not know what you did. Now desist from these evil lusts. Here you see how St. Peter traces all misfortune to ignorance. For where faith and the knowledge of Christ are lacking, nothing but error and blindness remain, so that one does not know what is right and what is wrong. Then people fall into vices of all kinds.

This is what has happened up to now. When Christ vanished and was eclipsed, error began. Then the whole world asked how one could be saved. This in itself is a sign of blindness or ignorance; it shows that the proper understanding of faith has disappeared and that no one any longer knows anything about it. For this reason the world is so full of many kinds of sects, and there is nothing but division; for everyone wants to devise his own way to heaven. From misfortune we must sink ever deeper into blindness, because we are helpless. Therefore St. Peter says: You have now been fools long enough. Now that you know and have come to a proper understanding, put an end to this.

But as He who called you is holy, be holy yourselves in all your conduct, since it is written: You shall be holy, for I am holy.

Here St. Peter cites a verse from the Old Testament, from Lev. 19:2, where God says: "You shall be holy; for I the Lord your God am holy." That is, because I am your Lord and God, and you are My people, you must be like Me. For a true lord brings it about that his people are like him, walk in obedience, and are guided by his will. Now just as God our Lord, is holy, so His people are also holy. Therefore we are all holy if we walk in faith. Scripture does not say much about the deceased saints; it speaks about those who are living on earth. Thus the prophet David glories in Ps. 86:2: "Preserve my life, for I am godly."

But here our men of learning have misinterpreted the verse again.[23] They say that the prophet called himself holy because he had a special revelation. In this way they themselves admit that they lack faith and do not have the revelation of Christ. Otherwise they would surely feel this. For he who is a Christian feels such a revelation in himself. But those who do not feel this are not Christians. For he who is a Christian enters with the Lord Christ into a sharing of all His goods. Now since Christ is holy, he, too, must be holy, or he must deny that Christ is holy. If you have been baptized, you have put on the holy garment, which is Christ, as Paul says (Gal. 3:27).

The little word "holy" designates that which is God's own and is due to Him alone. In German we use the word *geweihet*. Thus Peter says: You have now given yourselves to God as His own. Therefore see to it that you do not let yourselves be led again into the worldly lusts. But let God alone reign, live, and work in you. Then you are holy, just as He is holy.

So far the apostle has described the grace that is offered to us through the Gospel and the preaching about Jesus Christ, and he has taught us what our attitude toward this should be, namely, that we should hold to a pure and unchanged meaning of faith, in such a way that we know that no work we are able to do or devise can be of any help to us. Now when this is preached, reason comes along and says: "Ah, if this is true, then I need not do a single good work!" Thus stupid minds seize upon this and change Christian life into carnal liberty. They think they should do what they please. St. Peter confronts these people here, anticipates them, and teaches them that Christian liberty must be exercised solely over against God. For here nothing else is necessary than faith, that I give God His due honor and regard Him as my God, who is just, truthful, and merciful. Such faith liberates us from sin and all evil. Now when I have given God this honor, then whatever life I live,

---

[23] For Luther's own exegesis of this passage, see his *Dictations on the Psalter* (W, IV, 20).

I live for my neighbor, to serve and help him. The greatest work that comes from faith is this, that I confess Christ with my mouth and, if it has to be, bear testimony with my blood and risk my life. Yet God does not need the work; but I should do it to prove and confess my faith, in order that others, too, may be brought to faith. Then other works will follow. They must all tend to serve my neighbor. All this God must bring about in us. Therefore we should not make up our minds to begin to lead a carnal life and to do what we please. For this reason St. Peter now says:

17. *And if you invoke as Father Him who judges each one impartially according to his deeds, conduct yourselves with fear throughout the time of your exile.*

18. *You know that you were ransomed from the futile ways inherited from your fathers, not with perishable things such as silver or gold,*

19. *but with the precious blood of Christ, like that of a lamb without blemish or spot.*

20. *He was destined before the foundation of the world but was made manifest at the end of the times for your sake.*

21. *Through Him you have confidence in God, who raised Him from the dead and gave Him glory, so that your faith and hope are in God.*

Thus St. Peter says: By faith you are now children of God, and He is your Father. You have acquired an imperishable inheritance in heaven· [as he stated above]. Therefore nothing remains now but that the veil be taken away and that what is now hidden be revealed. You must still wait until you see this. It is now possible for you to address God confidently as Father; but though He is your Father, He is so just that He gives to everyone according to his deeds and does not respect the person. Therefore even though you have the great distinction to be called a Christian and a child of God, you dare not think that God will spare you on this account if you live without fear and imagine that it is now sufficient for you to boast of such a distinction. To be sure, the world judges according to the person. It does not punish all in the same way. It spares those who are friends, rich, beautiful, learned, wise, and powerful. But God has no regard for this. No matter how great the person is, all this is immaterial to Him. Thus in Egypt He slew the son of King Pharaoh just as readily as He slew the son of a common miller.

The apostle wants us to expect such judgment of God and to be in fear, lest we boast of being called Christians and depend on it, as if God would be more indulgent with us on this account than He would be with others. In times past the Jews, too, were deluded by this assumption; they boasted of being Abraham's seed and the people of God. Scripture does not differentiate according to the flesh; it differentiates according to the spirit. It is true that God had promised that Christ should be born from Abraham and that a holy people should come from him; but it does not follow from this that all who are born from Abraham are God's children. God also promised that the heathen shall be saved. But He did not say that He would save all the heathen.

But a question now arises here. Since we say that God saves us solely through faith and without regard to works, why, pray, does St. Peter say that God does not judge according to the person, but that He judges according to the works? Answer: What we have taught, that faith alone justifies before God, is undoubtedly true, since it is so clear from Scripture that it cannot be denied. Now what the apostle says here, that God judges according to the works, is also true. But one should maintain with certainty that where there is no faith, there can be no good works either, and, on the other hand, that there is no faith where there are no good works. Therefore link faith and good works together in such a way that both make up the sum total of the Christian life. As you live, so you will fare. God will judge you according to this. Therefore even though God judges us according to our works, it nevertheless remains true that the works are only the fruits of faith. They are the evidence of our belief or unbelief. Therefore God will judge and convict you on the basis of your works. They show whether you have believed or have not believed, just as one cannot condemn and judge a liar better than from his words. Yet it is evident that the words have not made him a liar, but that he has become a liar before he tells a lie; for the lie must come into the mouth from the heart. Therefore the only way to understand this is the simplest way, namely, that the works are fruits and signs of faith and that God judges people according to these fruits, which certainly have to follow, in order that one may see publicly where belief or unbelief is in the heart. God will not judge according to whether you are called a Christian or have been baptized. No, He will ask you: "If you are a Christian, then tell Me: Where are the fruits with which you can show your faith?"

Therefore St. Peter now says: Since you have the kind of Father who does not judge according to the person, conduct yourselves with fear throughout the time of pilgrimage. That is, do not fear the Father because of pain and punishment, as non-Christians and also the devil fear; but be afraid lest He forsake you and withdraw His hand, as a pious child is afraid that it may anger its father and do something displeasing to him. This is the kind of fear God wants us to have, in order that we may guard against sins and serve our neighbor while we sojourn here on earth.

As we have heard, a sincere Christian believer has all the possessions of God and is a child of God. The time of his life, however, is but a pilgrimage. For through faith the spirit is already in heaven, and this makes him lord over all things. But God permits him to remain alive in the flesh and lets his body walk the earth in order that he may help others and bring them to heaven too. Therefore we must use everything on earth in no other way than as a guest who travels across country, comes to an inn where he must spend the night, and takes nothing but food and lodging from the innkeeper. He does not say that the innkeeper's property belongs to him. Thus we must also deal with temporal goods as if they did not belong to us. We must limit our enjoyment of them to what is necessary for the preservation of the body. With the rest we must help our neighbor. Thus the Christian life is only a night's lodging; "for here we have no lasting city" (Heb. 13:14), but we must go where the Father is, namely, to heaven. Therefore we should not indulge in riotous revelry here; but, as St. Peter says, we must conduct ourselves with fear.

You know that you were ransomed from the futile ways inherited from your fathers, not with perishable things such as silver or gold, but with the precious blood of Christ.

The apostle means that this should draw you to the fear of God with which you should conduct yourselves, that you think of how much your redemption has cost. Formerly you were citizens in the

world and subjects of the devil, but now God has torn you from
that kind of life and has put you in another position, so that you
are citizens in heaven but strangers and guests on earth. And you
see how much God has spent on you and how rich the treasure is
with which you were ransomed and made children of God. Therefore conduct yourselves with fear, and see to it that you do not
despise this and lose the noble, precious treasure.

Now what is the treasure with which we have been redeemed?
It is not perishable gold or silver; it is the precious blood of Christ,
the Son of God. This treasure is so costly and noble that the mind
and reason of no man can comprehend it. Just one drop of this
innocent blood would have been more than enough for the sin of
the whole world.[24] Yet the Father wanted to pour out His grace on
us so abundantly and to spend so much that He let His Son Christ
shed all His blood and gave us the entire treasure. Therefore He
does not want us to make light of and think little of such great
grace; but He wants us to be moved to conduct ourselves with
fear, lest this treasure be taken away from us.

Mark well that St. Peter says: "You were ransomed from the
futile ways inherited from your fathers." In this way he beats down
every excuse on the basis of which we think that our position
must be correct because it has existed from time immemorial and
all our forefathers, among whom there were also wise and pious
people, held this view. For St. Peter says: Everything our fathers
instituted and did was evil, and what you learned from them regarding the worship of God is also evil, so that it cost the Son of
God His blood to redeem the people from it. Now everything
that is not washed with the blood is poisoned and condemned because of the flesh. From this it follows that the more man presumes
to acquire piety without Christ, the more he stands in his own way,
and the deeper he sinks into blindness and wickedness and makes
himself guilty of profaning the precious blood (cf. 1 Cor. 11:27).[25]

External, gross sins are relatively insignificant when compared
with the doctrine that one should become pious by means of works
and by worshiping God according to our reason. For this dishonors
and blasphemes the innocent blood more than anything else. The

---

[24] This is an allusion to the medieval idea, expressed most familiarly in the
hymn *Adoro Te devote* of Thomas Aquinas, that "one drop [of the blood of Christ]
can save the entire world from every crime."

[25] Luther's words are *und sich an dem thewren blütt verdampt.*

heathen committed a far greater sin by praying to the sun and the moon, which they regarded as the proper worship of God, than by sinning in any other way. Therefore the piety of man is sheer blasphemy of God and the greatest sin a man commits. Thus the ways now current in the world – the ways which the world regards as worship of God and as piety – are worse in the eyes of God than any other sin. This applies to the priests and the monks and to what seems good in the eyes of the world yet is without faith. Therefore it is better for him who does not want to obtain grace from God through the blood never to appear before the eyes of God. For by doing so he only angers the Majesty more and more.

Like that of a lamb without blemish or spot.

Here, however, St. Peter expounds Scripture. For in spite of its brevity this is a powerful, rich epistle. Thus now, when speaking of "the futile ways inherited from the fathers," he is in agreement with many statements in the prophets, as, for example, with Jer. 16:19, where we read: "To Thee shall the nations come from the ends of the earth and say: 'Our fathers have inherited nought but lies, etc.'" It is as if St. Peter were saying: "The prophets also proclaimed that you should be delivered from the futile ways of the fathers."

Thus here, too, he wants to direct us to Scripture when he says: "You were ransomed . . . with the precious blood of Christ, like that of a lamb without blemish or spot" and explains what is stated in the prophets and in Moses. In Is. 53:7, for example, we read: "Like a lamb that is led to the slaughter." Likewise the figure of the paschal lamb in Ex. 12:3ff. St. Peter explains all this here and says: The lamb is Christ, and just as the former had to be without blemish, so this Lamb, whose blood was shed for our sin, is also spotless and innocent.

He was destined before the foundation of the world but was made manifest at the end of the times.

That is, we did not merit this and never asked God that the precious blood of Christ be shed for us. Therefore we have nothing to boast of. The glory belongs to no one but God alone. God promised us this without any merit on our part; and He also revealed or made known what He ordained and decreed from eternity, before the creation of the world. To be sure, this was also promised in the prophets, but in a veiled manner and not openly. Now, however, after the resurrection of Christ and the sending of the Holy Spirit, it has been preached publicly and has resounded throughout the world.

St. Peter calls the era in which we are now living, the period from Christ's ascension to the Last Day, "the end of the times." Thus the apostles, the prophets, and Christ Himself also call it the last hour.[26] This does not mean that the Last Day was to come immediately after Christ's ascent into heaven, but the reason is that after this proclamation of the Gospel concerning Christ there will be no other proclamation and that it will not be revealed and set forth better than it has been set forth and revealed. For of this there has always been one revelation after the other. Therefore God says in Ex. 6:3 "By My name the Lord I did not make Myself known to them." For although the patriarchs knew God, yet at the same time they did not yet have as clear a proclamation from God as was made later through Moses and the prophets. But now no more glorious and no clearer proclamation has come into the world than the Gospel. Therefore this is the last one. All the times have come and gone, but now the Gospel has been revealed to us for the last time.

In the second place, the end of the world is not far away so far as time is concerned. St. Peter explains this in 2 Peter 3:8 when he says: "With the Lord one day is as a thousand years, and a thousand years as one day." He wants to give us this guidance concerning the reckoning of time in order that we may judge according to God's way of looking at it, namely, that "the end of the times" is already at hand. But the fact that there is still some time left means nothing before God. Salvation has already been revealed and completed; but God permits the world to continue to stand in order that His name may be honored and praised more widely, even though in His own eyes it has already been revealed most perfectly.

For your sake. Through Him you have confidence in God, who raised Him from the dead and gave Him glory, so that your faith and hope are in God.

[26] The only explicit reference to "the last hour" seems to be 1 John 2:18, on which see Luther's comments, p. 251.

He says that the Gospel has been revealed for our sakes. For God and the Lord Christ did not need this; they did it for our benefit, in order that we might believe in Him, not through ourselves but through Christ, who intercedes for us before the Father. Him the Father raised from the dead in order that He might rule over all things. Thus he who believes in Him has all His blessings and ascends to the Father through Him. Thus we have faith in God and through that faith also a hope. Faith alone has to save us. But there must be a faith in God. For if God does not help, you have no help at all. Therefore even if you had the friendship of all men, this is not enough. No, you must have the friendship of God, in order that you may be able to speak proudly of Him as your Father and of yourself as His child, and also have greater confidence that He will help you in all your troubles than you have that your physical father and mother will do so. All this solely through the one Mediator and Savior, the Lord Christ. Such faith, he says, does not come from the power of man. No, God creates it in us because Christ has merited this with His blood—Christ, to whom He has given the glory and whom He has placed at His right hand to create faith in us through the power of God.

So far we have heard St. Peter exhort us to gird our minds, in order that we may remain pure and live in faith; then, since it has cost so much, to "conduct ourselves with fear" and not to rely on the fact that we are called Christians, since God is a Judge who does not care about anybody but judges one as He judges the other, without respect of persons. Now Peter continues and concludes the first chapter.

22. *Having purified your souls by your obedience to the truth for a sincere love of the brethren, love one another earnestly from the heart.*

23. *You have been born anew, not of perishable seed but of imperishable, through the living and abiding Word of God;*

24. *for All flesh is like grass and all its glory like the flower of the grass. The grass withers, and the flower falls,*

25. *but the Word of the Lord abides forever. That Word is the good news which was preached to you.*

In Gal. 5:22-23 Paul enumerates the fruits that follow from faith. "The fruit of the Spirit," he says, "is love, joy, peace, patience, kindness, goodness, faithfulness, gentleness, self-control." Thus here St. Peter also speaks of the fruits of faith, namely, that we should purify our souls by obedience to the truth through the Spirit. For where faith is genuine, it subdues the body and constrains the lust of the flesh. Even though it does not slay the body, it nonetheless makes it subject and obedient to the Spirit and holds it in check. This is what St. Paul also means when he speaks of fruits of the Spirit. It is a great work that the Spirit is lord over the flesh and curbs the evil lust that is innate in us from our father and mother. For without grace it is impossible for us to live properly in wedlock, let alone out of wedlock.

But why does the apostle say that we should purify our souls? He is well aware of the fact that after Baptism the lust of the flesh abides in us until death. Therefore it is not enough for one to abstain from the deed, to remain chaste outwardly, and to let evil lust stay in the heart. No, one must strive to purify the soul, so that evil lust and desire depart from our heart and the soul is hostile to them and constantly fights against them until it is rid of them.

And now St. Peter makes a beautiful addition, namely, that one should purify the soul by obedience to the truth in the Spirit. Many sermons have been preached and many books have been written about chastity. There they have said that one should fast for a certain length of time, not eat meat, not drink wine, etc., in order to get rid of the affliction. Although this has helped to some extent, it has not been enough; it has not subjugated lust. Thus St. Jerome writes about himself that he abused his body until it resembled that of an Ethiopian, but that this did not help and that he still dreamed he was singing and dancing among harlots in Rome.[27] Thus St. Bernard also hurt and ruined his body until it stank, as I have said above.[28] These men were sorely tried, and they undertook to subdue this by external means. But since this is external, the poultice has been applied only on the outside, not on the inside. Therefore it does not suffice to quell lust.

But here St. Peter has given a real remedy for this, namely,

[27] Jerome to Eusochium, *Epistolae,* XXII, 7, 1–2, *Patrologia, Series Latina,* XXII, 398, 399; cf. *Luther's Works,* 22, p. 266.

[28] See p. 27, note 16.

obedience to the truth in the Spirit. Scripture gives the same remedy in other passages, as, for example, in Is. 11:5: "Faithfulness shall be the girdle of his loins." This is the right poultice; it girds the loins. The evil must come out, not go in; for it has grown inside in the flesh and blood, in the marrow and the veins, not outside in the cloth or in the garment. Therefore it is useless to attempt to curb lust with external means. To be sure, one can weaken and mortify the body with fasting and work; but one does not expel evil lust in this way. Faith, however, can subdue and restrain it, so that it gives room to the Spirit.

Thus the prophet Zechariah speaks in chapter 9:17 about a wine which Christ has. He gives it to maidens to drink, and they flourish. Other wine tends to incite to evil lust; but this wine, that is, the Gospel, subdues lust and makes chaste hearts. This is what St. Peter says: When one takes hold of the truth with the heart and is obedient to it in the Spirit, this is the right help and the most powerful remedy. Otherwise you will find no remedy that could quell all evil thoughts in this way. For when it enters the heart, the evil inclination soon departs. Let him who wants to, try this. He will find that this is true, and those who have tried it are well aware of this. But the devil does not easily let anyone come to the point of taking hold of and enjoying the Word of God; for he knows well what power it has to subdue evil lust and thoughts.

Thus St. Peter now wants to say: If you want to remain chaste, you must take hold of obedience to the truth in the Spirit; that is, one must not only hear and read the Word of God, but one must take it to heart. Consequently, it is not enough to preach or hear the Gospel once. No, one must constantly move forward and progress. For the Word has such grace that the more one deals with it, the sweeter it becomes. Although the doctrine of faith is always one and the same, one cannot hear it too often, unless there are impertinent and coarse hearts.

Now the apostle adds:

For a sincere love of the brethren.

To what end should we now lead a chaste life? To be saved by doing so? No, but for the purpose of serving our neighbor. What should I do to check my sin? I must take hold of the obedience

to the truth in the Spirit, that is, faith in God's Word. Why do I
check sin? To enable me to be of service to others. For first I must
hold body and flesh in subjection through the Spirit. Then I can
also be of service to others.

We read on:

Love one another earnestly from the heart.

The apostles Peter and Paul differentiate between brotherly
love and love in general.[29] Brotherhood means that Christians
should all be like brothers and make no distinction among them;
for since we all have one Christ in comon, one Baptism, one faith,
one treasure, I am no better than you are. For what you have I
also have, and I am just as rich as you are. The treasure is the same
except that I may have understood it better than you, so that I
have it lying in gold, while you have it in a plain bit of cloth. Therefore just as we have the grace of Christ and all spiritual blessings
in common, so we should also have body and life, property and
honor in common, so that one serves the other with all things.

Now Peter speaks clearly of sincere brotherly love. The apostles
like to use this little word. They undoubtedly saw that we would
call one another Christians and brothers, but that this would be
false, colored, feigned, and nothing but hypocrisy. We have
established many brotherhoods in the world; but they are sheer
humbug and deception invented and brought into the world by
the devil.[30] They are antagonistic to true faith and genuine brotherly love. Christ belongs to me as well as to St. Bernard. He belongs
to you as well as to St. Francis. If someone comes along and says
that I will go to heaven if I am a member of this or that brotherhood,
tell him: "That is a lie! For Christ cannot put up with it. He wants
no other brotherhood than the one we all have in common. So you
come along, you fool, and want to establish your own brotherhood."
Of course, I would sanction the establishment of a brotherhood
which did not propose to help the soul but represented an agreement on the part of some to contribute to a fund from which those
who needed it would be helped.

Thus in Baptism we Christians have all obtained one brotherhood. From this no saint has more than I and you. For I have been

---

[29] Luther is thinking particularly of Rom. 12:9-10 and 2 Peter 1:7 (cf. p. 157).
[30] On "brotherhoods" cf. *Luther's Works*, 35, p. 67, note 41.

bought with just as high a price as he has been bought. God has spent just as much on me as He has spent on the greatest saint. The only difference is that the saint may have grasped the treasure better and may have a stronger faith than I have.

Love, however, is greater than brotherhood; for it extends also to enemies, and particularly to those who are not worthy of love. For just as faith is active where it sees nothing, so love should also not see anything and do its work chiefly where nothing lovable but only aversion and hostility is seen. Where there is nothing that pleases me, I must put up with it for this very reason. And this, says St. Peter, should be done fervently and with all one's heart, just as God loved us when we were unworthy of love. Now Peter continues:

You have been born anew.

In the third place, this should be done because you are no longer what you formerly were, he says, but are new persons. Works have not brought this about, but for it a birth has been required. For you cannot make the new man. No, he must grow or be born. Just as a carpenter cannot make a tree, but the tree itself must grow out of the earth, and just as we all were not made children of Adam but were born as such and have inherited sin from our father and mother, so we cannot become children of God by means of works but must be born again. This is what the apostle wants to say: Since you are now new creatures, you must also conduct yourselves differently now and lead a new life. Just as you formerly lived in hatred, so you must now walk in love, contradictory in every respect. But how did the new birth come about? In the following way:

Not of perishable seed but of imperishable, through the living and abiding Word of God.

We have been born anew through a seed. For, as we see, the only way anything grows is through a seed. Now if the old birth originated from a seed, the new birth must also be from a seed. But what is the seed? Not flesh and blood. What then? It is not perishable, but it is an eternal Word. This is everything from which we live put together, food and nourishment. But it is chiefly the seed from which we are born anew, as the apostle says here.

How does this take place? In the following way: God lets the Word, the Gospel, go forth. He causes the seed to fall into the hearts of men. Now where it takes root in the heart, the Holy Spirit is present and creates a new man. There an entirely new man comes into being, other thoughts, other words and works. Thus you are completely changed. Now you seek everything from which you formerly fled; and what you formerly sought, that you flee. Physical birth takes place in the following way: When man has received the seed, the seed is changed, so that it is no longer seed. But this is a seed that cannot be changed; it remains eternally. But it changes me in such a way that I am changed into it and what evil there is in me because of my nature disappears completely. Therefore this is an extraordinary birth—a birth from an unusual seed. Now St. Peter continues:

All flesh is like grass and all its glory like the flower of the grass. The grass withers, and the flower falls, but the Word of the Lord abides forever.

This verse is taken from Is. 40:6-8, where the prophet says: "A voice says: 'Cry!' And I said: 'What shall I cry?' All flesh is grass, and all its beauty is like the flower of the field. The grass withers, the flower fades, but the Word of our God will stand forever." These are the words quoted here by St. Peter. For, as I have said,[31] this is a rich epistle and one that is well interlarded with Scripture passages. Thus Scripture now says that God's Word abides forever. That which is flesh and blood is as perishable as grass, even though it is young and therefore flourishing. When it is rich, powerful, clever, pious, and therefore flourishing—all this pertains to the flower—the flower nonetheless begins to wither. What is young and beautiful becomes old and ugly. What is rich becomes poor, etc. Everything has to perish through the Word of God. But this seed cannot pass away.

Now St. Peter finishes:

That Word is the good news which was preached to you.

It is as though the apostle were saying: You need not open your eyes wide when you come to the Word of God. You have it before

---

[31] Cf. pp. 18–21.

your eyes. It is the Word which we are preaching. With it you can subdue all evil lusts. You need not search far. Do no more than take hold of it when it is preached. For it is so near that one can hear it, as Moses also says in Deut. 30:11-14: "For this commandment which I command you this day is not too hard for you, neither is it far off. It is not in heaven; neither is it beyond the sea. But the Word is very near to you; it is in your mouth and in your heart." To be sure, it is quickly spoken and heard; but when it enters the heart, it cannot die or pass away. Nor does it let you die. It holds you as long as you cling to it. Thus when I hear that Jesus Christ died, took away my sin, gained heaven for me, and gave me all that He has, I am hearing the Gospel. The Word is soon gone when it is preached; but when it falls into the heart and is grasped by faith, it can never slip away. No creature can invalidate this truth. The depths of hell can do nothing against it; and even if I am already in the jaws of the devil, I must come out and remain where the Word remains, if I can take hold of it. Therefore St. Peter says with good reason that you need not look for anything else than what we have preached.

St. Paul also says in Rom 1:16: "I am not ashamed of the Gospel; it is the power of God for salvation to everyone who has faith." The Word is a divine and eternal power; for although the voice or speech soon fades away, yet the core remains, that is, the meaning, the truth expressed with the voice. Thus when I put a cup of wine to my lips, I drink the wine even though I do not force the cup down my throat along with the wine. Thus the Word which the voice speaks enters the heart and comes to life even though the voice remains outside and passes away. Therefore it is surely a divine power. Indeed, it is God Himself. For thus God says to Moses in Ex. 4:12: "I will be with your mouth." And in Ps. 81:10 He says: "Open your mouth wide"; that is, "Preach boldly. Speak out, be hungry; I will fill you. I will be present there and say enough." Thus Christ says in John 14:6: "I am the Way and the Truth and the Life." He who clings to this is born of God (cf. 1 John 5:1). Thus the seed is our Lord God Himself. All this points out that we cannot be helped with works. Although the Word is unimposing and seems to be nothing while it proceeds from the mouth, yet there is such boundless power in it that it makes all who cleave to it children of God, as John 1:12 says. It is on such a precious blessing that our salvation rests.

This is the first chapter of this epistle. In it you see how master-fully St. Peter preaches faith and treats of it. Hence one sees clearly that this epistle is the true Gospel.[32] Now the second chapter follows. It will teach us how we should conduct ourselves toward our neighbor so far as deeds are concerned.

[32] Cf. p. 4.

CHAPTER TWO

1. *So put away all malice and all guile and insincerity and envy and all slander.*

2. *Like newborn babes, long for the pure spiritual milk, that by it you may grow up to salvation;*

3. *for you have tasted the kindness of the Lord.*

4. *Come to Him, to that Living Stone, rejected by men but in God's sight chosen and precious;*

5. *and like living stones be yourselves built into a spiritual house, to be a holy priesthood, to offer spiritual sacrifices acceptable to God through Jesus Christ.*

Here the apostle begins to teach us what the works and fruits of a Christian life should be. For we have said often enough that a Christian life is composed of two parts: faith in God and love toward one's neighbor.[1] Likewise, that the Christian faith is given in such a way that many evil lusts still remain in the flesh as long as we live, since there is no saint who is not in the flesh. But that which is in the flesh cannot be completely pure. Therefore St. Peter says: Be armed in such a way that you guard against sins which still cling to you, and that you constantly fight against them. For our worst foes are in our bosom and in our flesh and blood. They wake, sleep, and live with us like an evil guest whom we have invited to our house and cannot get rid of. Therefore since the Lord Christ is now completely yours through faith, and you have received salvation and all His blessings, you must henceforth let it be your concern to cast off all wickedness, or all that is evil, and all guile. This means that no one should deal unfaithfully and falsely with the other person. The world has a proverb which says: "The world is full of perfidy." This is true. But we Christians must deal

---

[1] See, for example, *Luther's Works*, 31, pp. 364–368 and passim.

uprightly and with purity of heart, not perfidiously, with people as well as with God, fair and square,[2] so that no one overreaches the other person in selling, buying, or promising, and the like.

Thus St. Paul also says in Eph. 4:25: "Therefore putting away falsehood, let everyone speak the truth with his neighbor." It is the truth when yes means yes and no means no. But it is hypocrisy when the outward bearing belies one's thoughts. For it is important to behave according to what is in the heart. A Christian must act in such a way that he can let everybody see and know what he thinks in his heart. In all his behavior and in everything he does he must think only of praising God and serving his neighbor. He should fear no one. And at heart everyone should be what he appears to be. He should not resort to dissimulation and in this way cause people to gape.

Furthermore, St. Peter says that we must put away envy and slander. Here he strikes a telling blow at the common vices that are prevalent among people in their dealings with one another. Slander is very common and reckless. Since people are quick to engage in slander, no one becomes aware of it. Therefore guard against it, says St. Peter, even though you are spiritual and know what the fruits of the Spirit are.

Like newborn babes, long for the pure spiritual milk.

Here the apostle employs an analogy. He wants to say: Through the Word of God you are now born anew. Therefore conduct yourselves like newborn babes, who seek nothing else than milk. Just as they long for the breasts and milk, so you, too, should yearn for the Word, strive for it, and have a liking for it, in order that you may imbibe the pure spiritual milk.

These, too, are figurative words. For the apostle has neither physical milk nor physical longing in mind, just as he is also not speaking of a physical birth. No, he is speaking of another milk, that is, a spiritual milk which is taken with the soul and which the heart must imbibe. This milk must be unadulterated. It must not be like the false commodity that is usually sold. It is truly very important and decidedly necessary to give the newborn young Christians milk that is pure and unadulterated. But the milk is nothing but the Gospel, which is also the very seed by which we

[2] Luther's words are *schlecht und recht.*

were conceived and born, as we heard above.[3] This is also the food that nourishes us when we grow up; it is the armor which we put on and with which we equip ourselves. Yes, it is everything put together. But the admixture is the human doctrines with which the Word of God is adulterated. Consequently, the Holy Spirit wants every Christian to see what kind of milk he drinks; he himself must learn what to think of all teachings.

But the breasts which give this milk and which the babes suck are the preachers in Christendom, as the groom says to the bride in Song of Sol. 4:5:[4] "Your two breasts are like two fawns." They should have a bag of myrrh hanging around them, as the bride says in Song of Sol. 1:13: "My beloved is to me a bag of myrrh that lies between my breasts." This means that one must always preach Christ. The groom must constantly be between the breasts. Otherwise things are not as they should be. The milk is adulterated if anything but Christ is preached.

This is what happens: When one preaches that Christ died for us and rescued us from sin, death, and hell, this is pleasing and sweet like milk. But then one must also preach the cross, so that one suffers as Christ did. This is a strong potion and strong wine. Therefore one must give Christians the softest food first, that is, the milk. For one cannot preach better to them than one can do by first preaching Christ alone. He is not bitter. No, He is nothing but sweet, fat grace. Here you need not yet suffer any pains at all. This is the true, pure, and unadulterated milk.

And here St. Peter has again delved extensively in Scripture, just as he has a very rich fund of Scripture passages. In the Old Testament the following words are recorded in Ex. 23:19 and in Deut. 14:21: "You shall not boil a kid while it is still at its mother's milk." My dear friend, why did God have this committed to writing? Of what importance is it to Him that no kid be slaughtered while it is still sucking milk? Because He wants to state the same thing St. Peter teaches here. He means: Preach gently to the young and weak Christians. Let them enrich themselves and grow fat in the knowledge of Christ. Do not burden them with strong doctrine, for they are still too young. But later, when they grow strong, let them be slaughtered and sacrificed on the cross.

Thus we also read in Deut. 24:5 that if a man was newly married,

---

[3] Cf. pp. 43–44.

[4] The original has "Song of Solomon 3."

he was not allowed to go out with the army during the first year, lest he be killed. He was to be happy at home with his wife. All this means that to those who are still young Christians one must give time and that one must deal gently with them. When they are grown up, God leads them to the sacred cross and also lets them die like the other Christians. Then the kid is slaughtered.

Now Peter continues:

That by it you may grow up to salvation; for you have tasted the kindness of the Lord.

It is not enough to hear the Gospel once; one must study it constantly, in order that we may grow up. Then, when faith is strong, one must provide for and feed everyone. But this is not said to those who have never heard the Gospel; they know neither what is milk nor what is wine. Therefore St. Peter adds: "For you have tasted the kindness of the Lord." It is as if he were saying: It does not touch the heart of him who has not tasted it; to him it is not sweet. But those who have tried it—they always eat this food and busy themselves with the Word. To them it tastes right; to them it is sweet.

But to have tasted means when I believe in my heart that Christ gave Himself to me and became my own, that my sin and my misery are His, and that His life is now mine. If this goes to the heart, then one relishes it. For how could I not derive joy and delight from it? Surely I rejoice heartily if a good friend gives me 100 guldens. But he whose heart is not touched by this cannot rejoice over it. But those who are lying in the throes of death or are oppressed by an evil conscience relish it most. Then hunger is a good cook, as the saying goes. It makes the food taste good, for the heart and the conscience can hear nothing more delightful. When they feel their misery, they long for this food; they smell the roast from afar and cannot be satisfied. Thus Mary says in the *Magnificat:* "He has filled the hungry with good things" (Luke 1:53). But those hardened people who live in their own holiness, rely on their works, and do not feel their sin and misery—they do not relish it. Everything tastes good to him who sits at table and is hungry. But he who is sated beforehand relishes nothing; to him the very best food gives gray hair. Therefore the apostle says: "For you have tasted the kindness of the Lord." It is as if he were saying: "If you have not tasted it, I am preaching in vain."

He continues:

Come to Him, to that Living Stone.

Here he again reaches back into Scripture and quotes from the prophet Isaiah, who says in chapter 28:14-16: "Therefore hear the Word of the Lord, you scoffers . . . you have said: 'We have made a covenant with death, and with Sheol we have an agreement. . . . We have made lies our refuge. . . .' Therefore thus says the Lord God: 'Behold, I am laying in Zion for a foundation a Stone . . . a precious Cornerstone, of a sure foundation, etc.'" St. Paul cites this verse too (Rom. 9:33). It is also an exceedingly important Scripture passage. For Christ is the precious Cornerstone on which we must be built.

And look how St. Peter takes these words and applies them to Christ. Then what Isaiah says about putting one's trust in Him means, as St. Peter states, to build on Him. This is the proper interpretation of Scripture. The builders place the cornerstone where it lies firmly and securely, so that it can support the entire structure. Thus the Living Stone, which is Christ, supports the whole building. To build, therefore, means that we all intertwine our trust and confidence and put them in Him.

Rejected by men but in God's ˈsight chosen and precious.

Here the apostle quotes a statement made by the prophet David in Ps. 118:22-23: "The Stone which the builders rejected has become the chief Cornerstone. . . . It is marvelous in our eyes." Christ, too, cites this statement in Matt. 21:42. Likewise Peter in Acts 4:11, where he says: "This is the Stone which was rejected by you builders." You are builders, he says. For they taught the people, delivered long sermons, and issued many laws; but they produced only work-righteous people and hypocrites. So Christ comes along and says (Matt. 23:33): "You are hypocrites and a brood of vipers!" He passes many terrible judgments on them and associates with the sinners, not with the great saints. This they cannot bear. They even reject Him and say: "You are a heretic! Do you forbid people to perform good works? Ah, you must die!" This is why Peter says here: This is the Cornerstone which is rejected in this way by men—the Cornerstone on which you must be built through faith. This is now marvelous in our eyes, as the prophet declares (Ps. 118:23). It seems strange to us, and if the Spirit does not teach it, one nowise understands it. Therefore Peter says that this Stone is chosen and precious in God's sight, that it is a select, precious Stone powerful enough to remove death, pay for sin, rescue from hell, and, in addition, to give the kingdom of heaven.

And like living stones be yourselves built into a spiritual house.

How can we build ourselves? Through the Gospel and preaching. The preachers are the builders. The Christians, who hear the Gospel, are those who are built and the stones one must join to this Cornerstone, so that we place our confidence in Him and our hearts rest and repose on Him. Then I must also be prepared to retain the form of this Stone; for if I am placed on Him through faith, I and everyone with me must do the kind of works He did and lead the kind of life He led. It is now a fruit of faith and a work of love that we all should accommodate ourselves to one another and become one building. Thus St. Paul also speaks of this, although in another way, when he says in 1 Cor. 3:16: "Do you not know that you are God's temple?" The house of stone or wood is not His house. He wants to have a spiritual building, that is, the Christian congregation, in which we are all equal in one faith, one like the other, and are all placed and fitted on one another and joined together through love without malice, guile, hypocrisy, hatred, and slander, as the apostle has said.

To be a holy priesthood.

Here He has abolished both the external, physical priesthood and the external church which existed previously in the Old Testament. All this He takes away and wants to say: All the externals of the priesthood have now come to an end. Therefore another priesthood begins and offers other sacrifices. This means that everything is spiritual. We have argued extensively that those who are called priests today are not priests in the sight of God. And we have substantiated this with what Peter says here.[5] Therefore understand it well, and if someone comes along and wants to explain it—as

[5] For example, Luther had quoted 1 Peter 2:9 in support of his doctrine of the universal priesthood in *The Freedom of a Christian, Luther's Works,* 31, p. 354.

[W, XII, 307, 308]

some have done — by saying that Peter is speaking about a twofold priesthood, namely, about external and spiritual priests,[6] then ask him to put spectacles on to be able to see and take hellebore to sweep out his brain. St. Peter says: Be yourselves built to be a spiritual or holy priesthood. Now ask those priests whether they, too, are holy. Their life shows, as one sees, that the wretched people are up to the ears in greed, whoring, and vices of all kinds. He who has the priesthood must, of course, be holy; but he who is not holy does not have it. Therefore St. Peter is speaking here of only one priesthood.

We ask further whether St. Peter is differentiating between spiritual and secular, as today one calls the priests the clergy[7] and the other Christians the laity. They must admit against their will that here St. Peter is addressing all those who are Christians, namely, those who put away all malice, guile, hypocrisy, hatred, etc., who are like newborn babes and drink the unadulterated milk. Thus the lie must overreach itself.[8] Therefore this is certain: Since St. Peter is addressing all those who are Christians, it is evident that they are lying and that he is not saying anything about their priesthood, which they have fabricated and which they apply to themselves alone. Consequently, our bishops are nothing but St. Nicholas' bishops;[9] and their laws, sacrifices, and works are just like their priesthood. This would be fine sport for Shrove Tuesday, except that God's name is blasphemed under the mask.

Thus only those are the holy and spiritual priesthood who are true Christians and are built on the Stone. For since Christ is the Groom and we are the bride, the bride has everything that the Groom has, even His own body. When He gives Himself to the bride, He gives Himself entirely as what He is; and the bride, in turn, also gives herself to Him. Now Christ is the High and Chief Priest anointed by God Himself. He also sacrificed His own body for us, which is the highest function of the priestly office. Then He

[6] This distinction had been urged by Luther's antagonist Jerome Emser; cf. *Luther's Works*, 40, p. 22.

[7] The German word "spiritual" *(geistlich)* was, and still is, used as both an adjective and a noun for the clergy.

[8] Luther's sentence, which is certainly colloquial and probably proverbial, is *Also muss sich die lügen selbs yns maull beyssen.*

[9] A "St. Nicholas' bishop" was "a boy bishop elected by choirboys or scholars on St. Nicholas' Eve (Dec. 5)," *Oxford English Dictionary*, VII, 129.

prayed for us on the cross. In the third place, He also proclaimed the Gospel and taught all men to know God and Him Himself. These three offices He also gave to all of us. Consequently, since He is the Priest and we are His brothers, all Christians have the authority, the command, and the obligation to preach, to come before God, to pray for one another, and to offer themselves as a sacrifice to God. Nevertheless, no one should undertake to preach or to declare the Word of God unless he is a priest.

To offer spiritual sacrifices acceptable to God through Jesus Christ.

A spiritual sacrifice is not money contributed as a sacrifice to the pope. Nor is it, as in the Old Testament, the obligatory sacrificing of the tenth part of everything. Such physical sacrifices and such a priesthood have all ceased now. Today everything is new and spiritual. Christ is the Priest, and we are all priests. Just as He sacrificed His body, so we, too, must sacrifice ourselves. Here everything foreshadowed by the external sacrifices as they took place in the Old Testament is now fulfilled. Briefly stated, all this means that the Gospel is preached. He who preaches the Gospel practices and does all this. He slaughters the calf, namely, the carnal mind; he strangles the old Adam. For one must slay with the Gospel what is irrational in the flesh and blood. Then we let ourselves be sacrificed and put to death on the cross. The true priestly office is practiced when we sacrifice that villainous rogue, the lazy old ass, to God. If the world does not do this, we must do it ourselves; for in the end we must put aside every vestige of the old Adam, as we heard above in the first chapter.[10] This is the only sacrifice that is acceptable and pleasing to God. From this you can now see where our fools and blind leaders have taken us and how this text has been neglected.

Now you might say: "What kind of situation will arise if it is true that we are all priests and should all preach? Should no distinction be made among the people, and should the women, too, be priests?" Answer: In the New Testament no priest has to be tonsured. Not that this is evil in itself, for one surely has the right to have the head shaved clean. But one should not make a distinction between those who do so and the common Christian. Faith cannot

---

[10] Cf. p. 40

tolerate this. Thus those who are now called priests would all be laymen like the others, and only a few officiants would be elected by the congregation to do the preaching. Thus there is only an external difference because of the office to which one is called by the congregation. Before God, however there is no distinction, and only a few are selected from the whole group to administer the office in the stead of the congregation. They all have this office, but nobody has any more authority than the other person has. Therefore nobody should come forward of his own accord and preach in the congregation. No, one person must be chosen from the whole group and appointed. If desired, he may be deposed.[11]

Now those people have created a special estate and say that it was established by God. They have acquired such freedom that almost in the midst of Christendom there is a greater distinction than there is between us and Turks. As St. Paul says in Gal. 3:28, you must pay no attention to distinctions when you want to look at Christians. You must not say: "This is a man or a woman; this is a servant or a master; this person is old or young." They are all alike and only a spiritual people. Therefore they are all priests. All may proclaim God's Word, except that, as St. Paul teaches in 1 Cor. 14:34, women should not speak in the congregation. They should let the men preach, because God commands them to be obedient to their husbands. God does not interfere with the arrangement. But He makes no distinction in the matter of authority. If, however, only women were present and no men, as in nunneries, then one of the women might be authorized to preach.

This is the true priesthood. As we have heard, it embraces these three things: to offer spiritual sacrifices, to pray for the congregation, and to preach. He who can do this is a priest. They are all obliged to preach the Word, to pray for the congregation, and to sacrifice themselves before God. Let those fools go their way who call the spiritual estate "priests," who, after all, exercise no other office than being tonsured and anointed. If shaving the head and anointing made one a priest, I could even oil and anoint the hoofs of an ass and make him a priest too.

Finally St. Peter says that we must offer up spiritual sacrifices that are acceptable to God through Jesus Christ. Since Christ is the Cornerstone on whom we are built, all our dealings with God

[11] See Luther's specific suggestions from about this same time, *Luther's Works*, 40, pp. 40–42.

must be carried on through Him, as we have heard exhaustively above.[12] Otherwise God would not regard my cross, even if I tortured myself to death. But He does regard Christ. Through Him my works have validity before God. Otherwise they would not be worth a blade of straw. Therefore Scripture fittingly calls Christ a precious Cornerstone who imparts His virtues to all who are built on Him through faith. Thus in the verse which speaks of Christ as the Living Stone, St. Peter teaches us what Christ is. This is a fine figure of speech from which one can readily understand how one should believe in Christ. Now the text continues:

6. *For it stands in Scripture: Behold, I am laying in Zion a Stone, a Cornerstone chosen and precious, and he who believes in Him will not be put to shame.*

7. *To you therefore who believe, He is precious, but for those who do not believe, The very Stone which the builders rejected has become the Head of the corner,*

8. *and A Stone that will make men stumble, a Rock that will make them fall; for they stumble because they disobey the Word, as they were destined to do.*

9. *But you are a chosen race, a royal priesthood, a holy nation, God's own people, that you may declare the wonderful deeds of Him who called you out of darkness into His marvelous light.*

10. *Once you were no people, but now you are God's people; once you had not received mercy, but now you have received mercy.*

I have stated before that St. Peter interlards and protects his epistle well with Scripture passages, as all preachers should do, in order that they may be fully founded on God's Word.[13] Thus here the apostle quotes four or five verses consecutively. The first he has taken verbatim from the prophet Isaiah (28:16), where it is stated that Christ is "a precious Cornerstone, of a sure foundation." It is the very same verse we have just discussed and have explained to some extent. It is truly a cardinal statement of the doctrine of

[12] Cf. p. 29.
[13] See, for example, p. 44.

faith, which should be the foundation if someone wanted to preach
where Christ had not been preached before. For one must begin
with the fact that Christ is the Stone on which faith must be built
and must stand.

But the words that follow—"He who believes in Him will not
be put to shame"—show that the prophet is not speaking of a
physical stone. If I am to believe in Him, this must be a spiritual
Stone; for how can I believe in stone and wood? Furthermore, He
must be true God, since in the First Commandment God has forbidden belief in anything but Him alone. Because the Stone is
laid as the foundation on which we should trust, this must be God
Himself. On the other hand, He cannot be God alone but must at
the same time be man, because He must be part of the building,
and not only a part but also the Head. Now when one constructs
a building, one stone must be like the other, so that every stone
has the character, nature, and form of the other. Therefore since
we are built on Christ, He must be like us and of the very same
nature as the other stones that rest on Him, namely, a true man
as we all are. Thus Scripture expresses such great things with
simple and plain words, namely, the sum and substance of our
faith. In such brief statements it includes more than any man can
express.

Now I have also stated what the building is.[14] It is faith. Through
faith we are placed on Christ, put our trust in this Stone, and thus
become like Him. And this must take place in such a way that the
building fits together; for the other stones must all be adjusted and
arranged according to this Stone. This is love, a fruit of faith.

But why does the prophet call Christ a Stone "of a sure foundation"? Because no building can be erected unless such a stone
is first put in place, for the other stones that go into the building
are not stable unless they rest on a stone of this kind. Thus we
must all be founded on Christ, and we must acknowledge Him as
a Stone "of a sure foundation." Then we cannot boast that this
Stone must take anything from us, but we must receive benefit
from Him alone. For we do not bear Him, but He bears us. Sin,
death, hell, and everything we have lie on Him, so that all this
and whatever happens to us cannot harm us if we are placed on
this Foundation. For if we remain this way on Him and trust in

[14] Cf. p. 52.

Him, we must also remain where He is, just as natural stones must be dependent on their foundation stone.

Besides, the prophet also calls Christ a "Cornerstone." The Holy Spirit has a way of saying a great deal in a few words. Christ is a Cornerstone because He brought the Gentiles and the Jews, who were mortal enemies, together. Thus the Christian Church was gathered from both. The apostle Paul writes extensively about this (cf. Eph. 2:19-22). The Jews gloried in the Law of God, boasted that they were God's people, and despised the Gentiles. But now Christ appeared, deprived the Jews of their glory, and also summoned us Gentiles. Thus He made us both one through one faith and dealt with us in such a manner that we must both confess that we have nothing of ourselves but are all sinners, that we must expect piety and heaven from Him alone, and that we Gentiles hold that Christ came to save us as well as the Jews. Therefore He is the Cornerstone who joins two walls together, the Jews and the Gentiles, so that one building and one house results.

Now the prophet concludes as follows: "He who believes in Him will not be put to shame." By saying that those who believe in Christ are not put to shame the Holy Spirit tells us what He has in mind, namely, that He has already pronounced judgment and has decided that the whole world must be put to shame and made to blush. Yet He wants to except some from the great multitude. Only those who believe in Christ can escape the shame. This is the way Christ Himself explains it in Mark 16:16 when he says: "He who believes and is baptized will be saved; but he who does not believe will be condemned." These words agree with what the prophet says here. Therefore Peter has aptly stated in the first chapter of this epistle that the prophets "searched and inquired about this salvation" (v. 10) and prophesied concerning the future grace. Thus one should now proclaim that it was Christ who delivered us from this shame in which we all were.

Now let him who wants to do so step forth to praise free will and defend the powers of man. If you want to invalidate all the works of man, everything he teaches, and whatever owes its origin to him, you have enough in this verse alone. It knocks all this to the ground, so that it has to fall as dry leaves drop from a tree. For it is ordained that what does not rest on this Stone is already lost. Any desire on your part to accomplish anything with works is intolerable to Him. The Spirit and the Divine Majesty speak so simply that no one pays heed, yet the words are so powerful that they knock everything to the ground. Who will act contrary to this, or who will not be frightened by it? Therefore God wants us to despair completely of ourselves, to boast only of His goods, and to build on the foundation which no creature can upset. No one should rely on his own piety, but one should trust only in Christ's righteousness and in everything Christ has. But what does reliance on His righteousness mean? Nothing else than that I despair of myself and remember that my righteousness and my truth must collapse and that I depend on the eternal existence of His righteousness, His life, His truth and all His goods. That is the foundation on which I stand. Everything that does not rest on this foundation will have to fall. But only he who relies on it will not be put to shame; he will remain, and no power can harm him. Therefore Christ should not only be a Stone, but God also wants to make Him the Foundation. With this we should comfort ourselves. God has said it. He will not be able to lie.

Now this Stone does not serve itself, but it lets itself be trampled on and buried in the ground, so that one does not see it. The other stones rest on it and are visible. Therefore He has been given to us in order that we should take from Him, rely on Him, and believe that all He has is ours, that all He can do has been done for our benefit, so that I can say: "This is my own possession and treasure with which my conscience can comfort itself." Now St. Peter continues:

> *To you therefore who believe, He is precious, but for those who do not believe, The very Stone which the builders rejected has become the Head of the corner, and A Stone that will make men stumble, a Rock that will make them fall.*

To be sure, says Peter, the good and precious Stone is precious and honorable to some. On the other hand, many do not regard It as precious but look upon It as offensive and as a Stone over which one stumbles. How does this happen? Scripture speaks about It in two ways, namely, that some believe in It and, on the other hand, that many do not believe. To those who believe, It is precious. My heart must rejoice when I put my trust and comfort in It. Therefore the apostle says: "To you therefore who believe, He is precious." This means that you hold Him in high esteem. For even though He is precious and good in Himself, this does not profit me and does not help me. Therefore He must be precious to us by bestowing many precious goods on us, like a precious gem which does not keep its power to itself but breaks forth and radiates all its power, so that I have everything it is.

The unbelievers, however, do not regard Christ as such a precious Stone. No, they reject Him and are offended by Him. Therefore He is not a source of comfort to them but is harmful and offensive, even though in Himself He is comforting. These are not only the gross public sinners but rather the great saints, who rely on their free will, on their works and piety. They must run into and collide with this Stone. Here God decrees that those who enter without works will come to righteousness solely through faith. But the others do not attain this; for, as St. Paul says in Rom. 10:3, they want to acquire it through their own piety.

St. Peter says that this has become "the very Stone which the builders rejected." Here he condenses Scripture, but he quotes the passage from Ps. 118:22 to which he referred above: "The Stone which the builders rejected has become the chief Cornerstone." I have explained sufficiently who the builders are. They are those who teach, preach the Law, and want to make people pious through works. They agree with Christ as winter and summer agree. Therefore the preachers who preach about works must reject this Stone.

Moreover, the apostle takes another statement, one from the prophet Isaiah, who wrote in chapter 8:13-14 that what St. Peter says here would happen. The prophet says: "Let Him [the Lord of hosts] be your fear, and let Him be your dread. And He will become a sanctuary, and a stone of offense, and a rock of stumbling to both houses of Israel." This is what the prophet means: The Lord shall become a sanctuary unto you, that is, He shall be sanctified in your hearts. You need have no other holiness, neither this nor that, except that you believe. To the others He will be a Stone of stumbling and of offense.

But what is meant by offense and colliding or stumbling? This is what is meant: When one preaches Christ and says: "Behold, this Stone is placed as a foundation in order that you may despair completely of yourself and lose heart, regard your own works and piety as something altogether damnable, rely solely on Him, and believe that Christ's righteousness is your righteousness." When those people hear this, they recoil, stumble, and are offended. They say:

"What? Do you mean to say that chastity, celebrating Mass, and similar good works amount to nothing? The devil tells you to say this." They cannot adjust themselves to the thought that what they undertake to do is not good, but they think that it is pleasing to God. They even quote passages from Scripture and say: "God has commanded us to do good works." When one chooses to refute them, they begin to shout: "Heretic! Heretic! Fire! Fire!" Therefore they cannot endure the Stone and want to overturn It. Thus they collide with this Stone and cannot avoid being crushed by It, as Christ says in Matt. 21:42, 44: "Have you never read in the Scriptures: 'The very Stone which the builders rejected has become the Head of the corner?' . . . And he who falls on this Stone will be broken to pieces; but when It falls on anyone, It will crush him." Therefore do as you please, this Stone is no joke. It has been laid, and It will remain in position. He who wants to collide with It and scoff at It will have to cave in.

This is the stumbling and the offense about which Scripture says a great deal. Thus the Jews stumble over this Stone to this day, and they will continue to do so until the Last Day comes. Then this Stone will fall on all unbelievers and crush them. Therefore even though Christ is such a choice and precious Stone, yet through no fault of His He must also be called "a Stone that will make men stumble, a Rock that will make them fall." And just as the Jews have done, so we also always do today. For just as they boasted with God's name that they were God's people, so it happens today too. Christ is denied today under the name of Christ and the Christian Church, and the precious Stone is rejected. He comes because they should reject their works. But this they cannot endure, and they reject Him. Therefore the apostle continues:

For they stumble because they disobey the Word, as they were destined to do.

When one says that their works are not good and have no validity before God, they can and will not hear this. Now God made Christ the Foundation on which they should be laid and through whom they should derive all bliss. He has let Him be proclaimed to the whole world in order that through the preaching of the Gospel they might be founded on Him. But they refuse to accept Him; they reject Him and persist in their notion and works. For if they let themselves be placed on Him, their honor, riches, and power would topple, so that one would no longer lift them up.

St. Peter goes on:

> *But you are a chosen race, a royal priesthood, a holy nation, God's own people.*

Here the apostle gives the Christians a proper title. He took this statement from Moses, who tells the Jews in Deut. 7:6: "You are a people holy to the Lord your God; the Lord your God has chosen you to be a people for His own possession, out of all the peoples that are on the face of the earth." And in Ex. 19:5-6 we read: "You shall be My own possession among all peoples . . . and you shall be to Me a kingdom of priests and a holy nation." Here you see what Peter is speaking about. I repeat what I said earlier, namely, that one must become accustomed to the way Scripture is wont to speak about priests.[15] Let no one be concerned about those whom people call priests. Let everyone call them what they choose. You must remain with the pure Word of God. What it calls priests, you, too, must call priests. We will permit those whom the bishops and the pope consecrate to call themselves priests. They may call themselves what they choose, provided that they do not call themselves "priests of God"; for they cannot adduce a single word from Scripture in defense of this.

But if they come along with this verse and say that it is speaking to them, answer them as I taught above, and ask them to whom Peter is speaking here. Then they will have to confess the truth to their shame. For it is certainly clear and manifest enough that the apostle is addressing the whole multitude, all Christians, when he says: "You are a chosen race . . . a holy nation." Up to this point, of course, he has spoken about no one except those who are built on the Stone and believe. Therefore it must follow that he who does not believe is no priest. Then they say: "Ah, one must explain the words as the saintly fathers interpreted them!" Then you must say: "Let the fathers and teachers, whoever they may be, explain as they choose. This is what St. Peter tells me. He has greater testimony from God than they have. Besides, he is older. Therefore I will agree with him." Thus this verse requires no commentary; for it speaks explicitly of those who believe. Now not only those

---

[15] Cf. p. 53.

who are anointed and tonsured are believers. Therefore we are
willing to let them call themselves priests, for we do not care how
they want to be dubbed. No, the question at issue is whether they
are called priests in Scripture and whether God calls them priests.
Some can be selected from the congregation who are officeholders
and servants and are appointed to preach in the congregation and
to administer the sacraments. But we are all priests before God if
we are Christians. For since we have been laid on the Stone who
is the Chief Priest before God, we also have everything He has.

It would please me very much if this word "priest" were used
as commonly as the term "Christians" is applied to us. For priests,
the baptized, and Christians are all one and the same. For just as
I should not put up with it when those who have been anointed
and tonsured want to have exclusive right to the terms "Christians"
and "baptized," so I should also not put up with it when they alone
want to be called priests. Yet they have monopolized this title.
Thus they have called "the church" what the pope, together with
his pointed hats, decrees. But Scripture turns this around. Therefore note this well, in order that you may know how to differentiate
between those whom God calls priests and those who call themselves priests. For it must be our aim to restore the little word
"priests" to the common use which the little word "Christians"
enjoys. For to be a priest does not belong in the category of an
external office; it is exclusively the kind of office that has dealings
before God.

The same thing is true with regard to the fact that we are all
kings. "Priests" and "kings" are all spiritual names just as "Christians," "saints," and "church" are. And just as you are not called
a Christian because you have a great deal of money and property
but because you have been built on the Stone and believe in Christ,
so you are not called a priest because you are tonsured or wear
a long coat but because you may approach God. In like manner,
you are not a king because you wear a golden crown and have many
lands and people under you, but because you are a lord over all
things, death, sin, and hell. If you believe in Christ you are a king
just as He is a King. Now He is not a King after the manner of
earthly monarchs. He does not wear a golden crown. Nor does He
ride along with great pomp and many horses. No, He is a King
over all kings — a King who has power over all things and at whose

feet everything must lie. Just as He is a Lord, so I, too, am a lord. For what He has, that I, too, have.

Now someone may say: "St. Peter declares here, too, that the Christians also are kings. On the other hand, it is evident that we are not all kings. Therefore this verse cannot be understood to mean that he is speaking about all in general. For he who is a Christian is not a king in France or a priest in Rome." So I also ask now whether the king of France is also a king before God. This he concedes, for God will not judge according to the crown. To be sure, he is a king on earth and before the world; but when death comes, his rule has ended. Then he will have to lie at the feet of those who believe. We are speaking of an eternal kingdom and priesthood. Here every believer is truly a king before God. But who does not know that we are not all tonsured and anointed priests? The fact that those men are anointed does not make them priests before God. Thus they are not kings before God either because they have been crowned. Crowned kings and anointed priests belong in the world and have been made kings and priests by men. The pope may make as many priests of that kind as he pleases, provided that he does not make priests before God; for God wants to make these Himself.

Therefore when St. Peter says here: "You are a royal priesthood," this is tantamount to saying: "You are Christians." If you want to know what kind of title and what kind of power and praise Christians have, you see here that they are kings and priests and a chosen race. But what is the priestly office? The answer follows:

That you may declare the wonderful deeds of Him who called you out of darkness into His marvelous light.

A priest must be God's messenger and must have a command from God to proclaim His Word. You must, says Peter, exercise the chief function of a priest, that is, to proclaim the wonderful deed God has performed for you to bring you out of darkness into the light. And your preaching should be done in such a way that one brother proclaims the mighty deed of God to the other, how you have been delivered through Him from sin, hell, death, and all misfortune, and have been called to eternal life. Thus you should also teach other people how they, too, come into such light. For you must bend every effort to realize what God has done for you.

[W, XII, 319, 320]

Then let it be your chief work to proclaim this publicly and to call everyone into the light into which you have been called. Where you find people who do not know this, you should instruct and also teach them as you have learned, namely, how one must be saved through the power and strength of God and come out of darkness into the light.

And here you see that Peter states clearly that there is only one light and concludes that all our reason, no matter how clever, is utter darkness. For although reason can count one, two, three, can also see what is black or white, large and small, and can judge about outward things, yet it cannot see what faith is. Here it is stone-blind. And even if all men were to put all their wisdom together, they could not understand one letter of the divine wisdom. Therefore St. Peter is speaking here of another light, a light that is marvelous; and he tells us bluntly that we are all in darkness and in blindness if God does not call us into His true light.

Experience also teaches us this. For when one preaches that we cannot come before God with works, but that we must have a Mediator who could come before God and reconcile us to Him, then reason must admit that it could have absolutely no knowledge of this. Therefore it must have a different light and knowledge if it is to understand this. Consequently everything that is not God's Word and faith is darkness. For there reason gropes about like a blind man, always falls from one thing upon another, and does not know what it is doing. If we tell this to the learned and wise in the world, they do not want to hear it and begin to cry out and rage against it. Therefore St. Peter is truly a bold apostle. What everybody calls light he designates as darkness.

Thus we see that the first and foremost duty we Christians should perform is to proclaim the wonderful deeds of God. Now what are the wonderful deeds and the noble works God has done? They are the deeds and works we have often mentioned, namely, that by the power of God Christ has swallowed up death, devoured hell, drunk sin to the dregs, and placed us into eternal life. These are such great deeds that man cannot understand them, let alone perform them. Therefore it is completely useless to preach human doctrines to us Christians. No, one should preach to us about the kind of power that overcomes the devil, sin, and death. And here St. Peter has again referred to many Scripture passages, just as throughout his writings he nearly always quotes one verse after the other. For all the prophets say that God's name and honor, and His arm or power, should be honored and praised, and that He would perform a deed of which the whole world would sing and speak. The prophets are full of this everywhere. Here St. Peter points to all these places. Moreover, the prophets also said much about light and darkness. They said that we must be illumined with the light of God. In this way they also show that all human reason is darkness. St. Peter continues:

> *Once you were no people, but now you are God's people; once you had not received mercy, but now you have received mercy.*

This verse is found in Hos. 2:23. St. Paul also quoted it in Rom. 9:25, where he says: "Those who were not My people I will call My people." All this points to the fact that Almighty God chose the people of Israel in particular, conferred great honor on them, gave them many prophets, and also performed many miraculous deeds with them because He wanted Christ to become man from this nation. All this took place for the sake of the Child. For this reason they are called God's people in Scripture. But the prophets amplify this and said that this promise should become known and should also concern the Gentiles.

Therefore St. Peter says here: "Once you were no people, but now you are God's people." From this it is clear that he wrote the epistle to the Gentiles, not to the Jews. With these words he now wants to point out that the statement of the prophet has now been fulfilled, that they are now a holy nation, God's own people, the priesthood and kingdom, and that they have everything Christ has — provided that they believe. Thus we read further in Peter:

11. *Beloved, I beseech you as aliens and exiles to abstain from the passions of the flesh that wage war against your soul.*

12. *Maintain good conduct among the Gentiles, so that in case they speak against you as wrongdoers, they may see your good deeds and glorify God on the day of visitation.*

Here St. Peter's way of speaking is a little different from Saint Paul's. Paul would not speak this way, as we shall hear. For every apostle, just as every prophet, has his own way of speaking. So far

St. Peter has now properly laid his foundation of the Christian faith, with which the chapter deals. Now he continues and teaches how we should conduct ourselves toward all men. This is a proper way to preach: first to emphasize faith, what it does and what its power and nature are, namely, that it gives us enough of everything necessary for piety and salvation, that one can do nothing except through faith, and that through it we have everything God has. Now if God has dealt this way with us, has given us everything that is His, and has become our own, so that we have all blessings and enough of everything through faith, what are we to do now? Are we to be idle? To be sure, it would be best for us to die. Then all this would be ours. But since we are still living here, we should do for our neighbor as God has done us and give ourselves to him as God has given Himself to us. Thus it is faith that saves us. But it is love that prompts us to give ourselves to our neighbor, now that we have enough. That is, faith receives from God, love gives to the neighbor. This is a brief discussion of the subject. Of course, one can preach a great deal about it and amplify it, as St. Peter does here.

This is what the apostle means when he says: "Beloved, I beseech you as aliens and exiles." Since you are now one with Christ and wholly one cake,[16] since His goods are your goods, since what harms you harms Him, and since He cares about everything you have, therefore you should tread in His footsteps and conduct yourselves as though you were no longer citizens in the world; for your possessions are now in heaven and not on earth. Even though you have lost all your temporal goods, you still have Christ, and He is worth more than all that. The devil is a prince of the world, and he rules it; his citizens are the people of the world. Therefore since you are not of the world, you must act like a stranger in an inn who does not have his possessions there but only takes food and gives his money for it. For here there is only a stopover where we cannot remain. We must proceed on our journey. Therefore we should use temporal goods for no other purpose than clothing and food. Then we depart for another land. We are citizens in heaven; on earth we are pilgrims and guests.

I beseech you to abstain from the passions of the flesh that wage war against your soul.

16 Cf. *Luther's Works*, 23, p. 149, note 109.

It is not my purpose here to decide whether St. Peter is speaking of outward indecency, as St. Paul is wont to do. Paul calls everything carnal that physical and carnal man does without faith. But it is my opinion that St. Peter has a way of speaking that is a little different. Nor do I believe that Peter is using the little word "soul" in the sense of "spirit," as St. Paul does. No, Saint Peter, as I think, has conformed more to the common Greek language than St. Paul has done. But it is of no consequence whether one takes this word to mean all kinds of lusts or only carnal lust and indecency. Here, however, St. Peter wants to point out that no saint on earth can be wholly perfect and pure. The schools of higher learning have also trampled this verse underfoot. They do not understand it either. They think that it refers only to sinners, as though the saints no longer had any evil lust.[17] But he who studies Scripture properly must grasp a distinction, for the prophets occasionally speak of saints as though they were pure in every respect, and on the other hand, they speak of them as still having evil lust and as contending with sin. Those people cannot adjust themselves to these two facts. Therefore you must understand it to mean that Christians are divided into two parts: the inner being, which is faith, and the outer being, which is the flesh. Now when one looks at a Christian according to faith, he is pure and completely clean; for the Word of God finds no uncleanness in him. And when it enters the heart so that the heart clings to it, it must also make the heart completely clean. Therefore all things are perfect in faith. Accordingly, we are kings and priests, and God's people, as has been said above. But since faith is in the flesh and we are still dwelling on earth, we sometimes feel evil inclinations, such as impatience, fear of death, etc. All these are still weaknesses of the old man, for faith has not yet completely permeated him and still does not have full power over the flesh.

You can understand this from a parable in Luke 10:34ff. concerning the man who went down from Jerusalem to Jericho and fell among the murderers, who beat him and left him half-dead. Later the Samaritan attended to him, bound up his wounds, looked after him, and had him cared for. Here you see that since this man is now being cared for, he is no longer mortally ill but is now sure to live. Only one thing is lacking: he is not completely well. Life is there, but he does not yet have perfect health but is still in the

[17] On Luther's criticism of this exegesis cf. *Luther the Expositor*, pp. 75–77.

care of the physicians. He must continue to be cared for. Thus we also have the Lord Christ completely and are certain of eternal life. Nevertheless, we do not yet enjoy perfect health. Something of the old Adam still remains in the flesh.

A similar parable is recorded in Matt. 13:33. There Christ says: "The kingdom of heaven is like leaven which a woman took and hid in three measures of meal, till it was all leavened." When dough is prepared from flour, all the leaven is in it; but the leaven has not yet completely permeated the dough and has not worked through it. The flour has to be worked until it is leavened through and through. Now no more leaven should be added. Thus through faith you also have everything you should have to grasp the Word of God. But the Word has not yet penetrated completely. Therefore it must work until you are fully renewed. This is the way you should discern Scripture, lest you also distort it as the papists do.

Therefore I say: When one reads in Scripture about saints that they were perfect, you must understand this to mean that they were entirely pure and sinless according to faith. Nevertheless, the flesh was still present. It could not be wholly pure. For this reason Christians desire and pray that the body, or the flesh, be mortified in order that they may become completely pure. Those who teach differently have not felt or tasted this. Consequently, they speak as they think and understand with their reason. This makes error inevitable. Here indeed the great saints who taught and wrote a great deal stumbled. Origen does not have a single word about this in his books. Jerome never understood it. If it had not been necessary for Augustine to have so many controversies with the Pelagians, he, too, would have had little understanding of it. When they speak of saints, they eulogize them as though they were different from and better than other Christians, just as though the saints had not felt the flesh and complained about it as we do.

Therefore St. Peter says here: You are entirely pure and in full possession of righteousness. Therefore fight from now on against the evil lusts. Thus Christ also says in John 13:10: "He who has bathed does not need to wash, except for his feet." It is not enough that the head and the hands are clean. Therefore even·though Christ says that they are entirely clean, He still wants them to wash their feet.

But what does St. Peter mean when he says: "Abstain from the passions of the flesh that wage war against your soul"? This is what he wants to say: You dare not think that this will happen if you play and sleep. To be sure, sin has been removed through faith; yet you still have the flesh, which is foolish and furious. Therefore see that you suppress it. You will have to have strength to quell and subdue lust, and the greater your faith is, the greater the trials will be. Therefore you must be prepared and armed, and you must combat lusts without ceasing; for they will assail you with large numbers and try to take you captive.

For this reason St. Paul also says in Rom. 7:22-23: "I delight in the Law of God, in my inmost self; but I see in my members another law at war with the law of my mind and making me captive to the law of sin, so that I do what I do not want to do." It is as if he were saying: "To be sure, I struggle against it; but it refuses to stop. Therefore I would like to be rid of it, but this will not happen. My wishing does not help. What, then, shall I do?" And later (verse 24) he exclaims: "Wretched man that I am! Who will deliver me from this body of death?" All saints cry out this way. But those who do not have faith the devil leads in such a way that they just go along in their sins and follow them unconcernedly. "The others," the devil thinks, "I have already taken captive with unbelief. Now I will let them go along in such a way that they commit no gross sins and have no great trials. Thus I will cover up the abscess and the rascal." The believers, on the other hand, always have trials enough; they must wage war constantly. Those who are without faith and the Spirit do not feel this; or they fall behind, run away, and follow evil lust. But as soon as the Spirit and faith enter the heart, man becomes so feeble that he imagines that he cannot suppress the faintest thoughts and extinguish the smallest sparks. He sees nothing but sin in himself from the crown of his head to the soles of his feet. For before he believed, he went his way as he pleased. But now that the Spirit has come and wants to make him pure, the battle begins. Then the devil, the world, and the flesh assault the. faith. Throughout Scripture all the prophets also bemoan this.

Therefore St. Peter now says that the struggle takes place in the believers, not in sinners. And he also gives comfort by saying that we can fend off the evil lusts if only we resist them. Even if you have evil thoughts, you should not despair on this account. Only see to it that you are not taken captive by them. Our teachers wanted to help matters by saying that people should torture them-

[W. XII, 325, 326.

selves until they no longer had evil thoughts and finally became mad and insane. But if you are a Christian, you must learn that you will undoubtedly feel all kinds of trials and evil inclinations in your flesh. For if faith is present, a hundred more evil thoughts and a hundred more trials come than there were before. Only see to it that you are a man and do not let yourself be taken captive by them. Resist constantly, and say: "I will not! I will not!" For here things must go just as they go between an evil husband and an evil wife who constantly grumble against each other. The one does not want what the other wants.

Now a true Christian life is never at rest. This does not mean that one should feel no sin. Indeed, one should feel it. Only one should not yield to it. One should fast, pray, and work, in order to subdue and suppress lust. Therefore you dare not think that in this way you will become a saint, as those fools speak about this. As long as flesh and blood remain, so long sin also remains. Consequently, constant warfare is necessary. He who does not experience this dare not boast of being a Christian.

Formerly we were taught that if we had gone to confession or had entered a spiritual vocation, we were now completely pure and no longer had to wage war against sins. Furthermore, they also said that Baptism made one so clean and pure that no evil remained in a person. Then they thought: "Now I will be at peace." Then the devil came along and toppled them worse than before. Here, therefore, you must get a proper understanding. If you want to go to confession and be absolved, you must act like a soldier who takes the lead in battle when this is really important and the war begins. Now one must fight in earnest, just as though previously this had been sport. Now one must draw the sword and lay about with a vengeance. But there must be vigilance as long as the battle lasts. Thus even if you are baptized, you must realize that you are never safe from the devil and from sin. Indeed, you must remember that now you will have no peace. Thus the Christian life is nothing but a battle and a camp, as Scripture says. Therefore our Lord God is also *Dominus Sabaoth* (Ps. 24:10), that is, a Lord of hosts. Likewise, *Dominus potens in proelio*, "the Lord mighty in battle" (Ps. 24:8). He shows His might by letting His people wage war constantly and by letting them take the lead where the trumpets always sound. They must constantly remember to exclaim: "To the defense here! To the defense there! Thrust here! Strike there!" Thus this is an everlasting struggle, and you must do all you can to strike the devil down with the Word of God. Here one must always resist, call upon God, and despair of all human powers. We read on:

> *Maintain good conduct among the Gentiles, so that in case they speak against you as wrongdoers, they may see your good deeds and glorify God on the day of visitation.*

Look at the excellent sequence St. Peter observes here. He has just taught us what we should do to subdue our flesh with all its evil lusts. Now he also teaches us why this should be done. Why should I subdue my flesh? That I may be saved? No, but in order to maintain good conduct before the world. For good conduct does not make us pious, but we must be pious and believe before we begin to maintain good conduct. But I should not maintain this good conduct in my own interest; I must do so in order that the Gentiles may mend their ways and be attracted by it, that they may also come to Christ through us, which is a true work of love. They malign and chide us; they regard us as the worst scoundrels. Therefore we should exemplify such fine conduct that they have to say: "Ah, one can find no fault with them!"

We read that when the emperors reigned and persecuted the Christians, one could find no fault with the Christians except that they worshiped Christ and regarded Him as a god. Thus Pliny writes to the emperor Trajan that he knew of no wrong the Christians committed except that they assembled early every morning and sang some hymns of praise, with which they honored their Christ, and that they partook of the Sacrament. Otherwise no one could find any fault with them.[18] Therefore St. Peter now says: You must endure being spoken against as wrongdoers. Consequently, you must maintain such conduct that you harm no one. Then you will cause them to mend their ways. "On the day of visitation," that is, you must endure their chiding until it becomes manifest and is revealed how unjustly they have treated you, and they have to glorify God in you.

Now St. Peter continues:

13. *Be subject for the Lord's sake to every human institution, whether it be to the emperor as supreme,*

---

[18] Pliny, *Epistles*, X, 96.

14. *or to governors as sent by him to punish those who do wrong and to praise those who do right.*

15. *For it is God's will that by doing right you should put to silence the ignorance of foolish men.*

16. *Live as free men, yet without using your freedom as a pretext for evil; but live as servants of God.*

17. *Honor all men. Love the brotherhood. Fear God. Honor the emperor.*

Thus St. Peter proceeds in the proper order and teaches us how we should conduct ourselves in every situation. So far he has spoken only in general terms and has told us how one should conduct oneself in all positions in life. Now he begins to teach how one should conduct oneself toward the secular government. For since he has now said enough in the first place about how one should act toward God and for oneself, he now tells us how one should conduct oneself toward all people. This is what he wants to say: In the first place and above all, you should walk in a true faith and keep your bodies under discipline, lest they follow evil lusts. Therefore let obedience to the government be your first concern.

The Greek for what I have translated into German with *aller menschlicher ordnung*, "to every human institution," is κτίσις. The Latin word is *creatura*. Our men of learning did not understand this either.[19] The German language expresses well what the little word means when one says: *Was der Furst schaffet, das soll man hallten,* "One must do what the prince commands." That is how the apostle uses the little word here. It is as if he were saying: "What the government commands, obey it." For *schaffen* means "to command," and *ordnung* is a creature of man. Those people have interpreted *creatura* to mean an ox or an ass, as the pope also speaks about it. If that is what Peter meant, then one would also have to be subject to a servant. But the apostle calls laws or commands human institutions. What they command, that one should do. What God commands, requires, and wants, that is His institution, namely, one's faith. Now there is also a human or secular command, namely, an institution comprising injunctions, as should be true of the

[19] See, for example, Martin of Leon (an Augustinian), *Expositio in epistolam B. Petri, Patrologia, Series Latina,* CCIX, 227-228.

external government. To this we should be subject. Therefore you must understand the little words *creatura humana* to mean *Quod creat et condit homo,* "What man creates and institutes."

For the Lord's sake.

We do not owe the government obedience for its own sake, says St. Peter, but for the sake of God, whose children we are. This must induce us to be obedient, not the thought that our obedience is a meritorious deed. For what I do for God's sake, this I must do without recompense and to serve Him. Therefore I must be willing to do for nothing everything His heart desires. But why should one be subject to the government for God's sake? Because it is God's will that malefactors be punished and that benefactors be protected, in order that in this way unity may remain in the world. Therefore we should further external peace. God wants us to do this. For since we are not all believers but the great majority are unbelievers, God has regulated and ordained matters this way in order that the people of the world might not devour one another. The government should wield the sword and restrain the wicked if they do not want to have peace. Then they have to obey. This He accomplishes through the government, so that in this way the world is ruled well everywhere. Thus you see that if there were no evil people, one would not need a government.[20] Therefore St. Peter adds the words "to punish those who do wrong and to praise those who do right." Pious people are to be commended for doing what is right. The secular government should praise and honor them, in order that the others may have their conduct as an example. But it should not be one's purpose to merit anything before God for this. Thus Paul also says in Rom. 13:3: "Rulers are not a terror to good conduct, but to bad. Would you have no fear of him who is in authority? Then do what is good, and you will receive his approval."

For it is God's will that by doing right you should put to silence the ignorance of foolish men.

With these words St. Peter stops the mouths of the good-for-nothing babblers who boast of the Christian name and estate. He

---

[20] At other times Luther traced the origin of government to the original creation of God rather than to the fall of man; see, for example, *Luther's Works,* 13, pp. 47, 48.

refutes any argument they might adduce as they say: "Since a Christian's faith is sufficient, and works do not make a man pious, why, then, is it necessary to obey the secular authority and pay taxes or tribute?" This must be your reply: "Although we derive no benefit from this, we should nevertheless do it for God without recompense to stop the mouths of God's enemies, who chide us. Then they cannot charge us with anything and must say that we are pious and obedient people." Thus one reads of many saints that they went to war under pagan princes, slew the enemy, and were subject and obedient to these princes, just as we owe obedience to Christian governments, even though the opinion is current today that we could not be Christians under the Turk.[21]

Here you might say: "Yet Christ gave the command (Matt. 5:39) not to resist evil, but that if anyone strikes us on one cheek, we should turn to him the other cheek also. How, then, can we strike and kill people?" Answer: This is what the heathen formerly cast into the teeth of the Christians. They said: "If anything like this should happen, their rule would have to come to an end."[22] But to this we say: "It is true that the Christians do not resist evil for their own sakes. Nor should they take vengeance when they are harmed. But they should suffer injustice and violence. For this reason they also cannot be hard on the unbelievers." But this does not mean that the government is forbidden to wield the sword. For although pious Christians do not need the sword and law — since they live in such a way that no one can complain about them, and since they wrong nobody but do good to all and gladly suffer everything done to them — yet the sword must be wielded for the sake of the non-Christians, to punish them for the harm they inflict on the others. Public peace must be preserved, and the pious must be protected. Here God has established another method of government,[23] which should use force to compel those who are unwilling of their own accord to abstain from doing wrong to refrain from doing harm.

---

[21] In the preface to his treatise *On War Against the Turk*, dated October 9, 1528, Luther said that people had been importuning him "for the past five years" to write something about war against the Turks (W, XXX-2, 107). He may be reflecting the beginnings of that importuning here.

[22] This was a stock argument of anti-Christian polemics; for example, the emperor Julian asked: "Can anyone praise this teaching when, if it be carried out, no city, no nation, not a single family will hold together?" (Fragment 5.)

[23] The term used here is *regiment;* cf. p. 20, note 10.

Therefore God has instituted government for the sake of the unbelievers. Consequently, Christians, too, may exercise the power of the sword. They have the obligation to serve their neighbors and to restrain the wicked with it, in order that the pious may remain in peace among them. Yet the injunction of the Lord not to resist evil remains in force, so that even if a Christian wields the sword, he does not use it for himself and does not avenge himself but uses it solely for others. Thus it is also a work of Christian love to protect and defend a whole community with the sword and not to let the people be abused. Christ gives His teaching only to those who believe and love. And they observe it. But since the great multitude in the world does not believe, it does not keep the commandment either. Consequently, it is necessary to rule these as non-Christians and to check their arrogance. For if one permitted their power to run riot, no one would be able to live among them.

Thus there are two kinds of government in the world, just as there are two kinds of people, namely, believers and unbelievers. Christians let the Word of God rule them; for themselves they have no need whatever of the secular government. But non-Christians need another rule, namely, the secular sword, because they refuse to be guided by the Word of God. Otherwise, if we were all Christians and followed the Gospel, it would not be necessary or profitable at all to wield the secular sword and power. For if there were no transgressors, there could be no punishment either. But since we cannot all be pious, Christ has entrusted the wicked to the government to be ruled as they must be ruled. But the pious He keeps for Himself and rules them Himself with His Word alone.

Therefore the Christian rule is not opposed to the secular rule. Nor is the secular government in opposition to Christ. The secular rule has nothing at all to do with the office of Christ but is an external matter, just as all other offices and estates are. And just as these are outside the pale of Christ's office, so that a non-Christian administers them as well as a Christian, so it is not the office of the secular sword to make people either Christians or non-Christians. But I have often said enough about this elsewhere.[24]

---

[24] See, for example, *Luther's Works*, 45, pp. 114–117.

Now St. Peter continues:

Live as free men, yet without using your freedom as a pretext for evil; but live as servants of God.

This is said especially to us who have heard about Christian liberty, lest we rush in headlong and misuse this liberty, that is, lest under the name and the pretext of Christian liberty we do everything we please, so that liberty becomes impudence and carnal arrogance, which, as we see, is happening in our day. This began to take place even in the times of the apostles. From the epistles of St. Peter and St. Paul one can note that at that time people did what the great multitude does today. By God's grace we have now again become acquainted with the truth, and we know that what pope, bishops, priests, and monks have so far taught, instituted, and practiced is sheer fraud. Our conscience has been rescued and liberated from the human laws and all the compulsion they imposed on us, so that we are not obligated to do what they have commanded us to do on pain of losing salvation. To this freedom we must now cling firmly, and we must never let ourselves be torn from it. In addition, however, we must also be very careful not to make this freedom a pretext for evil.

The pope did wrong by attempting to force and compel the people with laws. For in a Christian people there should and can be no compulsion, and if one begins to bind consciences with external laws, faith and the Christian way of life soon perish. For Christians must be guided and governed only in the Spirit, so that they know that through faith they already have everything by which they are saved, that they need nothing else for this, that they are not obligated to do anything more than serve and help their neighbor with everything they have, just as Christ helped them. All their works are performed without compulsion and for nothing; they flow from a happy and cheerful heart, which thanks, praises, and lauds God for all the good things it has received from Him. Thus St. Paul writes in 1 Tim. 1:9 that "the Law is not laid down for the just"; for of their own accord they do without recompense and unbidden everything God wants.

Now when such compulsion of the teaching of men is abolished and Christian liberty is preached, reprobate hearts, which are without faith, rush in and want to be good Christians by refusing to observe the pope's laws. They use this liberty as an excuse and say that they have no such obligation. Yet they also fail to do what genuine Christian liberty demands, namely, to serve their neighbor with a cheerful heart, as true Christians do, regardless of the fact that this is commanded. Thus they make Christian liberty only a pretext under which they do nothing but disgraceful things. They sully the noble name and title of the liberty which Christians have.

St. Peter now forbids this here, for he wants to say: Even though you—if you are Christians—are free in all external matters and should not be compelled by law to be subject to the secular government, since, as we have said, no law is laid down for the just (1 Tim. 1:9), yet of your own accord you should be willing and unconstrained. It is not that you must obey the law out of necessity, but you must do so to please God and to serve your neighbor. Christ Himself did this, as we read in Matt. 17:24ff. He paid the tax, even though He did not have to do so but was free and a Lord over all things. Thus He also submitted to Pilate and let Himself be judged, even though He Himself said to Pilate: "You would have no power over Me unless it had been given you from above" (John 19:11). With these words He Himself confirms this power. Yet He submits to it because this was pleasing to His Father.

From this you see that that great multitude of those who do neither what the world nor what God wants have nothing at all in common with Christian liberty. They persist in the old careless way of life, even though at the same time they boast of the Gospel. To be sure, we are free from all laws; but we must also be considerate of the weak and unschooled Christians. This is a work of love. Therefore St. Paul says in Rom. 13:8: "Owe no one anything, except to love one another." Therefore let him who wants to boast of liberty first do what a Christian should do, namely, serve his neighbor. Then let him use his freedom in the following way: When the pope or anyone else presents his commands to him and wants to insist that they be obeyed, he should say: "Dear Junker Pope, I refuse to obey for the simple reason that you are ordering me to do so and are interfering with my freedom." For, as St. Peter says here, in our freedom we should conduct ourselves as servants of God, not as servants of men. Otherwise if someone desires from me a service I can render him, I will gladly do it out of goodwill, regardless of whether it is commanded or not. I will do so for the sake of brotherly love and because service to my neighbor is pleasing to God. Therefore I do not want to be compelled to be subject to secular princes and lords; but I will be subject to them of my own accord, not because they command me but to render a service to my neighbor. All our works should be of such a nature that they flow from pleasure and love, and are all directed toward our neighbor, since for ourselves we need nothing to make us pious. Next come the words:

Honor all men.

This is not a command; it is a sincere exhortation. We owe everybody honor, even though we are free. For liberty does not extend to wrongdoing but only to welldoing. Now we have often said that through faith every Christian attains what Christ Himself has and thus becomes His brother.[25] Therefore just as I accord Christ all honor, so I must also do this for my neighbor. This is not confined to external gestures, such as bowing before him and the like. No, it is rather inwardly, in the heart, that I esteem him highly as I esteem Christ highly. We are the temple of God, as St. Paul says in 1 Cor. 3:16; for the Spirit of God dwells in us. Now if we kneel before a monstrance and the picture of the holy cross, why should we not be far more inclined to do this before a living temple of God?

Thus in Rom. 12:10 St. Paul tells us to "outdo one another in showing honor." Everyone should place himself below the other person and exalt him. The gifts of God are manifold and different, so that one person is in a higher position than another. But no one knows who is highest before God. For one who is in the very lowest position here He can easily elevate to the highest position there. Therefore everyone, even if he occupies a high position, should humble himself and honor his neighbor.

Love the brotherhood.

I have stated above how the apostles differentiate between ordinary and brotherly love.[26] It is our duty to love even our enemies. This is ordinary Christian love. But it is brotherly love when we Christians love one another as brothers and one person looks after the other person, since we all have the same blessings

[25] Cf. *Luther's Works*, 31, pp. 351–352 for one instance.
[26] See, p. 42, note 29.

from God. It is this love that St. Peter demands here in particular.

Fear God. Honor the emperor.

The apostle does not say that one should esteem lords and kings highly. No, he says that one should honor them even though they are heathen. Christ did this too. So did the prophets, who fell at the feet of the kings of Babylon.[27] But here you might say: "Here you see that one must also be obedient to the pope and fall at his feet." Answer: Yes, if the pope assumes secular power and acts like another overlord, one must also obey him. If, for example, he were to say: "I order you to wear a cowl or to be tonsured, likewise to fast on this day—not that this has any validity before God or that it is necessary for salvation, but because I, as a secular lord, want it this way." But when he comes along and says: "I, as God's vicegerent, command you to do this. You must accept this as if it came from God Himself, and you must do so on pain of excommunication and at the risk of committing a mortal sin," then say: "Gracious junker, I will not do it."

We should be subject to power and do what they order, so long as they do not bind our conscience and so long as they give commands that pertain to external matters only, even though they deal with us as tyrants do. For if anyone takes our coat, we should let him have our cloak as well (Matt. 5:40). But if they want to encroach on the spiritual rule and want to take our conscience captive where God alone must sit and rule, one should by no means obey them and should sooner let them have one's life. Secular domain and rule do not extend beyond external and physical matters. But the pope arrogates not only this to himself but also wants the spiritual rule. Yet he has neither the one nor the other. For his commands pertain solely to clothing, food, foundations, and prebends, which belong neither in the secular nor in the spiritual rule. For how is the world improved by them? Moreover, he acts contrary to God's command when he makes noncompliance with his orders a sin and makes good works where God does not command. Therefore Christ cannot put up with this. But He can put up with the secular government, since it does not concern itself with sins or good works and

---

[27] It is not clear which passages from the Old Testament Luther has in mind here; for the closest to what he is saying seems to be Dan. 2:46, in which, however, the king did homage to the prophet.

spiritual matters but has to do with other things, such as how to secure and fortify cities, build bridges, fix toll, levy taxes, provide protection, defend the land and its people, and punish evildoers. Therefore a Christian can surely be obedient to such a prince, provided that the prince does not give any commands that do violence to a Christian's conscience. A Christian does this without compulsion, since he is free in all things.

Therefore if an emperor or a prince were to ask me now what my faith is, I would have to tell him, not because of his command, but because it is my duty to confess my faith publicly before everybody. But if he wanted to go beyond this and commanded me to believe this or that, I would have to say: "My dear lord, attend to your secular rule. You have no authority to meddle in God's kingdom. Therefore I refuse to obey you. You surely cannot put up with any meddling in your domain. If anyone trespasses on your territory without your consent, you shoot at him with guns. Do you suppose that God should tolerate your desire to dethrone Him and to put yourself in His place?" St. Peter calls the secular government merely a human institution. Therefore they have no power to interfere in God's arrangement and to give commands concerning faith. Let what I have just said be enough about this subject. Now the epistle goes on:

18. *Servants, be submissive to your masters with all respect, not only to the kind and gentle but also to the overbearing.*

19. *For one is approved if, mindful of God, he endures pain while suffering unjustly.*

20. *For what credit is it if when you do wrong and are beaten for it, you take it patiently? But if when you do right and suffer for it, you take it patiently, you have God's approval.*

So far St. Peter has taught us that we must be submissive to secular authority and show it honor. In this connection we have stated how far this power extends and that it should not meddle in matters pertaining to faith. This is stated about government in general and is a teaching for everyone. But now the apostle continues and speaks of the kind of power that does not extend to a community but pertains only to particular persons. Here he teaches, in the first place, how servants should conduct themselves toward their masters. This is what he means:

Manservants and maidservants are Christians just as other people are; for they share the Word, faith, Baptism, and all blessings with everyone else. Therefore before God they are just as great and high as others. But according to their outward way of life and before the world there is a difference. They are in an inferior station and must serve others. Therefore since they are called to this estate by God, they must let it be their duty to be subject to their masters, to look up to them, and pay attention to them. From this the prophet David draws an excellent analogy and points out how they should serve. "Behold," he says in Ps. 123:2, "as the eyes of servants look to the hand of their master, as the eyes of a maid to the hand of her mistress, so our eyes look to the Lord our God." That is, manservants and maidservants should fulfill the wishes of the master or the mistress with humility and fear. God wants this. Therefore it should be done gladly. You can be sure and confident that this is pleasing and acceptable to God if you do it in faith. Consequently, these are the best good works you can perform. You need not go far afield and search for others. What your master or mistress commands, this God Himself has commanded you to do. It is not a command of men, even though it is given through men. Therefore you should not consider what kind of master you have, whether good or bad, friendly or irritable and angry; but you must think as follows: "The master may be as he wants to be, I will serve Him and do his bidding in honor of God, because He wants me to do this, and because my Lord Christ Himself became a Servant for my sake."

This is the true doctrine. It should be taught constantly. Today, unfortunately, it is disregarded and suppressed. But only those who are Christians teach it. For the Gospel preaches solely to those who accept it. Therefore if you want to be a child of God, impress this on your heart, so that you serve as if Christ Himself were ordering you to do so, as St. Paul, too, teaches in Eph. 6:5-7: "Slaves, be obedient to those who are your earthly masters, with fear and trembling, in singleness of heart, as to Christ; not in the way of eye-service, as men-pleasers, but as servants of Christ, doing the will of God from the heart, rendering service with a good will as to the Lord and not to men, etc." Thus he also says in Col. 3:24: "You are serving the Lord Christ." Would that priests, monks, and nuns were in such a station! How they would thank God and rejoice! For not one of them can say: "God commanded me to celebrate Mass, to sing matins, to observe the seven canonical hours with prayer, and the like." For they do not have a single word in Scripture about this. Therefore when one asks them whether they are certain and convinced that their station is pleasing to God, they say no. But if you ask a lowly housemaid why she washes dishes or milks the cow, she can say: "I know that what I do is pleasing to God, for I have God's word and command." This is a great blessing and a precious treasure of which no one is worthy. A prince should thank God for being able to do work of this kind. It is true that in his position he can also do what God wants, namely, punish the wicked. But when can he perform such a service properly? How rarely it happens! But in this station everything is ordained in such a way that if they do what they are ordered to do, all this is pleasing to God. God does not consider how small the works are; He considers the heart which serves Him with such small works. But here, too, it happens as it does in other matters. No one does what God has commanded. But when man institutes something, and God does not command, then everybody comes running.

So you say: "What indeed am I to do if I have a queer and ill-tempered master whom no one can serve satisfactorily? One finds many people like this." St. Peter answers: If you are a Christian and want to please God, you must not ask how eccentric and rude your master is; but you must always turn your eyes to what God commands you to do. Therefore this is what you should think: "In this way I shall be serving my Lord Christ. He wants me to be obedient to this rude man." If God were to order you to polish the shoes of the devil or the worst rogue, you would have to comply. And this work would be just as good as the greatest work of all, because God orders you to do it. Therefore you should have no regard for any person in this matter, but you should regard only what God wants. Then the most insignificant work, if it is done properly, is better in the sight of God than the works of all the priests and monks put together. If a person is not persuaded that this is God's will and good pleasure, then nothing else will help. You can do no better than to comply; you can do no worse than not to comply. Therefore one should do this "with all respect," as

St. Peter says. One should proceed in the proper manner, since it is God's command, not the command of men.

And here, of course, St. Peter is speaking of servants as they were at that time, when they were slaves. In some places one still finds people of this kind. One sold them like cattle. They were mistreated and beaten by their masters, and the masters had so much freedom that they were not punished, even if they killed the slaves. For this reason it was necessary for the apostles to admonish and console such slaves by telling them that they could serve even irritable masters and even suffer harm and injustice from them. He who is a Christian must also bear a cross. And the more you are wronged, the better it is for you. Therefore you must accept such a cross willingly from God and thank Him. This is the true suffering that is pleasing to God. For what would your boasting of the cross amount to if you were severely beaten and had deserved it? Therefore St. Peter says: "For one is approved if, mindful of God, he endures pain while suffering unjustly." Such suffering is pleasing and acceptable to God. It is a real service to God. Behold, here the truly precious good works we should do are described, and we fools have trampled this teaching underfoot and have invented and proposed other works. We should lift up our hands, thank God, and rejoice that we now know this. The apostle continues:

21. *For to this you have been called, because Christ also suffered for you, leaving you an example, that you should follow in His steps.*

22. *He committed no sin; no guile was found on His lips.*

23. *When He was reviled, He did not revile in return; when He suffered, He did not threaten; but He trusted to Him who judges justly.*

24. *He Himself bore our sins in His body on the tree, that we might die to sin and live to righteousness. By His wounds you have been healed.*

25. *For you were straying like sheep, but now have returned to the Shepherd and Guardian of your souls.*

This is what we have said, namely, that servants should impress it on their hearts and be moved to do and suffer willingly what they must, because Christ did so much for them. They must think as follows: "Since my Lord served me even though He was not obliged to do so, and since He sacrificed life and limb for me, why would I refuse to serve Him in return? He was completely pure and without sin. Yet He humbled Himself so deeply, shed His blood for me, and died to blot out my sins. Ah, should I then not also suffer something because it pleases Him?" Now he who contemplates this would surely have to be a stone if it did not move him. For if the master takes the lead and steps into the mire, it stands to reason that the servant will follow.

Therefore St. Peter says: "To this you have been called." To what? To suffer wrong, as Christ did. It is as if he were saying: "If you want to follow Christ, you dare not argue and complain much when you are wronged; but you must suffer it and be forgiving, since Christ suffered everything without any guilt on His part. He did not appeal to justice when He stood before the judge. Therefore you must tread justice underfoot and say: 'Thank God, I have been called to suffer injustice. For why should I complain when my Lord did not complain?'"

And here St. Peter has taken a few words from the prophet Isaiah, who says in chapter 53:9: "Although He had done no violence, and there was no deceit in His mouth." Likewise: "With His stripes we are healed" (v. 5). Christ was so pure that not a single evil word was on His tongue. Had He been treated as He deserved, everybody would have fallen at His feet and held Him in affection. Furthermore, He surely had the power and the right to avenge Himself. Yet He permitted Himself to be reviled, scorned, blasphemed, and even killed; and He never opened His mouth. Why, then, should you, too, not suffer this, since you are nothing but sin? You should praise and thank God for being worthy of becoming like Christ. You should not murmur or be impatient when you are wronged, since the Lord neither reviled nor threatened but even prayed for His enemies.

So you might say: "Do you mean to say that I should justify those who wrong me and say: 'They have done well?'" Answer: No. But you should say: "I will suffer this very willingly, even though I have not deserved it and you are doing me an injustice. I will suffer it for my Lord's sake. He also suffered injustice for me." You should leave the matter to God, just as Christ leaves it to His heavenly Father. God is a just Judge. He will reward it richly. St. Peter says: "He Himself bore our sins in His body on the tree"; that is, He did not suffer for Himself. No, He suffered for our benefit. We crucified Him with our sins. We are still far from suffering what He suffered. Therefore if you are a pious Christian, you should tread in the footsteps of the Lord and have compassion on those who harm you. You should also pray for them and ask God not to punish them. For they do far more harm to their souls than they do to your body. If you take this to heart, you will surely forget about your own sorrow and suffer gladly. Here we should be mindful of the fact that formerly we, too, led the kind of unchristian life that they lead, but that we have now been converted through Christ, as St. Peter concludes when he says:

You were straying like sheep, but have now returned to the Shepherd and Guardian of your souls.

But this is a quotation from the prophet Isaiah, who says: "All we like sheep have gone astray; we have turned everyone to his own way" (53:6). But we have now acquired a Shepherd, says St. Peter. The Son of God came for our sakes, to be our Shepherd and Bishop. He gives us His Spirit, feeds and leads us with His Word, so that we now know how we have been helped. Consequently, if you realize that your sins have been removed through Him, you are His sheep, and He is your Shepherd. Moreover, He is your Bishop, and you are His soul. This is now the comfort all Christians have.

Thus in this epistle we have two chapters in which St. Peter has taught us in the first place the true faith and then the true works of love. He has spoken about two kinds of works. First he has told us about the duty we all owe the government, then how servants should conduct themselves toward their masters. And what Saint Peter says here about servants also applies to some other persons, namely, to craftsmen, day laborers, and hired help of all kinds. Now he will go on to teach how husband and wife should conduct themselves toward each other.

CHAPTER THREE

1. *Likewise you wives, be submissive to your husbands, so that some, though they do not obey the Word, may be won without a word by the behavior of their wives,*

2. *when they see your reverent and chaste behavior.*

3. *Let not yours be the outward adorning with braiding of hair, decoration of gold, and wearing of robes;*

4. *but let it be the hidden person of the heart with the imperishable jewel of a gentle and quiet spirit, which in God's sight is very precious.*

5. *So once the holy women who hoped in God used to adorn themselves and were submissive to their husbands,*

6. *as Sarah obeyed Abraham, calling him lord. And you are now her children if you do right and let nothing terrify you.*

Here St. Peter is speaking primarily of the women who at that time had heathen and unbelieving husbands. On the other hand, he is also speaking of believing men who had heathen wives. For in those days, when the apostles were proclaiming the Gospel among the Gentiles, it often happened that the one became a Christian and the other did not. Now since at that time wives were commanded to be submissive to their husbands, how much more this should be observed today! Therefore St. Peter wants to say that it is the wife's duty to be submissive to her husband, even though he is a heathen or an unbeliever. And he gives the reason for this.

So that some, though they do not obey the Word, may be won without a word by the behavior of their wives, when they see your reverent and chaste behavior.

That is, when a husband sees that his wife conducts and adapts herself properly, he may be induced to believe and to regard the Christian estate as proper and good. Even though women have no command to preach, yet they should deport themselves in such a way in the matter of gestures and conduct that they induce their husbands to believe, as we read about St. Augustine's mother, who converted her heathen husband before his death. Later she also converted her son Augustine.[1] This, of course, is an external thing, which should not be done for the purpose of becoming pious in this way. Obedience does not save you, for it may well be that you can find an obedient wife who is nevertheless an unbeliever. But you must obey for the purpose of serving your husband in this way. For this is the order established by God when He says to the woman in Gen. 3:16: "Your desire shall be for your husband, and he shall rule over you." This is also one of the penalties God imposed on women. But such conduct, I say, is external; it pertains to the body, not to the spirit.

But it is important to know what kind of works one must perform to please God. We should strive hard to achieve this, just as we see that the world has striven to accomplish what it has invented. It is a high and noble treasure for a woman to have when she conducts herself in such a way that she is submissive to her husband, for then she knows that she is doing a God-pleasing work. What greater joy can come to her? Therefore a woman who wants to be a Christian wife should think as follows: "I will not consider what kind of husband I have, whether he is a Gentile or a Jew, whether he is pious or wicked; but I will take into account that God has placed me in the state of matrimony and wants me to be submissive and obedient to my husband." If she renders such obedience, then all her works are golden.

But if she does not let herself be induced by this, she will not be helped in any other way. For you will accomplish nothing with blows; they will not make a woman pious and submissive. If you beat one devil out of her, you will beat two into her, as the saying goes. Oh, if married people knew this, how well they would fare! But no one enjoys doing what God has commanded. On the other hand, everybody hastens to do what men have invented. God insisted to such an extent on obedience to this command that He

---

[1] Augustine, *Confessions*, Book IX, ch. 9, par. 22.

authorized husbands to annul vows made by their wives if the husbands express disapproval, as we read in Num. 30:8. The reason for this is that God wants peace and quiet to reign in a household. This is one point. Now the apostle goes on to tell how a woman should conduct herself toward other people.

Let not yours be the outward adorning with braiding of hair, decoration of gold, and wearing of robes; but let it be the hidden person of the heart with the imperishable jewel of a gentle and quiet spirit, which in God's sight is very precious.

Not only a wife but also a husband should have this internal treasure. Here someone might ask whether or not what St. Peter says about adornment is commanded. We read about Esther that she wore a golden crown and precious adornment, as befits a queen (Esther 2:12, 17). The same thing is said about Judith (Judith 10:3-4). But it is also written here that they disdained adornment and were compelled to wear it (Esther 14:16). Therefore we say: A woman must be so minded as to pay no regard to adornment. Otherwise, when people acquire ornaments, they do not know when to stop. This is the way they are by nature. Therefore a Christian wife should disdain it. But if the husband wants it, or if there is any other proper reason for her to adorn herself, it is all right. Yet, as St. Peter says here, she must be adorned "in the hidden person of the heart with a gentle and quiet spirit." You are adorned beautifully enough when you are adorned for your husband. Christ does not want you to adorn yourself to please others and be called a pretty wench. But you must see to it that you wear the hidden treasure and precious ornament imperishably in your heart, says St. Peter, and that you lead a chaste and decent life. It is a good sign that there is not much spirit when so much stress is placed on adornment. But if faith and spirit are there, they will trample adornment underfoot and say, as Queen Esther said (Esther 14:16): "Thou knowest my necessity—that I abhor the sign of my proud position, which is upon my head on the days when I appear in public. I abhor it like a menstruous rag, and I do not wear it on the days when I am at leisure." Such a wife will be all the more pleasing to her husband. Therefore, as St. Peter says, wives must be intent on adorning "the hidden person" where an imperishable, quiet spirit dwells. Not only should they shun extravagance, lest they be pushed aside and come to shame; but he means that they should see to it that the soul within them remains in the true faith, lest their faith be harmed.

This leads to a heart that does not start thinking about how it appears before the world. Such a heart is a glorious thing before God. If a woman were to adorn herself with nothing but gold, gems, and pearls down to her feet, this would be extraordinarily splendid. But you could not hang so much on a woman that it could be compared to the sumptuous adornment of the soul that is magnificent in the sight of God. Gold and precious stones are magnificent in the eyes of the world, but before God this is a stench. But that woman is attired well and gloriously before God who goes her way in a gentle and quiet spirit. Therefore since God Himself considers this magnificent, it must be something glorious. A Christian soul has all that Christ has. For, as we have said, faith brings us all Christ's possessions put together.[2] This is a great and precious treasure and an adornment such as no one can praise sufficiently. God Himself also regards it highly. Therefore one should keep and restrain women from adornment, since otherwise they are inclined in this direction. If a Christian woman hears this, takes it to heart, and thinks: "I will pay no attention to adornment, since God pays no attention to it either; but if I must wear it, I will do so to please my husband," then she is properly adorned and decorated in the spirit. Next St. Peter also cites an example of saintly women for the purpose of urging them to lead a Christian life. He says:

So once the holy women who hoped in God used to adorn themselves and were submissive to their husbands, as Sarah obeyed Abraham, calling him lord.

As these women adorned themselves, he wants to say, so you do too, just as Sarah obeyed Abraham and called him her lord. Thus Scripture says in Gen. 18:10, when the angel came to Abraham and said: "A year from today Sarah shall have a son." Then she laughs and says (v. 12): "After I have grown old, and my lord is old, shall I have pleasure?" St. Peter undoubtedly had these words in mind when he mentioned Sarah as an example here. For she would not have called Abraham a lord if she had not been

[2] Cf. p. 11

submissive to him and had not called this to his attention. Therefore the apostle continues:

*And you are now her children if you do right and let nothing
terrify you.*

What does he mean by this? This is what he means: It is commonly the nature of women to be timid and to be afraid of everything. This is why they busy themselves so much with witchcraft
and superstition. One teaches the other, so that it is impossible
to tell what kind of hocus-pocus they practice. But a Christian
woman should not do this. She must go along freely and with
confidence and not be so timid. She should not practice witchcraft
and superstition and run hither and thither, uttering a magic
formula here and a magic formula there. Whatever her lot, she
should let God rule, and she should remember that she cannot
fare badly. For since she knows how she is faring and that her
position in life is pleasing to God, why should she fear? If your
child dies, if you become ill, be of good cheer; commit it to God.
You are in a God-pleasing station. What better lot can you desire?
These are words preached to wives. Now the apostle tells what
husbands should do.

7. *Likewise you husbands, live considerately with your wives,
bestowing honor on the woman as the weaker vessel, since you
are joint heirs of the grace of life, in order that your prayers
may not be hindered.*

Woman is also God's vessel or tool, says the apostle; for God
uses her to conceive, bear, feed, and look after children, and to
manage the house. The woman should do works of this kind. Therefore she is God's tool and vessel. God created her for this purpose
and implanted this in her. This is the way the husband should
regard his wife. Therefore St. Peter says: "You husbands, live considerately with your wives. Do not rule them recklessly." To be
sure, they should live as the husband rules. What he commands
and orders, this should be done. But the husband should also see
to it that he treats his wife with kindness and consideration. He
should be tender, and he should honor her as God's weakest vessel.

A man is also God's vessel, but he is stronger than a woman.
She is weaker physically and also more timid and downhearted

in spirit. Therefore you should deal with her and treat her in such a way that she can bear it. You must take care of her as you take care of another tool with which you work. For example, if you want to have a good knife, you must not hack into stone with it. Now it is impossible to give a rule for this. God leaves it to everyone to treat his wife considerately according to each wife's nature. You must not use your authority arbitrarily; for you are her husband to help, support, and protect her, not to harm her. It is impossible to set specific bounds for you. Here you yourself must know how to proceed thoughtfully.

Thus with regard to husbands we also know what God-pleasing works they should do. They should dwell with their wives, make a living, and treat their wives with kindness. It will not always be possible for things to go exactly as you would like to have them go. Therefore see to it that you are a man and that the less thoughtful your wife is, the more thoughtful you are. At times you must be lenient, slacken the reins a bit, give in, and also accord your wife the honor that is her due.

Honor has been interpreted in I do not know how many ways. Some have explained it to mean that the husband should provide food, drink, and clothing for his wife; others have referred it to the conjugal duty.[3] In my opinion, it means what I have said, namely, that a husband must bear in mind that his wife is a Christian too and is God's work or vessel. Both should conduct themselves in such a way that the wife holds her husband in honor and that the husband, in turn, gives his wife the honor that is her due. If this were observed, peace and love would reign. Otherwise, where this understanding is lacking, there is nothing but aversion in marriage. For this reason it happens that if a man and a woman take each other solely for the purpose of sensual pleasure and are intent on having happy days and sensual pleasure, they find nothing but heartache. But if you have regard for God's work and will, you can lead a Christian life in matrimony. Then you will not live as the heathen live. They do not know what God wants.

Since you are joint heirs of the grace of life.

The husband must not appraise his wife by the fact that she is

---

[3] Cf. Martin of Leon, *Expositio in epistolam B. Petri, Patrologia, Series Latina,* CCIX, 232.

weak and frail. No, he must bear in mind that she is also baptized and has exactly what he has, namely, all blessings from Christ. For inwardly we are all alike; there is no difference between a man and a woman. Externally, however, God wants the husband to rule and the wife to be submissive to him.

In order that your prayers may not be hindered.

What does St. Peter mean by this? This is what he means: If you do not act thoughtfully but want to bluster, growl, and insist on having your own way, and if she is also frail, so that neither can excuse or forgive the other, then you will not be able to pray and say: "Father, forgive us our trespasses as we forgive." With this prayer we must fight against the devil. Therefore we must be in agreement with one another. These are the truly precious good works that we should do. If this were preached and known, then we would all abound in good works in our homes. Thus we have now heard how a Christian should conduct himself in all walks of life, particularly how one person should conduct himself toward the other person.

Now we are told how we, one and all, should lead a Christian life in our relations with others.

8. *Finally, all of you, have unity of spirit, sympathy, love of the brethren, a tender heart, and a friendly mind.*

9. *Do not return evil for evil or reviling for reviling; but, on the contrary, bless, for to this you have been called, that you may obtain a blessing.*

10. *For he that would love life and see good days, let him keep his tongue from evil and his lips from speaking guile;*

11. *let him turn away from evil and do right; let him seek peace and pursue it.*

12. *For the eyes of the Lord are upon the righteous, and His ears are open to their prayer. But the face of the Lord is against those that do evil.*

All this says nothing else than that we should love one another. For here what Scripture ordinarily compresses into a few words is set forth in detail. St. Peter means to say: This is the sum and substance of the kind of outward life you should lead. You should have unity of spirit. The apostles Peter and Paul often employ this expression.[4] It means that we should all have one mind, one spirit, one conviction. What seems right and good to one should also be regarded as right and good by the others. This is a powerful, noteworthy word. One should understand it well. St. Paul, in particular, wrote much about it.

We cannot all do work of the same kind. Everyone must do his or her own kind of work. A man's work is different from that of a woman, a servant's from that of the master, etc. It is stupid to teach that we should all do the same kind of work, as those foolish preachers have taught. They proclaim the legends of the saints, that this saint performed one work and that saint performed another work. And they proceed to say that we, too, should do these works. Abraham undoubtedly did a good and precious work when he sacrificed his son, because God had given him a special command to do so. Then the heathen came along and wanted to sacrifice their children too. This was an abomination before God. Thus King Solomon did well by building the temple, and God rewarded him well for this. Now our blind fools also come along and proclaim that one must build churches and temples for God, even though we have no command about this from God. Thus today the very opposite is said, namely, that one and the same work should be done. And there are various opinions. This is directly contrary to the Gospel.

But one should teach that there should be one mind and many works, one heart and many hands. All should not do one and the same work, but everyone should attend to his own duties. Otherwise one and the same mind and one and the same heart do not remain. One must let what is external remain varied, so that everybody stays with what has been entrusted to him and with the kind of work he has at hand. This is a proper teaching, and it is altogether necessary to understand it well. For the devil pays special attention to this matter. He has brought it about that works are stressed and that everyone thinks his work is better than that of the other person. This is why people have come to be at such odds with one another,

---

[4] Although the Greek term used here appears nowhere else in the New Testament, the Latin term *unanimes* appears also in Rom. 15:6, in Phil. 1:27, and in Phil. 2:2.

monks against priests, one order against the other. For everyone claimed to be doing the best work. Then people proceeded to join orders. They thought that this order was better than that one. Then the Augustinians were against the Dominicans, the Carthusians against the Franciscans. As a result, there is general disagreement, and nowhere is there greater discord than that which exists among the orders.

If people had been taught that before God no work is better than the other, but that through faith they are all alike, then the hearts would have remained in harmony, and we would all be of like mind and say: "Before God the bishop's order or position is no better than that of the common man. Nor is the position of a nun better than that of a married woman, and so on in positions of all kinds." But they do not want to hear this, but everyone wants to be the best. They say: "Ah, why is my position in the order not better and greater than that of the common man?"

Therefore to have "unity of spirit" means that everyone regards his own work equal to that of the other person, that the estate of matrimony, for example, is just as good as that of a virgin. Thus before God everything is equal. He judges according to the heart and faith, not according to the person or according to the works. Therefore we should judge as God judges. Then we are of one mind, unity remains in the world, and hearts remain undivided and are not torn apart by external matters. I must esteem everything as good and must approve of the kind of work everyone does, provided that it is not a sin in itself.

Concerning this St. Paul also says in 2 Cor. 11:3: "But I am afraid that as the serpent deceived Eve by his cunning, your thoughts will be led astray from a sincere and pure devotion to Christ"; that is, that the devil will also deceive you and tear your guileless spirit asunder. And in Phil. 4:7 Paul says: "And the peace of God, which passes all understanding, will keep your hearts and your minds in Christ Jesus." Why does the apostle set such great store by the spirit? Ah, this is all-important! For if I have a wrong spirit, all is lost. If, for example, I am a monk and have the notion that my work has greater value before God than the work of the others and say: "Thank God, I have become a monk, and my station is now better than that of the common married estate," then haughtiness must result from this notion, and I cannot fail to regard myself as more pious than another person and to look down on others. Then I deceive myself. For a married woman who believes is better in the sight of God than I am with my order. Therefore if one knows that faith brings with it everything a Christian should have, then we all have one spirit and are of one mind, and there is no distinction among works.

Therefore this statement by St. Peter must be understood as referring to a spiritual and not an external sense, and to an inner opinion or thought pertaining to the things that have validity before God. Both teaching and life must be one and the same. I must regard as good what you regard as good, and by the same token what is pleasing to me must be pleasing to you, as I have said. This is the spirit Christians have, and to this spirit we must hold firmly, lest it be led astray, as St. Paul says. For if the devil leads the spirit astray, he has led true virginity astray. Then all is lost.

Have sympathy, love of the brethren, a tender heart, and a friendly mind.

To have sympathy means that one person should look after the other person and take his neighbor's trouble to heart. If your neighbor is in trouble, you should not think: "Ah, it serves him right! Too bad he doesn't have more trouble! He has surely deserved it." If there is love, he looks after his neighbor; if his neighbor is in trouble, he takes this to heart as though it were happening to him himself.

To have love of the brethren means to regard the other person as one's brother. This is easy to understand, for nature itself teaches it. Here you see what true brothers are. They cling together much more closely than any friends do. We Christians should also do this, for we are all brothers through Baptism. After Baptism even my father and my mother are my brother and my sister, for through faith I have the very same blessing and inheritance from Christ that they have.

A tender heart. *Viscerosi.* I cannot explain this expression in any other way than by giving an illustration. Observe how a mother or a father acts toward a child. When a mother sees her child in distress, all her bowels and the heart are stirred in her body. From this comes the way of speaking used in many places in Scripture. There is also a story about this in 1 Kings 3:16ff., where two women were at odds regarding a child before King Solomon, and each woman wanted to have the child. Now when the king wanted to find out who the true mother of the child was, he had to have recourse to nature. Then he hit upon the right way and said to both women: "You say that the child is yours. You, too, say that it is yours. All right, bring a sword, and divide the child into two parts, and give one part to this woman and one part to that woman." Then he found out who the true mother was. Here the text says that "her heart yearned for her son" and that she said: "Oh, my lord, give her the living child, and by no means slay it" (v. 26). Then the king came to a decision and said: "This is the real mother. Take the child, and give it to her." From this you can deduce what the expression "a tender heart" means here.

St. Peter wants us to treat one another as sincere bosom friends. Just as the heart, the marrow, the veins, and all powers are stirred there, so it must also be here. A cordial and motherly feeling must pervade the heart. This is the kind of spirit one Christian should have toward the other person. But the aim is high indeed. One will find exceedingly few of those who have such heartfelt love for their neighbor that when they see that a person is in trouble, they are stirred as a mother is stirred for her child, in such a way that this feeling penetrates her heart and all her veins. There you see what the way of life of monks and nuns is, how far it is from such heartfelt love. If one melted them all together into one heap, one would not find a single drop of such Christian love. Therefore let us take care and pay attention to ourselves, whether we find that kind of love in ourselves. This is a short and quickly delivered sermon, but it goes deep and covers a great deal of ground.

To have a friendly mind means that outwardly one should lead a life full of love. Not only should one person look after the other person, as father and mother look after their child; but one person should also treat the other person with love and tenderness. Some people are queer and gnarled, like a tree with many branches. They are so unfriendly that no one wants to have anything to do with them. This results from the fact that they are generally full of suspicion and soon become angry. No one likes to associate with them. But there are fine people; they put the best construction on everything, are not suspicious, are slow to wrath and ready to forgive. They are called *candidi*. St. Paul calls this virtue χρηστότης [5] and praises it often.

[5] Cf. Rom. 2:4; 2 Cor. 6:6; Gal. 5:22; Col. 3:12.

Look at the Gospel. It portrays the Lord Christ in such a way that this virtue is particularly noticeable in Him. Sometimes the Pharisees attack Him in this way, sometimes in that way. They would like to trap Him. Yet He does not get angry. And even though the apostles often stumble and make fools of themselves here and there, yet He never snarls at them but is always friendly and attracts them to Himself in such a manner that they are sincerely glad to be with Him and to associate with Him. One also sees this among good friends and companions on earth, where there are two or three good friends who are well disposed toward one another. When one of them makes a fool of himself, the other can readily forgive him. This is an imperfect picture of what St. Peter has in mind here, even though it does not tell the whole story. For this friendliness should be offered to everybody. It lets you see the true nature of love and what fine people Christians are. This is how the angels in heaven live among one another. The same thing would be true on earth, but it very seldom happens.

Now just as St. Peter has said that maidservants and manservants, husbands and wives, should attend to their duties, so he wants us all to do this at all times. Therefore if you want to be certain and confident that you are doing a precious and God-pleasing work, then in God's name drop everything that has been preached in the devil's name—everything with which the world busies itself in an effort to merit heaven. But how can you be surer that you are pleasing God than by doing as He says here? The works one should do and the way of life everyone should follow comprise having sympathy, love of the brethren, a tender heart, and being friendly. Here the apostle does not say a word about the nonsense preached to us. He does not say: "Build churches, endow Masses, become a priest, don a cowl, vow celibacy, etc." No, he says: "Bear in mind that you must be friendly." These are truly precious, golden works, gems and pearls that please God.

But this the devil does not like to see, for he knows that it means the loss of his cause. Therefore he devises what he can to suppress such teaching. He causes monks and priests to cry out: "If you are saying that our cause amounts to nothing, the devil is telling you to say this!" Then say to them in reply: "Do you not know that the works St. Peter is speaking about here must be good, namely, to have love of the brethren, to have a tender heart, and to be friendly? If these are the best works, as one must admit, you cer-

tainly have to be lying when you think that your works are better."
I am greatly amazed that it has been possible for such blindness
to arise among us. Thomas, the Dominican monk, had the effrontery
to write that priests and monks are in a station better than that of
ordinary Christians.[6] The schools of higher learning endorsed this
and created doctors on this basis. Later the pope and his crowd
came along and elevated those who teach this to sainthood.

Now, therefore, understand this, as I have stated. Christ Himself and all the apostles taught that if you want to do the best works
and to be in the best way of life, you will find nothing else than
faith and love. This is the best of all ways of life. Therefore it must
be a lie if they want to say that their way is better than faith and
love. For if it is better than faith, it is better than God's Word. If it is
above God's Word, it is above God Himself. Therefore St. Paul
was right when he said that the Antichrist would exalt himself
above God (2 Thess. 2:4). You must know what opinion to have
concerning these matters. Where love and friendliness do not
prevail, there all works are surely condemned. Just trample it
all underfoot. Thus we see how forcefully St. Peter has set forth
what the external manifestations of a true Christian life should be.
Above he taught in a masterly manner what the attitude of the inner
life should be toward God. Therefore this epistle must be considered a truly golden epistle. Now St. Peter continues:

*Do not return evil for evil or reviling for reviling; but, on the
contrary, bless, for to this you have been called, that you may
obtain a blessing.*

But this is a further explanation of love. It tells us how we
should act toward those who wrong and persecute us. When you
are treated badly, he says, you should do good. When you are
reviled and cursed, you should bless. But this is a great part of
love. O Lord God, how rare such Christians are! But why should
we return good for evil? Because, says the apostle, you have been
called to this, that you may inherit the blessing. This should induce
you to do so.

In Scripture we Christians are called a people of blessing or
the blessed people; for God says to Abraham in Gen. 12:3: "In
your Seed shall all families of the earth be blessed." Now since

---

[6] Thomas Aquinas, *Summa Theologica*, II – II, Q. 184, Art. 5.

God has poured out this blessing so richly on us in order to remove from us every malediction and the curse which we have brought with us from our first parents and which Moses has also pronounced on the unbelievers, so that we are now filled with blessing, we should conduct ourselves in such a way that poeple will say: "Indeed, this is a blessed nation!" Therefore this is what the apostle means here: Behold, since God has been merciful to you and has removed the curse from you and has not charged you with or punished you for the blasphemy with which you dishonored Him but, instead, has lavished grace and blessings on you, although you deserved every curse for your incessant blaspheming of God—for where there is unbelief, there the heart must constantly curse God—you should also do as has been done for you. Do not curse, do not revile, do good, speak well even when you are wronged, and bear injustice. Now St. Peter quotes from Ps. 34:13ff., where the prophet David says:

For he that would love life and see good days, let him keep his tongue from evil and his lips from speaking guile.

That is, he who wants to have pleasure and joy in life and not die but wants to see good days and fare well, let him keep his tongue from speaking evil, not only against friends—for this is a small virtue, which even the worst people, yes, even serpents and vipers, can practice. No, he says: Be of good cheer, and guard your tongue even against your enemies even when you are provoked and have reason to revile and to speak evil.

Furthermore, the apostle says that you must keep your lips from speaking guile. Of course, there are many who speak good words and say "Good morning!" to their neighbors; but in their hearts they think: "May the devil take you!" Those people have not inherited this blessing. They are evil fruits from the evil tree. Therefore Peter has quoted a verse that deals with works and yet goes to the root, that is, inwardly to the heart. The prophet's statement continues:

Let him turn away from evil and do right; let him seek peace and pursue it. For the eyes of the Lord are upon the righteous.

When one person hits another person on the head for doing wrong, the world looks upon this as peace. But this never leads to peace. For no king has ever been able to be at peace with his enemies in this way. The Roman Empire was so powerful that it crushed everything that resisted it. Yet it could not preserve itself by doing this. Therefore this method of attaining peace is worthless. For even if one enemy is conquered and stunned, then 10 and 20 rise up, until it has to fall. But he who curbs his tongue, turns away from evil, and does good seeks peace in the right way and will also find it. This is a different way from the one pursued by the world. To turn away from evil and do right means to pass over evil words indulgently and to be able to overlook evil and injustice. Seek peace in this way, and you will find it. If your enemy has vented his wrath and has done everything he could, then, if you are forbearing, do not revile, and do not rage against him, he will have to subdue himself with his own power. For this is how Christ also overcame His enemies when He was on the cross, not with the sword or with might.

Accordingly, there is a proverb which should be written in letters of gold. It reads: "To strike back creates strife" and "He who strikes back is wrong." From this it must follow that not to strike back makes for peace. How does this happen? After all, it is contrary to human nature. Yes indeed, it is contrary to human nature. But if you suffer wrong in this way and do not strike back but let it pass, then what follows will happen:

The eyes of the Lord are over the righteous, and His ears are open to their prayer. But the face of the Lord is against those that do evil.

If you do not take vengeance and do not repay evil with evil, the Lord is up in heaven. He cannot tolerate wrong. Therefore he who does not strike back must be in the right. For these the Lord has regard. His ears are open to their prayer. He is our Protector. He will not forget us. Therefore we cannot be out of His sight. With this we should comfort ourselves. This should move a Christian to suffer all wrong with patience and not to requite evil. When I consider this in the right way, I see that the soul of him who wrongs me must burn eternally in the fire of hell. Therefore a Christian heart must say: "Dear Father, since this person incurs Thy anger so horribly and hurls himself so tragically into the everlasting fire, I implore Thee to forgive him and to do to him as Thou hast done to me when Thou didst save me from Thy wrath." How does this happen? Thus: Just as He has regard for the righteous with

His mercy, so He regards the wicked with displeasure, wrinkles His brow, and has turned it in anger against them. And since we know that He regards us with mercy and those people with disfavor, we should take pity on them, have compassion, and pray for them. St. Peter continues:

13. *Now who is there to harm you if you are zealous for what is right?*

14. *But even if you do suffer for righteousness' sake, you will be blessed. Have no fear of them, nor be troubled;*

15. *but in your hearts sanctify Christ as Lord. Always be prepared to make a defense to anyone who calls you to account for the hope that is in you, yet do it with gentleness and reverence;*

16. *and keep your conscience clear, so that when you are abused, those who revile your good behavior in Christ may be put to shame.*

If we are zealous for what is right, that is, do not repay evil with evil but are sincere and friendly, etc., then no one could harm us. For even if we are deprived of honor, life, and goods, yet we are unharmed, since we have a possession that cannot be compared to what can be taken away from us. But those who persecute us have nothing but their possessions on earth. Afterwards they have eternal damnation. We, on the other hand, have an eternal, imperishable possession, even if we lose a small temporal possession.

But even if you do suffer for righteousness' sake, you will be blessed.

Not only, he says, can no one harm you if you suffer for God's sake; but you are also blessed, and you should be glad that you have to suffer, as Christ also says in Matt. 5:11-12:[7] "Blessed are you when men revile you and persecute you and utter all kinds of evil against you falsely on My account. Rejoice and be glad." Now he who takes hold of the fact that the Lord addresses these words to our hearts so lovingly and in such a comforting manner is fortunate. But he who is not strengthened, comforted, and cheered by them will undoubtedly remain destitute of strength.

---

[7] The original has "Matt. 6."

Have no fear of them, nor be troubled; but in your hearts sanctify Christ as Lord.

But here St. Peter quotes a statement from Is. 8:12-13, where the prophet says: "Do not fear what they fear, nor be in dread. But the Lord of hosts, Him you shall regard as holy; let Him be your fear, and let Him be your dread, etc." Here we have great protection and support. On this we can depend. Therefore no one can harm us. Let the world frighten, challenge, and threaten as long as it wants to – this must come to an end. But our comfort and joy will not come to an end. Therefore we should not be afraid of the world. No, we should be courageous. Before God, however, we should humble ourselves and fear.

But what does St. Peter mean when he says that we should sanctify God? How can we sanctify Him? Must He not sanctify us? Answer: In the Lord's Prayer we also say: "Hallowed be Thy name," that we should hallow His name, even though He Himself hallows His name. Therefore this is the procedure: You must sanctify Him in your hearts, says St. Peter; that is, when our Lord God sends us something – whether good or bad, whether it benefits or hurts, whether it is shame, honor, good fortune, or misfortune – I should consider this not only good but also holy, and I should say: "This is pure precious holiness, and I am not worthy of being touched by it." Thus the prophet says in Ps. 145:17: "The Lord is just in all His ways, and holy in all His doings." When in such matters I give praise to God and regard such works as good, holy, and precious, I sanctify Him in my heart. But those who run to the lawbooks, complain of suffering wrong, and say that God is sleeping and does not want to aid what is right and to prevent what is wrong – they dishonor God and do not consider Him just or holy. But he who is a Christian should say that God is in the right and that he himself is in the wrong, and he should regard God as holy and himself as not holy. He should say that God is holy and right in everything He does. God wants this. Thus the prophet Daniel says in the third chapter:[8] "Lord, everything Thou hast done for us Thou didst do on the basis of right and truthful judgment, for we have sinned. Therefore let the shame be ours, and let the honor and the praise be Thine." If we sing "Thanks be to God" and

[8] Luther seems to be thinking of Dan. 3:27ff., but the words quoted actually come from Dan. 9:5, 7, 14.

"Thee, God, we praise," and say "God be praised and blessed" when misfortune strikes us—that is what Peter and Isaiah call sanctifying the Lord properly.

But by this the apostle does not want you to say that he who harmed you did right and well. For between God and me and between me and you there is a far different judgment. I can harbor anger, hatred, and evil lust in my heart without harming you. Then you are still not harmed, and you have nothing against me. But before God I am wrong. Therefore He is in the right. If He punishes me, I have surely deserved it. If He does not punish me, He is showing me mercy. Thus He is always right. But from this it does not follow that he who persecutes me is doing what is right; for I have done him no wrong the way I have done before God. When God sends the devil or evil people to punish you, He uses them to administer His justice. Hence rascals and wrong are a good thing too.

Thus we read in Ezek. 29:19-20 about King Nebuchadrezzar, where the Lord says through the prophet: "Do you not know that he was My servant and that he served Me? Now I must reward him. I have not yet paid him. All right, I will give him the land of Egypt as a recompense." The king had no right to the country, but God has the right to let those people be punished through him. For in order that rascals may also serve Him and not eat their bread for nothing, He gives them enough and also lets them serve Him by persecuting His saints. Here reason comes along and thinks they are doing what is right, although God pays them only here, gives them much land here, and does this in order that they may be His jailers and persecute pious Christians. But if you suffer this, sanctify God, and say: "Right, Lord," then you prosper. Then He casts those people into hell and punishes them for their wrongdoing. But He receives you in mercy and gives you eternal bliss. Therefore let Him manage things. He will surely repay.

Of this we have an example in saintly Job after all his cattle and also his sons had been slain and he had been stripped of all his property. Then he said (cf. 1:21): "The Lord gave, and the Lord has taken away. As it pleased Him, so it has happened. Blessed be the name of the Lord." And when his wife came, mocked and reviled him, and said: "Do you still hold fast your integrity? Curse God, and die," he replied (2:10): "You speak as one of the foolish women would speak. Shall we receive good at the hand of God, and

shall we not receive evil? Therefore He did as it pleased Him."
Job says: "God gave it, and God took it away." He did not say:
"God gave it, and the devil took it away," even though the devil
had taken it away. Now this man sanctified the Lord in the right
way. Therefore he was also praised and lauded so highly by God.
Now the apostle continues:

*Always be prepared to make a defense to anyone who calls you
to account for the hope that is in you.*

Here we shall have to admit that St. Peter is addressing these
words to all Christians, to priests, laymen, men and women, young
and old, and in whatever station they are. Therefore it follows from
this that every Christian should account for his faith and be able to
give a reason and an answer when necessary. Now up to this time
the laity has been forbidden to read Scripture. For here the devil
came up with a pretty trick for the purpose of tearing the people
away from Scripture. He thought: "If I can keep the laity from
reading Scripture, then I shall bring the priests from the Bible into
Aristotle." Then the priests can babble what they please, and the
laity has to listen to what they preach to them. Otherwise, if the
laity were to read Scripture, the priests would also have to study,
lest they be rebuked and overridden. But note that St. Peter tells
every one of us to be prepared to make a defense of our faith. When
the time comes for you to die, neither I nor the pope will be at your
side; and if you know no reason for your hope and say: "I want to
believe what the councils, the pope, and our fathers believed,"
then the devil will answer: "But what if they were in error?" Then
he has won, and he drags you into hell. Therefore we must know
what we believe, namely, what God's Word says, not what the pope
or the saintly fathers believe or say. For you must not rely on a
person. No, you must rely on the Word of God alone.

Hence if someone tackles you, as if you were a heretic, and
asks: "Why do you believe that you are saved through faith?" then
reply: "I have God's Word and clear statements of Scripture.
Thus St. Paul says in Rom. 1:17: 'He who through faith is righteous
shall live.' And above (1 Peter 2:6), when St. Peter, on the basis of
the prophet Isaiah (28:16), speaks of Christ, the Living Stone, he
says: 'He who believes in Him will not be put to shame.' I build
on this, and I know that the Word does not deceive me." But if, as

other fools do, you want to say: "Ah, we want to hear how the council decrees! To this we want to cling," then you are lost. Therefore you should say: "What do I care about what this or that person believes or decrees? If the Word of God is not preached, I do not want to hear what is said."

You may say: "There is such confusion that no one knows what to believe. Therefore it is necessary to wait until it is decreed what one should accept." Answer: Meanwhile you will also go to the devil. For when you are lying at death's door and do not know what to believe, neither I nor anyone else can help you. Therefore you yourself must know. You must pay no attention to anyone, and you must cling firmly to the Word of God if you want to escape hell. And it is also necessary for those who are not able to read to take hold of and retain several — at least one or two — clear passages from Scripture and to stand firmly on this ground. For example, there is Gen. 22:18,[9] where God says to Abraham: "And in your Seed shall all the nations of the earth be blessed." If you have understood this, you can rely on it and say: "Even if the pope, the bishops, and all the councils confronted me and said otherwise, I say: 'This is God's Word; for me it is certain; it does not lie. What is to be blessed must be blessed through the Seed. What does the blessing mean? It means to deliver from the curse, that is, from sin, death, and hell. Therefore it follows from this statement that he who is not blessed through the Seed must be lost. Accordingly, my works and merits cannot contribute anything toward salvation.'"

St. Peter's statement that he who believes in the Stone will not be put to shame (cf. 2:6) reaches the same conclusion. Now if someone tackles you and demands the reason for your faith, you must reply: "Here is the foundation; it cannot deceive me. Therefore I do not care about what the pope or the bishops teach and decide. If they were true bishops, they would have to teach the foundation of faith, in order that all Christians might know it. Yet they continue to cry out that one should not let the laity read the Scriptures!"

If someone asks you whether you want to have the pope as a head, you must answer: "Yes, I want to have him as a head, a head of scoundrels and rascals. And I have a statement made by St. Paul in 1 Tim. 4:1, 3, where he says that some will give heed to doctrines of demons, who forbid marriage and enjoin abstinence from foods

---

[9] The original has "Gen. 12," probably meaning Gen. 12:3; but Gen. 22:18 is the actual source of the words.

which God created. It is evident that the pope has forbidden marriage. Therefore he is the Antichrist. For he acts contrary to what Christ commands and teaches. What Christ sets free, this the pope binds. When Christ says that it is not sin, the pope says that it is a sin."

Therefore we must now learn to give an account for our faith, for it surely must come to this. If it does not happen here, it must happen when death comes. Then the devil will step forth and say: "Why have you called the pope an antichrist?" If you are not prepared to stand your ground and give a reason, then he has won. Therefore St. Peter now wants to say here: Now that you have become believers, you will encounter much persecution from now on. But in persecution you must have a hope and wait for eternal life. And when you are asked why you have this hope, you must have God's Word on which to be able to build.

The sophists have also perverted this text. They say that one must vanquish the heretics with reason and on the basis of the natural light of Aristotle, since the Latin expression *rationem reddere* is used here, as though St. Peter meant that this should be done by means of human reason.[10] Therefore they say that Scripture is far too weak to overthrow heretics. This, they say, must be done by reason and must come from the brain, which must be the source of the proof that faith is right, even though our faith transcends all reason and is solely a power of God. Therefore if people refuse to believe, you should keep silence; for you have no obligation to force them to regard Scripture as God's Book or Word. It is sufficient for you to base your proof on Scripture. This you must do when they take it upon themselves to say: "You preach that one should not hold to the teaching of men, even though Peter and Paul, yes, even Christ, were men too." If you hear people who are so completely blinded and hardened that they deny that this is God's Word or are in doubt about it, just keep silence, do not say a word to them, and let them go their way. Just say: "I will give you enough proof from Scripture. If you want to believe it, this is good; if not, I will give you nothing else." Then you may say: "Ah, in this way God's Word must needs be brought into disgrace!" Leave this to God. Therefore it is necessary to grasp this well and to know

[10] Cf. Anselm of Canterbury, *Cur deus homo*, Book I, ch. 1, on this use of 1 Peter 3:15; also Thomas Aquinas, *Summa Theologica*, II-II, Q. 2, Art. 10.

how to meet those who stand up now and make such allegations. Now there follows:

Yet do it with gentleness and reverence.

That is, when you are challenged and are questioned with regard to your faith, you should not answer with proud words and act defiantly and violently, as though you wanted to uproot trees. No, you should conduct yourself reverently and humbly, as though you were standing before God's tribunal and had to give an answer there. For if it should now happen that you are cited before kings and princes and for a time had fortified yourself well with verses for this of Scripture and thought: "Wait, I will answer them in the right way," then you will surely find out that the devil will take the sword out of your hand and give you a thrust. Then you will be disgraced, and you will discover that you have put on your armor in vain. It can easily happen that the devil will take the verses you have understood best out of your hands, so that this will not help you, even if you have it well in mind. For he has been aware of your thoughts beforehand. God now permits this to happen in order that He may subdue your pride and make you humble.

Therefore if this is not to happen to you, you must be reverent and not rely on your own strength. No, you must rely on the words and the promise of Christ in Matt. 10:19-20: "When they deliver you up, do not be anxious how you are to speak or what you are to say; for what you are to say will be given to you in that hour; for it is not you who speak but the Spirit of your Father speaking through you." It is proper for you to arm yourself well with verses from Scripture when you are to give an answer. But see to it that you do not boast proudly of this. Otherwise God will surely tear the right verse out of your mouth and memory, even if you have been armed beforehand with all the verses. Accordingly, reverence is needed here. But when you are prepared in this way, you can defend yourself before princes and lords, and even before the devil himself. Only see to it that it is the Word of God, not the trivialities of men.

And keep your conscience clear, so that when you are abused, those who revile your good behavior in Christ may be put to shame.

St. Peter has spoken about this above (2:12). We cannot escape being reviled and condemned by the world and being regarded as the most hopeless scoundrels if we want to cling to the Gospel. Therefore we should let nothing disturb us. We should just fear God and have a good conscience. Then let the devil and all the world rage and bluster, let them revile as they please; in the end they will be put to shame for having reviled and defamed us. When, as St. Peter has said above (2:12), the day of visitation comes, then we will be safe and have a good conscience. Now these are all beautiful and powerful verses. They can comfort and encourage us. Yet at the same time they can keep us reverent.

17. *For it is better to suffer for doing right, if that should be God's will, than for doing wrong.*

18. *For Christ also died for sins once for all, the Righteous for the unrighteous, that He might offer us to God, being put to death in the flesh but made alive in the spirit.*

It will not come about that those who are on the way to heaven will have good days on earth, since those who do not come into heaven cannot have good days either. For all men are subjected to what God says to Adam (Gen. 3:19)—"In the sweat of your face you shall eat bread"—and to the woman (Gen. 3:16)—"I will greatly multiply your pain in childbearing." Now since we are all sub-jected to misfortune, how much more it is necessary for those who want to come into eternal life to bear the cross! For this reason St. Peter says that because God wants it this way, it is better for you to suffer for doing right. Those who suffer for doing wrong have an evil conscience and a twofold punishment. But Christians have only half of this. Outwardly they suffer, but inwardly they are comforted.

Yet here the apostle has set a limit, as he did above (1:6), when he said that "for a little while you may have to suffer various trials." He has done so in order to check those who, like the Donatists, about whom Augustine writes, turned to verses that speak of suffer-ing and killed themselves. They hurled themselves into the sea.[11] God does not want us to search for misfortune and to choose it our-selves. Walk in faith and love. If the cross comes, accept it. If it

[11] Cf. Augustine, *De correctione Donatistarum,* ch. 3, par. 12.

does not come, do not search for it. Therefore those hotheaded spirits do wrong by scourging and beating themselves or by killing themselves and trying in this way to take heaven by storm.

Paul has also forbidden this in Col. 2:23,[12] where he speaks of those saints who walk in self-chosen "devotion and self-abasement and severity to the body." We should take care of the body in such a way thàt it does not become too licentious (cf. Rom. 13:14). Yet we should not destroy it either. We should suffer when another person inflicts suffering on us. But we should not do so of our own accord. This is what the words "if that should be God's will" mean. If God inflicts suffering on you, then it is better. Then the fact that you are suffering for doing right is a greater blessing for you and makes you happier.

For Christ also died for sins once for all, the Righteous for the unrighteous.

Here St. Peter again presents the Lord Christ to us as an example and always refers to the suffering of Christ. He says that we should all follow this example, in order that it may not be necessary for him to suggest a special illustration for every station in life. For just as the example of Christ is suggested to everyone in general, so the apostle points out that everyone, no matter in what station in life he is, should pattern his whole life, as it happens, according to this example. He means:

Christ was righteous. For doing right He also suffered for us, who were unrighteous. But He did not seek the cross. No, He waited until it was God's will that He should drink the cup. He should be the model for us to imitate. And here St. Peter's chief reason for citing this example is that he now intends to draw a conclusion and will now give a further explanation of the suffering of Christ.

Actually, however, St. Peter is saying here: Christ suffered for us once, that is, Christ bore many sins on Himself. But He did not do this in such a way that He died for each sin. No, He rendered satisfaction for all at one time. By doing so He took away the sin of all those who come to Him and believe in Him. They are now free from death, just as He is free.

---

[12] The original has "Col. 3."

"The Righteous for the unrighteous," says the apostle. It is as though he were saying: We should sooner suffer, since we die for the Righteous One, who has no sin. But He died for the unrighteous on account of our sin.

That He might offer us to God.

The apostle says all this for the purpose of giving instruction concerning the particular nature of Christ's suffering, namely, that He did not die for His own sake but to offer us to God. How is this done? Did Christ not offer Himself? It is true that He offered Himself on the cross for every one of us who believes in Him. But by this very act He at the same time also offers us, so that it is necessary for all those who believe in Him to suffer too and to be put to death according to the flesh, as happened in His case. In this way He presented us to God as living in the spirit yet dying in the flesh, as St. Peter says later (cf. 1 Peter 4:6). On the other hand, we are one sacrifice with Him. As He dies, so we, too, die according to the flesh; as He lives in the spirit, so we, too, live in the spirit.

Being put to death in the flesh but made alive in the spirit.

The little word "flesh" occurs frequently in Scripture. So does the little word "spirit." And the apostles commonly contrast the two with each other. This is now the meaning: Through His suffering Christ was taken from the life which is flesh and blood just like a human being on earth, who lives in flesh and blood, walks and stands, eats, drinks, sleeps, is awake, sees, hears, touches and feels, and, in short, does what the body does. This is transitory. To it Christ died. St. Paul calls it the *corpus animale,* the "physical body" (1 Cor. 15:44), that is, life like that of an animal. In the flesh, not according to the flesh, that is, in the natural functions of the body. To this life he has died, so that this life has ceased with Him, and He has now been transferred into another life, has been made alive according to the spirit, and has entered into a spiritual and supernatural life which embraces the whole life that Christ now has in body and soul. Consequently, He no longer has a physical body but has a body that is spiritual. This is the way Paul expresses it.

This is how we, too, shall be on the Last Day. Then flesh and blood will become spiritual life, so that my body and your body will live without food and drink, will not beget children, digest, throw off waste matter, and the like. But inwardly we shall live according to the spirit, and the body will be glorified and be like the sun today and be even more brilliant. There will be no natural flesh and blood, no natural or physical functions which animals perform.

This is how St. Paul speaks about the subject in 1 Cor. 15:45: "The first man Adam became a living being; the last Adam became a life-giving spirit." And he adds: "Just as we have borne the image of the natural man, so we shall also bear the image of the spiritual man (cf. v. 49). From Adam we, like irrational animals, have inherited all the natural functions according to the five senses. But Christ is spiritual flesh and blood, not according to the external senses. He does not sleep and does not wake. Yet He knows everything and is everywhere. This is how we, too, shall be. He is the First Fruits, the Beginning, and the First-born of the spiritual life, as St. Paul says (1 Cor. 15:20, Col. 1:18); that is, He is the first who rose and entered into a spiritual life. Thus Christ now lives according to the spirit; that is, He is true man, but He has a spiritual body. Therefore here the words should not be referred to the way spirit and flesh are differentiated. No, they mean that the body and the flesh are spiritual and that the spirit is in the body and with the body. For here St. Peter does not mean to speak about the fact that the Holy Spirit raised Christ from the dead. No, he is speaking in general. Thus when I speak of "the spirit" in contrast with "the flesh," I do not mean the Holy Spirit. No, I mean what the Spirit brings about inwardly and what comes from the Spirit.

Now the apostle continues:

19. *In which He went and preached to the spirits in prison,*

20. *who formerly did not believe when God's patience waited in the days of Noah, during the building of the ark, in which a few, that is, eight persons, were saved through water.*

21. *Baptism, which corresponds to this, now saves you, not as a removal of dirt from the body but as an appeal to God for a clear conscience, through the resurrection of Jesus Christ,*

22. *who has gone into heaven and is at the right hand of God, with angels, authorities, and powers subject to Him.*

This is a strange text and certainly a more obscure passage than any other passage in the New Testament. I still do not know for sure what the apostle means.[13] At first the words give the impression that Christ preached to the spirits, that is, to the souls who did not believe many years ago, when Noah was building the ark. I do not understand this. Nor can I explain it. Nor has anyone ever explained it. But if anyone chooses to maintain that after Christ had died on the cross, He descended to the souls and preached to them there, I will not stand in the way. These words could give such a meaning. But I do not know whether St. Peter wants to say this. On the other hand, these words could also be understood to mean that after the Lord Christ had ascended into heaven, He came in the spirit and preached, yet in such a way that His preaching was not physical. For He does not speak with a physical voice and no longer performs the natural functions of the body. Therefore if this meaning, which the words seem to express, is correct, namely, that He preached to the spirits in His spiritual life, such preaching must also be a spiritual preaching which He does inwardly in the heart and in the soul, so that it is not necessary for Him to go with the body and preach orally. The text does not state that He descended[14] to the souls and preached to them when He died; for it reads "in which," that is, when He was put to death according to the flesh and was made alive according to the spirit, namely, when He divested Himself of His existence in the flesh and of the natural functions of the body and entered into a spiritual existence and life such as He now has in heaven. Then He went and preached. Now He did not descend again into hell after He had assumed such a new existence. Therefore one must understand these words to mean that He did this after His resurrection.

Since these words tend to force one to conclude that spiritual preaching is spoken of, we shall cling to the opinion that St. Peter is speaking of the office which Christ administers through external

---

[13] Luther's hesitancy to commit himself to a particular theory about the descent into hell continued throughout his life, as his "Torgau sermon" of April 16–17, 1533, makes clear (W, XXXVII, 35–72).

[14] Some editions alter this to read: "The text does not state that He descended *in this way*, etc.," but there is no justification in the manuscript evidence for such an emendation.

preaching. For He commanded the apostles to preach the Gospel physically. But in addition to the preaching, He Himself comes, is spiritually present, and speaks and preaches to the hearts of the people, just as the apostles address their words orally and physically to the ears of the people. Then Christ preaches to the spirits who are in captivity in the prison of the devil. Thus the going, like the preaching, should be understood in a spiritual sense.

But the words that follow — "to the spirits in prison, who formerly did not believe" — we choose to interpret in accordance with the divine computation of time, namely, that in the existence in which Christ is, those who lived in the past and those who are living today are alike before Him. For His rule extends over both the dead and the living. And in that life the beginning, the middle, and the end of the world are all in one lump. But here in the world, of course, there is one way of measuring. Here time is consecutive, the son after the father, etc. Let me give an illustration. If a piece of wood is lying some distance away from you, or if you are looking at it lengthwise, then you cannot examine it well; but if it is lying close to you, or if you are standing on top of it and can look at it crosswise, then you have a full view of it. Thus we on earth cannot understand this life; for it is always moving along consecutively, step by step until the Last Day. But before God everything takes place in one moment. For before Him a thousand years are as one day, as St. Peter says in his second epistle (2 Peter 3:8; cf. Ps. 90:4). Thus for Him the first human being is just as close as the human being who is to be born last. And He sees everything at one time, just as the human eye can bring together in one moment two things that are far from each other. Therefore here the meaning would be that Christ no longer preaches physically but is present with the Word and preaches to the spirits in their hearts. But do not understand this to mean that He preaches this way to all spirits.

But to which spirits did He preach? To those "who formerly did not believe." This is the figure of speech which is called synecdoche, *ex parte totum,* "the whole from a part," that is, not to those very same spirits but to those who are like them and are just as unbelieving as those. Thus one must look from this life into that life.

Now in my opinion this is the best interpretation of these words of St. Peter. Yet I will not fight too hard for it. But I surely cannot believe that Christ descended to the souls and preached to them there. Scripture, too, is against this and states that everyone, when he comes to that place, will receive as he believed and lived. Moreover, since it is not certain what the condition of the dead is, we surely cannot apply this verse to them. But it is certain that Christ is present and preaches to the hearts wherever a preacher proclaims the Word of God to the ear. Therefore we can adopt this interpretation without danger. But let him to whom a better interpretation is revealed follow it. This is now the sum and substance of the interpretation I have pointed out: Christ ascended into heaven and preached to the spirits, that is, to human souls, and among these souls there were unbelievers in the days of Noah. Now the text continues:

When God's patience waited in the days of Noah, during the building of the ark, in which a few, that is, eight persons, were saved through water.

But here it is St. Peter's purpose to lead us into Scripture, in order that we may apply ourselves to the study of Scripture. From this source he mentions Noah's ark as an analogy, and he interprets this figure. For the presentation of an analogy with illustrations of this kind is an attractive procedure. St. Paul also resorts to it when he speaks of the two sons and the two wives of Abraham in Gal. 4:22. And in John 3:14 [15] Christ does so when He speaks of the serpent which Moses had raised aloft in the wilderness. One can understand analogies of this kind. In addition, they are attractive. Therefore St. Peter adduces this analogy here. By using a physical analogy it is possible to express briefly what faith is.

But the apostle means to say that what happened when Noah was building the ark also happens today. Just as at that time he, together with seven others, was saved in the ark which floated on the water, so you, too, must be saved in Baptism. That water drowned everything that had life. Thus Baptism drowns everything that is carnal and natural; it makes spiritual men. But we take ship in the ark, which represents the Lord Christ, or the Christian Church, or the Gospel which Christ preaches, or the body of Christ to which we cling through faith; and we are saved, just as Noah was saved in the ark. Thus you see that the analogy summarizes what

---

[15] The original has "John 5."

faith and the cross, life and death, are. Now where there are people who cling to Christ, there a Christian Church is sure to be. There everything that comes from Adam and is evil is drowned.

Baptism, which corresponds to this, now saves you, not as a removal of dirt from the body but as the covenant of a good conscience with God.

You are not saved by washing the dirt from the flesh in order that the body may be clean, as the Jews did. Such cleanliness no longer has any validity, but there must be "the covenant of a good conscience with God"; that is, you must feel in yourself a good and cheerful conscience — a conscience that is in league with God and can say: "He gave me this promise. He will keep it, for He cannot lie." When you cling and cleave to His Word in this way, then you must be saved. Now the covenant is faith, which saves us. No external work you can do accomplishes this.

Through the resurrection of Jesus Christ.

St. Peter adds these words for the purpose of explaining faith, which is based on Christ's death, His descent into hell, and His resurrection from the dead. If He had remained dead, there would have been no help for us. But because He rose from the dead, sits at the right hand of God, and has this proclaimed to us in order that we may believe in Him, we have a covenant with God and a sure promise. With this we are saved, just as Noah was saved in the ark. Thus St. Peter has made the ark completely spiritual. Here one does not find flesh and blood. No, one finds a good conscience toward God, that is, faith.

Who has gone into heaven and is at the right hand of God, with angels, authorities, and powers subject to Him.

The apostle says all of this to explain and strengthen our faith. For Christ also had to ascend into heaven and become Lord over all creatures and wherever there is power, in order that He might also lead us to heaven and make us lords. Now this is said for our comfort, in order that we may know that all power in heaven and on earth, even death and the devil, must serve and aid us, just as everything must serve the Lord Christ and lie at His feet. This is the third chapter. The fourth follows.

CHAPTER FOUR

1. *Since therefore Christ suffered in the flesh, arm yourselves with the same thought; for whoever has suffered in the flesh has ceased from sin,*

2. *so as to live for the rest of the time in the flesh no longer by human passions but by the will of God.*

3. *Let the time that is past suffice for doing what the Gentiles like to do, living in licentiousness, passions, drunkenness, revels, carousing, and lawless idolatry.*

S t. Peter continues on the same path. Just as so far he has exhorted us all to suffer if it is God's will and has presented Christ to us as an example, so he now confirms this further and repeats it. He wants to say: Since Christ, who is our Leader and Head, suffered in the flesh and gave us all an example — besides, He redeemed us through His suffering — we should imitate Him, equip ourselves in this way, and put on armor of this kind. For in Scripture the life of the Lord Christ, and particularly His suffering, is presented to us in a twofold manner. In the first place, as a gift, as St. Peter has already done in the third chapter. First he stressed faith and taught that we are redeemed by the blood of Christ, that our sins have been taken away, and how He has been given to us as a gift. This cannot be grasped in any other way than through faith. The apostle spoke about this when he said: "Christ also died for sins once for all" (3:18). This is the chief article and the best part of the Gospel.

In the second place, Christ is held up and given to us as an example and a pattern for us to follow, for if we now have Christ as a gift through faith, we should go forward and do as He does for us. We should imitate Him in our whole life and in all our suffering. That is the way St. Peter presents this here. But here St. Peter is not speaking primarily of the works of love with which we serve and benefit our neighbor, which are really good works — for he has said enough about this above—but he is speaking about works that relate to our bodies and serve us ourselves—works through which faith is strengthened, so that we mortify sin in the flesh and thus are able to serve our neighbor better. For if I subdue my body, so that it does not become lascivious, I can also let my neighbor's wife and child alone. Thus if I suppress hatred and envy, I become all the more willing to be kind and friendly to my neighbor.

Now we have stated often enough that although we are righteous through faith and have the Lord Christ as our own, we are nonetheless also obliged to perform good works and to serve our neighbor. For we never become perfectly pure while we are living on earth, and everyone still finds evil lust in his body. To be sure, faith begins to slay sin and to bestow heaven; but it has not yet become perfect and really strong, as Christ says about the Samaritan (Luke 10:33 ff.), whose wounds were not yet healed. But he was bandaged and looked after, in order that his wounds might be healed. This is also how it is here. If we believe, our sin, that is, the wound we have brought from Adam, is bandaged and begins to heal. But in one person this healing is less, and in another person it is more, the more each one chastises and subdues the flesh, and the more firmly he believes. Therefore if we have these two things, faith and love, we should henceforth devote ourselves to sweeping out sin entirely until we die completely.

For this reason St. Peter says: "Arm yourselves with the same thought"; that is, make a firm resolution, and strengthen your hearts with the thought you receive from Christ. For if we are Christians, we have to say: "My Lord suffered for me and shed His blood. He died for my sake. Should I, then, be so worthless as not to be willing to suffer?" For since the Lord steps to the front in the fray, how much more should His servants rejoice to step forward! In this way we gain courage to prevail and to arm ourselves in our thoughts, in order that we may go through with joy.

In Scripture the little word "flesh" means not only the body externally, where there is flesh and blood, bone and skin, but everything that comes from Adam. Thus God says in Gen. 6:3: "My Spirit shall not abide in man forever, for he is flesh." And in Is. 40:5 we read that all flesh shall see the glory of the Lord; that is, this glory will be revealed to all mankind. Thus we also confess in the Creed: "I believe in the resurrection of the flesh"; that is, that mankind will rise again. Accordingly, flesh means the whole man through and through, as he lives here in this life.

Now the works of the flesh are enumerated by Paul one by one in Gal. 5:19-21, not only the coarse, carnal works, such as unchastity, but also the costliest and most sublime vices, such as idolatry and heresy, which are not only in the flesh but also in reason. Therefore one must understand this to mean that man, together with his reason and will, internally and externally, together with body and soul, is called flesh because with all his powers, externally and internally, he sees only that which is carnal and which benefits the flesh. Accordingly, St. Peter now adds here that "Christ suffered in the flesh." Now it is certain that His suffering extended farther than into the flesh alone; for, as the prophet Isaiah says (53:11), His soul suffered the great travail.

In this way you must also understand what follows here: "Whoever has suffered in the flesh has ceased from sin." For this, too, refers not only to cutting off someone's head and to dismembering the body but to everything that can hurt man, to whatever misery and distress he suffers. For many people have sound bodies, and yet inwardly they feel much heartache and wretchedness. If this happens for Christ's sake, it is profitable and good. For, as Saint Peter says, "whoever has suffered in the flesh has ceased from sin." The holy cross is a good means with which to subdue sin. When it attacks you in this way, your tickling, envy, and hatred, and your other rascality, vanish. God has laid the holy cross on us in order that it may drive and compel us, so that we have to believe and to extend a helping hand to one another.

This is why the text adds:

So as to live for the rest of the time in the flesh no longer by passions but by the will of God.

From now on, as long as we live, we should take the flesh captive and mortify it by means of the cross, so that we do what is pleasing to God, not that by doing so we should or could merit anything. "No longer by human passions," he says; that is, we should not do what we or others feel a desire to do. For, as Paul says in Rom. 12:2, we should "not be conformed to this world." We must avoid what the world would have us do.

Let the time that is past suffice for doing what the Gentiles like to do, living in licentiousness, passions, drunkenness, revels, carousing, and lawless idolatry.

Before we came to faith, we went to extremes by living so shamefully, "doing what the Gentiles like to do." This is tantamount to living in human passions. Therefore as long as we live from now on, we must see to it that we do what pleases God. For we have our enemy in our flesh. He is the real rascal, not only the gross things but above all the illusion of reason, which Paul calls *prudentia carnis*, that is, "the mind of the flesh" (Rom. 8:6). If this rascality has been subdued, the rest is easily subdued. This rascality commonly harms our neighbor so furtively that one cannot notice it.

By "licentiousness" St. Peter means outward gestures or words with which one gives evil indications even if the deed is not done, and with which one reveals indecency in seeing and hearing. From this the lust and also the deed result. Then such abominable idolatry also follows. Therefore we can apply this to ourselves; for since we have now lost faith, we have surely also lost God; and if we look at it in the proper way, we are certainly practicing idolatry more abominable than the idolatry practiced by the Gentiles.

4. *They are surprised that you do not now join them in the same wild profligacy, and they abuse you;*

5. *but they will give account to Him who is ready to judge the living and the dead.*

That is, so far you have lived as the Gentiles do; but now that you have desisted, people find this strange and consider it disgraceful and foolish. They say: "Ah, what big fools they are to turn away from all worldly goods and pleasure!" But let them think it strange! And let them revile you! They will have to give account. Therefore leave this to Him who will judge.

6. *For this is why the Gospel was preached even to the dead, that though judged in the flesh like men, they might live in the spirit like God.*

7. *The end of all things is at hand.*

But this is another strange text. The words state clearly that the Gospel was preached not only to the living but also to the dead. Yet the apostle adds that they are "judged in the flesh like men." Now the dead certainly do not have flesh. Therefore this can be understood only of the living. No matter what it is, it is a strange way of speaking. Whether the text has come to us in its entirety or whether a part of it has been lost, I do not know. Yet I understand it in the following way: One need not be concerned about how God will condemn the Gentiles who died many hundreds of years ago, but one must be concerned about those who are living today. Therefore the text speaks about people on earth.

But, as I have stated above, you must understand the little word "flesh" to mean that the whole man, as he lives, is called flesh, just as the whole man is called spirit when he strives for what is spiritual. Now this is mixed up, just as I say of a person who is wounded that he is in good health and yet is wounded, but in such a way that the part that is in good health is larger than the part that is wounded. He may be termed wounded only according to the part that has been smitten. Thus here, too, the spirit should have precedence. Therefore the apostle says that they are condemned according to their outward being, but that they are saved and live according to the inner man, that is, according to the spirit.

But how can the apostle say that they are alive and yet add that they are dead? I shall interpret this according to my own understanding—yet without setting any bounds to the Holy Spirit—to mean that the apostle calls the unbelievers "dead." I cannot accept the interpretation that the Gospel should be preached to the dead, unless St. Peter means that the Gospel went out freely and resounded everywhere (cf. Col. 1:23), that it was concealed neither from the living nor from the dead, neither from the angels nor from the devils, and that it was not preached secretly in a corner but was proclaimed so publicly that all creatures, if they had ears to hear, could have heard it, as Christ commanded in Mark 16:15: "Go into all the world and preach the Gospel to the whole creation!" For when the Gospel is preached in this way, it finds people who are condemned according to the flesh but live according to the spirit.

The end of all things is at hand.

This is also a strange way of speaking. Almost 1,500 years have elapsed since St. Peter preached. This is surely neither a near nor a short time. Still the apostle says that "the end of all things is at hand" and is already here, just as 1 John 2:18 also says: "It is the last hour." If the apostle did not make this statement, one could say that it was a lie. But now one must maintain firmly that the apostle is telling the truth. Yet what he means he himself will explain in his second epistle. There he tells why the time is near and says: "With the Lord one day is as a thousand years" (2 Peter 3:8). I have spoken about this above.[1] So one must figure that it will not be so long until the end of the world as it had been from the beginning up to that time. It is not to be expected that mankind will still see two or three thousand years after the birth of Christ. The end will come sooner than we think. Therefore the apostle continues:

Therefore keep sane and sober for your prayers.

8. *Above all, hold unfailing your love for one another, since love covers a multitude of sins.*

Here you see why we should be "sane and sober," namely, that we may be fit for prayer both for ourselves and for our neighbor. Furthermore, love cannot be fervent unless you hold the body in check, so that you have room for love.

Here St. Peter has taken a verse from the Book of Proverbs, where we read in chapter 10:12: "Hatred stirs up strife, but love covers all offenses." And this is what St. Peter means: Curb your flesh and lust. If you do not do this, you will easily become angry with one another, and it will not be easy for you to forgive one another. Therefore see to it that you subdue the evil lust. Then you will be able to love and forgive one another, for love covers sin.

According to the interpretation of some, this verse militates against faith. Therefore they say: "You declare that faith alone makes one pious and that no one can be freed from sin through works. Then why do Solomon and St. Peter say that love covers

---

[1] Cf. p. 114.

sin?"[2] You must reply: "Solomon says that he who hates another person is unceasingly eager for strife and quarreling. But where there is love, it covers sin and is glad to forgive. Where there is anger, you will find a rude person who refuses to be reconciled and remains full of anger and hatred. On the other hand, a person who is full of love cannot be angered, no matter how greatly he is offended. He covers everything and pretends not to see it, so that this covering is meant with reference to the neighbor, not with reference to God. Only faith shall cover your sin before God. But my love covers my neighbor's sin, and just as God covers my sin with His love if I believe, so I must also cover my neighbor's sin. Therefore the apostle says that you should love one another in order that one person may be able to cover the other person's sin. And love does not cover one, two, or three sins. No, it covers the multitude of sins. It cannot suffer and do too much; it covers everything. Thus in 1 Cor. 13:7 St. Paul also says, and, as it were, interprets this text: 'Love bears all things, believes all things, hopes all things, endures all things.' It wants the very best for everybody. It can suffer and forgive everything that is inflicted on it." St. Peter goes on:

9. *Practice hospitality ungrudgingly to one another.*

10. *As each has received a gift, employ it for one another.*

The person who is glad to provide lodging is called hospitable. Thus when the apostles went jointly in the country to preach, and when they sent their disciples to and fro, then one person had to provide lodging for the other person. This is how it should still be. One should travel from one place to another to preach, from city to city, from house to house; and one should not tarry too long at one place. One should be able to see: if a person is weak, he should get help; if a person has fallen, he should be encouraged, and the like. This, says St. Peter, should be done ungrudgingly, and no one should let this be too much. Now this is also a work of love, as is also the injunction that follows, namely, that we should

[2] The passage figured prominently in the debates of the Reformation, as its appearance in the Apology of the Augsburg Confession, Art. IV, pars. 117-118, indicates. For one instance to which Luther may be referring here cf. Ambrosius Catharinus Politus, *Apologia pro veritate catholicae et apostolicae fidei ac doctrinae adversus impia ac valde pestifera Martini Lutheri dogmata* (1520), Book IV, Disp. XII, ed. Josef Schweizer, *Corpus Catholicorum*, XXVII (Münster i. W., 1956), 291.

serve one another. With what? With the gifts of God which everyone has received. The Gospel wants everyone to be the other person's servant and, in addition, to see that he remains in the gift which he has received, which God has given him, that is, in the position to which he has been called. God does not want a master to serve his servant, the maid to be a lady, a prince to serve the beggar. For He does not want to destroy the government. But the apostle means that one person should serve the other person spiritually from the heart. Even if you are in a high position and a great lord, yet you should employ your power for the purpose of serving your neighbor with it. Thus everyone should regard himself as a servant. Then the master can surely remain a master and yet not consider himself better than the servant. Thus he would also be glad to be a servant if this were God's will The same thing applies to other stations in life.

As good stewards of God's varied grace.

God did not give us all equal grace. Therefore everyone should pay attention to his qualifications, to the kind of gift given to him. When he is aware of this, he should use his gift in the service of his neighbor, as St. Peter explains further, saying:

11. *Whoever speaks, as one who utters oracles of God.*

That is, if someone has the grace to be able to preach and teach, let him teach and preach. Thus St. Paul also says in Rom. 12:3-6: "I bid everyone among you not to think of himself more highly than he ought to think, but to think with sober judgment, each according to the measure of faith which God has assigned him. For as in one body we have members, and all the members do not have the same function, so we, though many, are one body in Christ, and individually members one of another. Having gifts that differ according to the grace given to us, let us use them." He continues: "If prophecy, in proportion to our faith; if service, in our serving; he who teaches, in his teaching" (v. 7). He teaches the same thing in other places — in 1 Corinthians (12:12) and in Ephesians (4:7).

Accordingly, God has poured out varied gifts among the people. They should be directed to only one end, namely, that one person should serve the other person with them, especially those who are in authority, whether with preaching or with another office. Now St. Peter says here: "Whoever speaks, as one who utters oracles of God." One should note very well that no one should preach anything unless he is sure that it is God's Word. Here St. Peter has stopped the mouth of the pope. And lo, the pope wants to be St. Peter's successor! How beautifully he lives up to that obligation! The apostle continues:

Whoever renders service, as one who renders it by the strength which God supplies.

That is, he who rules in the Christian Church and has an office or a duty to care for souls should not proceed as he pleases and say: "I am an overlord here. I must be obeyed. What I command must be carried out." God wants us to do nothing except what He assigns. It must be God's work and arrangement. Therefore a bishop should do nothing unless he is sure that God is doing it, that it is God's Word or work. For God does not want us to regard what He does with the Christian Church as jugglery. Therefore we must be so sure that God is speaking and working in us that our faith can declare: "What I have said and done, this God has done and said. I stake my life on this." Otherwise, if I am not sure of this, my faith is founded on sand. Then the devil will take me. Thus here it is earnestly forbidden to take orders from any bishop unless he is certain that God is doing what he does and he can say: "Here I have God's Word and command." Where this is not the case, he must be regarded as a liar. For God has ordained that our conscience must rest on solid rock. This pertains to the general rule. Here no one should follow his own opinion and do something concerning which he is not sure that God wants it. From this you see that long ago St. Peter toppled the rule of the pope and the bishops as it is today. The apostle goes on:

In order that in everything God may be glorified through Jesus Christ. To Him belong glory and dominion forever and ever. Amen.

This, the apostle says, is why you should be so sure that God is saying and doing what you are saying and doing; for if you do a work concerning which you are not certain that God has done it, you cannot praise and thank Him. But if you are sure of this, you can thank and laud Him for the sake of His Word and work. Otherwise you deny Him and regard Him as a juggler. Therefore it is both shameful and harmful to desire to rule in Christendom without God's Word and work. Consequently, St. Peter was constrained to add these words in order to give instruction regarding what the nature of the rule in Christendom should be. He continues:

12. *Beloved, do not be surprised at the fiery ordeal which comes upon you to prove you, as though something strange were happening to you.*

But this is a way of speaking that is not common in our language. St. Peter, however, uses it for the purpose of reminding us of what Scripture says. For Scripture is wont to say about suffering that it is like an oven full of fire and heat. Thus above, in the first chapter (v. 7), St. Peter says: "So that the genuineness of your faith, more precious than gold which though perishable is tested by fire, etc." Thus we also read in Is. 48:10 that God says: "I have tried you in the furnace of affliction." and in Ps. 17:3 we read: "Thou hast tried me with fire." Likewise in Ps. 26:2: "Prove me, O Lord, and try me; test my heart and my mind with fire." Likewise in Ps. 66:12: "We went through fire and water." Thus Scripture customarily calls suffering "a penetration with fire" and "a testing with fire." In agreement with this custom St. Peter says here that we should not be surprised or think it odd and strange when heat or glowing fire come upon us to try us as gold is melted in fire.

When faith begins, God does not forsake it; He lays the holy cross on our backs to strengthen us and to make faith powerful in us. The holy Gospel is a powerful Word. Therefore it cannot do its work without trials, and only he who tastes it is aware that it has such power. Where suffering and the cross are found, there the Gospel can show and exercise its power. It is a Word of life. Therefore it must exercise all its power in death. In the absence of dying and death it can do nothing, and no one can become aware that it has such power and is stronger than sin and death. Therefore the apostle says "to prove you"; that is, God inflicts no glowing fire or heat—cross and suffering, which make you burn—on you for any other purpose than "to prove you," whether you also cling to His Word. Thus it is recorded in Wisd. of Sol. 10:12 of Jacob: "God sent him an arduous contest, so that he might know that godliness is more powerful than anything." God lays a cross on all believers in order that they may taste and prove the power of God—the power which they have taken hold of through faith.

13. *But rejoice insofar as you share Christ's sufferings.*

St. Peter does not say that we should feel Christ's sufferings in order to share them through faith. No, he wants to say: Christ suffered. Therefore bear in mind that you, too, suffer and are tried. When you suffer in this way, you have communion with the Lord Christ. For if we want to live with Him, we must also die with Him. If I want to sit with Him in His kingdom, I must also suffer with Him, as St. Paul often says (Rom. 6:5; 2 Tim. 2:11).

That you may also rejoice and be glad when His glory is revealed.

You should rejoice even if you come into suffering and into the glowing fire. For although this is a physical suffering, it should be a spiritual joy, in order that you may rejoice forever. For this joy begins here in suffering and lasts forever. Otherwise he who does not bear his suffering with rejoicing, becomes sullen, and wants to be angry with God, will suffer here and will suffer there forever. Thus we read about the saintly martyrs that they approached their suffering cheerfully and in this way gained eternal joy. When St. Agatha, for example, had to lie in prison, she was as happy as if she were going to a dance.[3] And the apostles went away rejoicing and thanked God that they were counted worthy to suffer for Christ's sake, as Acts 5:41 says.

When His glory is revealed.

Christ does not yet reveal Himself as a Lord but is still at work with us. To be sure, He is a Lord per se; but we, who are His members, are not yet lords. But we will become lords when His glory will be revealed before all men on the Last Day more clearly than the sun.

14. *If you are reproached for the name of Christ, you are blessed.*

[3] Luther referred to this legend frequently in his later writings as well; see, for example, *Luther's Works*, 24, pp. 118, 196, 277, 420

The name "Christ" is odious before the world. When one preaches about Him, one must put up with the fact that the best people on earth blaspheme and slander His name. And, what is more dangerous and flagrant, in our day they persecute us and also use Christ's name and say that they are Christians and are baptized. Yet they deny and persecute Christ with their deeds. This is a deplorable quarrel. They make use of Christ's name against us as emphatically as we make use of it. Therefore we are now surely in need of comfort, so that we may remain firm and be cheerful even though the wisest and most pious people persecute us. Why?

Because the Spirit of glory and of God rests upon you; on their part He is evil spoken of, but on your part He is glorified.

You, says the apostle, have a Spirit resting upon you, that is, God's Spirit and the Spirit of glory, namely, a Spirit that glorifies us. But He does not do this here on earth; He will do so when the glory of Christ will be revealed on the Last Day. Furthermore, He is not only a Spirit who makes us glorious; but He is also a Spirit whom we glorify. The work of glorification is ascribed especially to the Holy Spirit, just as He glorified Christ. Now the same Spirit, says the apostle, rests upon you, because the name of Christ rests upon you. This Spirit is evil spoken of by them. For He must endure the worst kind of blasphemy and slander. Therefore do not be concerned about this blasphemy; it is directed against the Spirit, who is a Spirit of glory. Do not worry. He will surely avenge it and will raise you to a position of honor. This is the comfort we Christians have. Therefore we can say: "After all, the Word is not mine; faith is not mine; these are all works of God. He who reviles me reviles God." Thus Christ says in Matt. 10:40: "He who receives you receives Me." And again (Luke 10:16): "He who rejects you rejects Me."

Therefore this is what St. Peter wants to say: Be it known to you that the Spirit, whom you have, is so strong that He will surely punish His enemy, as God also declares in Ex. 23:22: "If you hearken attentively to My voice and do all that I say, then I will be an enemy to your enemies." And Scripture often points out that the foes of the holy people are God's foes. Now when we are defamed because we are Christians and believe, then we are not the ones being slandered, but the slander is actually directed against

God Himself. Therefore He says: "Be happy and of good cheer, for this is done to the Spirit, who is not yours but God's." Now the apostle adds a warning:

15. *But let none of you suffer as a murderer, or a thief, or a wrong-doer, or a mischief-maker;*

16. *yet if one suffers as a Christian, let him not be ashamed, but under that name let him glorify God.*

St. Peter wants to say: You have heard that you are to suffer and what your attitude toward your suffering should be. But see to it that this does not happen because you have deserved it for your wrongdoing, but that you suffer for the sake of Christ. Yet this is not our lot today, for we must suffer regardless of the fact that those who persecute us also bear the name of Christ. And no one can die because he is a Christian, but he dies as an enemy of Christ. And those who persecute him say that they are true Christians and also that he who dies for Christ's sake is blessed. This only the Spirit can decide. Here you must be sure that you are a Christian in the sight of God. Here God's judgment is secret, for today He has made a change. He will no longer judge by the name, as He did at the time when the name "Christian" first came into use.

Now St. Peter says: When you suffer in this way, you should not blush. No, you should praise God. Here he makes suffering and pain precious, so that it is so important that we should praise God for it, since we are not worthy of this suffering. Today, however, everybody shrinks from it. What good does it do to put the cross in monstrances? Christ's cross does not save me. To be sure, I must believe in His cross; but I must bear my own cross. I must put His suffering into my heart. Then I have the true treasure. St. Peter's bones are sacred. But what does that help you? You and your own bones must become sacred. And this happens when you suffer for Christ's sake.

17. *For the time has come for judgment to begin with the house-hold of God; and if it begins with us, what will be the end of those who do not obey the Gospel of God?*

Here he quotes two verses of a prophet at one time. In the first place, the prophet Jeremiah says in chapter 25:29: "Behold, I begin to punish in the capital city where My name is uttered. There first of all I punish My dearly beloved children, who believe in Me. They are the first to be subjected to suffering and to be led into the glowing fire. And do you, who do not believe and are My enemies, think that you will escape punishment?" And in chapter 49:12 Jeremiah says: "If those who did not deserve to drink the cup must drink it, will you go unpunished?" This is to say: "I smite My dear ones to show you what I will do to My enemies." Consider what kind of words these are. The greater God's saints are, the more terribly He lets them be knocked about and perish. What, then, will happen to the others?

In Ezek. 9:6 we read that the prophet saw six armed men whom the Lord commanded to slay everyone. "Begin at My sanctuary!" He said. This is what St. Peter means here. Therefore he says: The time of judgment, foretold by the prophets, is at hand. When the Gospel is preached, God begins to punish sin, in order that He may kill and make alive. He whips the pious with a foxtail, which is primarily a mother's rod. But what will happen to those who do not believe? It is as if he were saying: If God deals so seriously with His dear children, you can figure out what kind of punishment will be inflicted on those who do not believe.

18. *If the righteous man is scarcely saved, where will the impious and sinner appear?*

This verse is also taken from the Book of Proverbs, chapter 11:31: "If the righteous is requited on earth, how much more the wicked and the sinner!" This is also what St. Peter says here, namely, that the righteous man can scarcely be saved. He escapes by a hair. The righteous man is he who believes. Faith still requires trouble and toil in order that he may come through and be saved, for he must pass through the glowing fire. Where, then, will he who does not believe remain? If God gives faith a jolt to make it struggle, how can he who is without faith remain standing? Therefore the apostle now concludes by saying:

19. *Therefore let those who suffer according to God's will do right and entrust their souls to a faithful Creator with good works.*

That is, those whom God afflicts with suffering which they themselves have not sought and chosen should entrust their souls to

[W, XII, 386]

Him. They do well, continue in good works, do not withdraw because of the suffering, and entrust themselves to their Creator, who
is faithful. This is a great comfort for us. God created your soul without any trouble and assistance on your part. He did so before you
came into being. Accordingly, He is surely able to preserve it.
Therefore entrust it to Him, but in such a way that it is done with
good works. You must not think: "Ah, I will die with no concern!"
You must see to it that you are a good Christian, and you must prove
your faith with your works. But if you go along without further ado,
you will find out what your fate will be. This is the last admonition
St. Peter gives to those who must suffer for God's sake. Now there
follows:

CHAPTER FIVE

1. *So I exhort the elders among you, as a fellow elder and a witness of the sufferings of Christ as well as a partaker in the glory that is to be revealed.*

2. *Tend the flock of God that is your charge, not by constraint but willingly, not for shameful gain but eagerly,*

3. *not as domineering over those in your charge but being examples to the flock.*

4. *And when the chief Shepherd is manifested, you will obtain the unfading crown of glory.*

Here St. Peter tells how those who are to govern in the spiritual realm should conduct themselves. Now in the previous chapter (1 Peter 4:11) he stated that no one should teach or preach anything unless he is sure that it is God's Word, in order that our conscience may rest on solid rock. For it is impressed on us Christians that we must know with certainty what is pleasing to God and what displeases Him. Where this is not the case, there are no Christians. Then the apostle also stated that everyone must regard whatever office or work he has as being performed for God. This verse, however, is really addressed to the bishops or pastors, to inform them what qualifications they should have and how they should conduct themselves.

But here you must familiarize yourself with the language and learn the meaning of the words. The little word πρεσβύτερος, or "priest," is Greek. In German it is *eyn Eltister* ("an elder"). In Latin the word *senatores* is used, that is, a number of old and wise men who should have a great deal of experience. These are the men whom Christ called His officials and council. They administer the spiritual rule; that is, they preach, and they care for a Christian congregation. Therefore do not be misled in case the priests are now designated otherwise, for Scripture knows nothing about those who are called priests today. Forget about the present state of affairs, and bear in mind that when St. Peter and other apostles came into a city in which there were believers or Christians, they selected an elderly man or two who were upright, were married and had children, and were versed in Scripture. These men were called πρεσβύτεροι. Later Paul and Peter also called them ἐπίσκοποι, that is, bishops. Therefore the words "bishop" and "priest" had one and the same meaning.

Of this we have another excellent example in the legend of St. Martin.[1] A number of people came to a place in Africa and saw a man lying in a hut. Not knowing who he was, they took him to be a peasant. Later, when the people congregated there, this man stood up and preached. Then they saw that he was their pastor or bishop. For at that time pastors or bishops did not have ways, clothing, and gestures to distinguish them from other people.

These elders, says St. Peter, who are to take care of and provide for the people, I exhort. I am one of them. Accordingly, you see clearly that he calls those men elders who have had an office and have preached. For this reason he also calls himself an elder. And here St. Peter humbles himself. He does not say that he is an overlord, although he could have done so, since he was an apostle of Christ. He calls himself not only a fellow elder but also "a witness of the sufferings of Christ." It is as if he were saying: I not only preach, but I am also one of the Christians who must suffer. In this way he points out that where there are Christians, they must suffer and be persecuted. This is a true apostle. If there were a pope or a bishop of this kind today who also bore this title, we would be glad to kiss his feet.

As well as a partaker in the glory that is to be revealed.

This is still higher, and naturally a bishop should not make this statement thoughtlessly; for here St. Peter makes himself a saint. He was certain that he would be saved, for he had many promises to this effect. Thus Christ says (John 15:16): "I chose you." But it cost the apostles much travail before they reached this stage. Before

---

[1] Sulpicius Severus, *Dialogues*, I, *Postumianus*, ch. 4–5, *Patrologia, Series Latina*, XX, 186–187.

this they surely had to be humbled and to become rascals. Now although St. Peter knows that he is a partaker of salvation, he is not proud. Nor does he exalt himself, even though he is saintly. Now what should the elders do? We read:

Tend the flock of Christ that is your charge.

Christ is the chief Shepherd, and under Him He has many shepherds as well as many flocks of sheep. These sheep He has assigned to His shepherds here and there in many lands, as St. Peter writes here. What are these shepherds to do? They are to lead Christ's flock to pasture. The pope has taken this upon himself and tries to prove in this way that he is the overlord who can deal with the sheep as he pleases. It is well known what leading to pasture means. It means that the shepherds give the sheep pasture and provide them with fodder to make them fruitful, likewise that they take care that wolves do not come and tear the sheep to pieces. It does not mean to slaughter and kill.

Now St. Peter is speaking in particular of the flock of Christ, as though he were saying: "Do not think that the flock belongs to you. You are only servants." On the other hand, our bishops now say defiantly: "You are my sheep." We are Christ's sheep, for the apostle also said above (2:25): "You have now returned to the Shepherd and Guardian of your souls." The bishops are servants of Christ. It is their duty to tend His sheep and give them pasture. Therefore to give pasture is nothing else than to preach the Gospel, by which souls are fed and made fat and fruitful, and that the sheep are nourished with the Gospel and God's Word. This alone is the office of a bishop. Thus Christ also says to Peter (John 21:16): "Tend My sheep," which is to say: "The sheep you are to tend are not yours; they are Mine." Yet these words have been twisted to mean that the pope has external power over all Christendom.[2] Nevertheless, not one of them preaches a single word of the Gospel. And I fear that no pope has preached the Gospel since the days of Peter. Indeed, not one has written and handed down anything containing the Gospel. To be sure, the pope called Saint Gregory was a saintly man; but his sermons are not worth a heller.[3]

[2] On the exegesis of this passage cf. *Luther's Works*, 32, pp. 71–73.

[3] For a similar estimate of Gregory more than 20 years later cf. *Luther's Works*, 8, p. 246.

Therefore it seems that the Roman See is particularly cursed by God. Several popes may have been martyred for the sake of the Gospel, but they wrote nothing that is the Gospel. Yet they go ahead and proclaim that they must lead to pasture. Still they do no more than take consciences captive and destroy them with laws of their own. They do not preach a word about Christ.

To be sure, among all Christians one finds many, both men and women, who can preach as well as the one who preaches at a particular place. But in the whole group there are always many who are not strong. Therefore someone must be selected to strengthen them, lest wolves come and tear the sheep to pieces. For a pastor must not only lead to pasture by teaching the sheep how to be true Christians: but, in addition to this, he must also repel the wolves, lest they attack the sheep and lead them astray with false doctrine and error. For the devil does not rest. Now today one finds many people who can let the Gospel be preached, provided that one does not cry out against the wolves and preach against the prelates. But even if I preach in the right way and tend and teach the sheep, this protecting and guarding does not suffice to keep the wolves from coming and leading the sheep astray. For what is built if I lay stones and watch someone else knock them down? The wolf can surely let the sheep have good pasturage. The fatter they are, the more he likes them. But he cannot bear the hostile barking of the dogs. Therefore to him who takes this to heart it is important to tend the sheep in the right way, as God has commanded.

"The flock that is your charge," he says; that is, the flock that is with you. This does not mean that the flock is at their feet. "And tend it, not by constraint but willingly, not for shameful gain." Here the apostle has completely expressed with one word what the prophet Ezekiel writes about shepherds or bishops in chapter 34:1 ff. This is the meaning: You should not only tend the flock, but you must also pay heed and observe where there is need and trouble. Here he uses the Greek word ἐπισκοποῦντες, that is, "Be bishops." It is derived from the little word ἐπίσκοπος, which in German is *eyn vorseher* or *wechter*, a man who watches or guards and looks round about him to see what everyone needs. Now note that a bishop and an elder are one and the same thing. Therefore it is a lie when they say today that the office of a bishop implies dignity and that he is a bishop who wears a miter on his head. It is not a position that implies dignity. No, it is an office requiring that the incumbent must take care of us, watch over us, and be our guardian. He must know what kind of weakness there is everywhere. If someone is weak, he must help and comfort. If someone falls, he must buoy him up, etc., in order that the Christians may be adequately provided for in body and soul, etc. Therefore I have often said that if there were a proper administration today, there would have to be three or four bishops in one city to take care of the congregation and pay heed to whatever need there is.[4]

And here St. Peter touches on two matters that might well make a person afraid to preside over the people. First of all, we find some pious people who are not willing to be persuaded that they are preachers; for it is a burdensome office to watch everywhere how the sheep live, in order to help them and to buoy them up. Here one must watch and be on guard day and night, lest the wolves break into the fold. Furthermore, one must hazard life and limb when doing this. Therefore the apostle says: "You should not do it by constraint." It is true that no one should force himself into this office without being called. But when he is called and required, he must go willingly and do what his office demands. For those who must do this by constraint and have no desire and love for it will not carry it out well.

The others, who preside over the people for shameful gain and to feed their bellies, are even worse than these. They look for the wool and the milk from the sheep and care nothing about the pasturage. This is what our bishops do today. Now this is an exceedingly harmful vice, for it is especially disgraceful when a bishop conducts himself in this manner. Therefore both apostles, Peter and Paul, often made mention of this (cf. Acts 20:33). Likewise the prophets. For this reason Moses also declares (Num. 16:15): "I have not taken one ass from them." And the prophet Samuel says (1 Sam. 12:3): "Whose ox have I taken? Or whose ass have I taken?" For if he who should lead to pasture is bent to such an extent on profit and is so greedy for gain, he will soon become a wolf himself.

But eagerly.

That is, a bishop must take pleasure in his office, be inclined in this direction, and do his work gladly. These are men who serve

[4] Cf. *Luther's Works,* 40, p. 40.

willingly and do not look for the wool from the sheep. Thus we have two kinds of false shepherds: some do not do their work willingly; others do it willingly but do it because of greed. The apostle continues:

Not as domineering over those in your charge.

These are the men who rule willingly for the sake of honor, in order that they may be able to domineer and be mighty tyrants. Therefore he exhorts them not to act as though the people were under them, that they may be able to be junkers and do as they please. For we have one Lord. He is Christ, who rules over our souls. The bishops should confine themselves to tending the flock. Thus St. Peter has now overthrown ·and condemned the whole present rule of the pope with one word, and he concludes clearly that the popes have no authority to command as much as a word, but that they should be no more than servants and say: "This is what your Lord Christ says. Therefore you must do it." Thus Christ also says (Luke 22:25-26): "The kings of the Gentiles exercise lordship over them; and those in authority over them are called benefactors. But not so with you." In opposition to this the pope now declares: "You must rule and have power."

But being examples to the flock. And when the chief Shepherd is manifested, you will obtain the unfading crown of glory.

That is, remember that you must take the lead and conduct yourselves in such a way that your life can be an example to the people and that they can follow in your footsteps. But our bishops say to the people: "Go and do this!" And they sit on cushions and are junkers. They impose burdens on us—burdens which they themselves do not touch (cf. Matt. 23:4), although they should not preach a single word and give orders to others if they themselves have not done what they command. But if one were to force them to do this, they would soon become tired of their power.

Now for this St. Peter does not mean to specify a temporal reward for the bishops. It is as if he were saying: Your office is so great that it cannot be rewarded here. But you will receive an eternal crown, which will follow of itself if you feed the sheep of Christ in this way. This is St. Peter's exhortation to those who are to care for souls. From it you can now conclude cogently and show clearly that the pope, together with his bishops, is an end-christ[5] or antichrist, since he does none of the things St. Peter requires here. He himself neither teaches nor does these things. Instead, he does the very opposite. He not only refuses to feed the sheep or to let them be fed, but he himself is the wolf and tears them to pieces. Yet he boasts that he is the vicar of the Lord Christ. Indeed, that he is when Christ is not present, just as the devil also sits and rules in Christ's place.

Therefore it is necessary for simple people to understand this passage and similar passages well and to contrast the pope's rule with these statements when one wants to question and examine them. Then they can answer and say: "Thus Christ spoke and did. But the pope teaches and does the very opposite. Christ says yes. But the pope says no. Now because they are at loggerheads, one of them must surely be lying. Now Christ surely does not lie. Therefore I conclude that the pope is a liar and, in addition, is the real Antichrist." Thus you must be so well armed with Scripture that you not only can call the pope an antichrist but know how to give clear proof of this, that you can confidently stake your life on this and prevail against the devil when you die. Now the apostle goes on:

5. *Likewise you that are younger be subject to the elders.*

Now these are the final admonitions in this epistle. St. Peter wants things to be ordered in such a way in Christendom that those who are young obey those who are old, in order that those who are in a subordinate position may always humbly obey those who are above them. If this were prevalent today, one would not need so many laws. This is exactly what the apostle wants. Those who are younger should be governed according to the understanding of those who are old and know best how this is to be done to the glory of God. St. Peter believes, however, that such old people should be endowed with knowledge and understanding in the Holy Spirit. But if they themselves are fools and understand nothing, no good government will result. But if they have understanding, it is good that they rule the youth. Here, however, St. Peter

---

[5] The German name is *Endchrist* (sometimes *Endechrist*), which, both in this treatise and in others, is often used in place of *Antichrist;* cf. also *Luther's Works,* 13, p. 190, note 51.

is not yet speaking of the secular rule; he is saying in general that the elders should rule the younger, whether these elders are priests or old men.

Clothe yourselves, all of you, with humility toward one another.

Here the apostle has proceeded in another direction. He has modified his statement and wants everyone to be subject to the other person. But how can this be in agreement with what he said before, if the elders are to rule and yet all are subject to one another? Should one turn the situation around? He who is so inclined may explain the words to mean that above St. Peter was speaking about the old people and that here he is speaking about those who are young. But we shall let his words stand as they are and say that a general statement is made, as Paul also says in Rom. 12:10: "Outdo one another in showing honor." Those who are young should be subject to those who are old, yet in such a way that the latter, who are above the former, do not consider themselves lords but deign to obey if a younger person happens to have more understanding and knowledge. Thus in the Old Testament God often appointed young men who excelled the old men in understanding.

Thus in Luke 14:8-10 Christ also teaches: "When you are invited by anyone to a marriage feast, do not sit down in a place of honor, lest a more eminent man than you be invited by him; and he who invited you both will come and say to you: 'Give place to this man,' and then you will begin with shame to take the lowest place. But when you are invited, go and sit in the lowest place, so that when your host comes he may say to you: 'Friend, go up higher.'" In addition, Christ quotes the verse He uses in many other places: "For everyone who exalts himself will be humbled, and he who humbles himself will be exalted" (Luke 14:11; 18:14; Matt. 23:12).

Therefore the young must indeed be subject to the elders. Yet the elders, on the other hand, must be so disposed that in his heart everyone considers himself the most insignificant. If this were done, we would have good peace, and things would go well on earth. Now we should do this, the apostle says, in order to show humility.

For God opposes the proud but gives grace to the humble.

That is, God humbles those who refuse to yield, and, on the

other hand, exalts those who humble themselves. This is a common saying. Would to God that it were also common in life!

6. *Humble yourselves therefore under the mighty hand of God.*

God wants everyone to be subject to the other person. Therefore do this willingly and gladly. Then He will exalt you. But if you do not do it willingly, you will be obliged to do it. God will cast you down nevertheless.

That in due time He may exalt you.

When God lets His own be cast down in this way, it appears as though He wanted to hold Himself aloof too long. This is why the apostle says: Do not be misled. Forget about it, and rely on the fact that you have a sure promise that this is the hand and the will of God. Therefore you should not think about how long you are subject; for even though God delays, He will nonetheless exalt you! Therefore he goes on to say:

7. *Cast all your anxieties on Him, for He cares about you.*

You have the kind of promise that makes you sure that God does not forsake you, but that He cares about you. Therefore forget about all your anxiety, and let Him manage. These are exceedingly delightful words. How could God act in a more pleasing and friendly manner? But why does He speak so alluringly? Because no one humbles himself gladly and forgets about his sentiments. Therefore St. Peter gives us the comfort that God not only sees us but also cares about us and has our best interests at heart. He goes on to say:

8. *Be sober, be watchful. Your adversary the devil prowls around like a roaring lion, seeking someone to devour.*

Here St. Peter gives us a warning and wants to open our eyes, and it would be worthwhile to write this verse in golden letters. Here you see what this life is and how it is portrayed, namely, that we should always wish we were dead. Here we are in the realm of the devil, not otherwise than if a pilgrim came into an inn where he knew that everybody in the house was a robber. If he had to go there, he would nevertheless arm himself and make the best provision possible. He would not sleep much. Today we are in this situation on earth, where the evil spirit is a prince, has the hearts of men in his power, and through them does what he pleases. This is terrible if one looks at it in the right way. Therefore St. Peter wants to warn us here to be on our guard. He acts as a faithful servant who knows what is going on here. This is why he says: "Be sober." For those who gorge, guzzle, and are sated sows are good for nothing. Therefore it is necessary for us to have this treasure with us at all times.

"Be watchful," he says — not only spiritually but also physically; for a lazy body that likes to sleep after it has gorged itself full and guzzled will not resist the devil, because this becomes difficult even for those who have faith and are spiritual.

Why should we be sober and vigilant? Because "your adversary the devil prowls around like a roaring lion, seeking someone to devour." The evil spirit does not sleep; he is cunning and malicious. He has determined to assail us, and he knows the right stratagem to employ to accomplish this. He prowls about like a hungry lion. He roars. He would like to devour everything. Here St. Peter gives us an excellent admonition. He reveals our enemy to us in order that we may be on our guard against him. Thus Paul also says (2 Cor. 2:11): "We are not ignorant of his designs." But the prowling around takes place in such a way that he makes us careless. Then wrath, quarreling, pride, unchastity, and contempt for God follow.

Note well here that he says: "The devil prowls around." He is not in your sight when you are armed; but he looks in front and behind, inside and outside, for a place at which to attack you. When he attacks you here now, he soon rushes there and attacks you at another place. He hastens from one side to the other and employs all kinds of cunning and trickery to make you fall. And even if you are well armed at one place, he pounces on you at another place. If he cannot knock you down there either, he attacks you somewhere else. Thus he never ceases but goes all around and gives no rest anywhere. But we are fools and pay no attention to it. We go our way and are not watchful. Thus it is easy for him to gain ground.

Now let everyone pay proper heed to this. Everyone will notice something in himself. He who has tried it is well aware of it. Therefore we are miserable people to go along so heedlessly. If we look at it in the right manner, we should cry murder against life. Thus

Job says (7:1): "Has not man a hard service upon earth, and are not his days like the days of a hireling?" Why, then, does God leave us in this life and misery? He does so in order that faith may be exercised and grow, that we may hasten from this life, that we may long for death and desire to die.

9. *Resist him, firm in your faith.*

You must be sober and vigilant, but in order that the body may be ready. But this does not yet vanquish the devil. It is done only in order that you may give the body less reason to sin. The true sword is your strong and firm faith. If you take hold of God's Word in your heart and cling to it with faith, the devil cannot win but must flee. If you can say: "This is what my God has said, and I take my stand on it," you will see that the devil will soon go away. Then aversion, evil lust, anger, greed, melancholy, and doubt all go away. But the devil is crafty and is unwilling to let this happen to you. He tries to wrest the sword from your hand. If he makes you lazy, so that the body becomes unfit and is inclined to rascality, he soon tears the sword out of your hand. This is what he did to Eve. She had God's Word. If she had clung to it, she would not have fallen. But when the devil saw that she held the Word in such low esteem, he tore it from her heart, and she let it go. Thus the devil won.

Thus St. Peter has given us adequate instruction as to how we should fight against the devil. This does not require much running to and fro or any work you can do; it requires only that you cling to the Word through faith. When the devil comes and wants to drive you into melancholy because of your sin, just take hold of the Word of God, which promises forgiveness of sin, and rely on it. Then the devil will soon desist.

St. Peter continues:

Knowing that the same experience of suffering is required of your brotherhood throughout the world.

That is, do not be surprised if you must be assailed by the devil; but take comfort in the fact that you are not alone, but that there are more. They, too, must suffer this way. And bear in mind that your brothers help you fight.

Now this is the epistle in which you have heard a genuine Christian doctrine adequately presented, how masterfully St. Peter has described faith, love, and the holy cross, and how he teaches and warns us how we should fight with the devil. Now he who understands this epistle undoubtedly has enough and needs no more, except that God does more than is required by teaching the same things richly in other books. But they contain nothing that is different, for here the apostle has forgotten nothing that a Christian must know.

In conclusion, he does what a good preacher should do, namely, that he should bear in mind that he must not only feed but must also take care of and pray for them. He closes with a prayer that God may give them grace and strength to take hold of the Word and retain it.

10. *And after you have suffered a little while, the God of all grace, who has called you to His eternal glory in Christ, will Himself restore, establish, and strengthen you.*

This is the wish with which he commends his listeners to God — to God, who alone gives grace, and not only a little grace but all grace piled up; who has called you through Christ to have eternal glory, not by reason of any merit on your part but through Christ. If you have Him, you have eternal glory and salvation, without any merit on your part. He will establish you, so that you become strong, grow, and stand firm, and are able to accomplish much. In addition, He will strengthen and support you, so that you are able to bear and suffer everything.

11. *To Him be the dominion forever and ever. Amen.*

The praise is the sacrifice we Christians should bring to God. Now in conclusion he adds something:

12. *By Silvanus, a faithful brother as I regard him, I have written briefly to you, exhorting and declaring that this is the true grace of God; stand fast in it.*

Although I know, he says, that you have heard this before and that by this time it is not necessary for me to instruct you in it, yet I have written this to you to exhort you, as true apostles must do, to remain in it, in order that you may teach and practice it and may not think that I am preaching anything different from what you have heard before.

13. *She who is at Babylon, who is likewise chosen, sends you greetings.*

This is the way it is customary to write "Good night!" in letters. She—namely, the congregation at Babylon—sends you greetings, he says. It is my opinion—but I am not sure—that here he means Rome, for it is believed that he wrote the epistle from Rome.[6] Otherwise there are two Babylons. One is in Chaldea; the other is in Egypt, where Cairo is situated today.[7] But Rome is called Babylon only in a spiritual sense. As the apostle has stated above (1 Peter 4:4), the "wild profligacy" is meant. For the Hebrew word "Babel" implies confusion (cf. Gen. 11:9). Perhaps the apostle called Rome a confusion because such profligacy and such a jumble of disgraceful living and wickedness of all kinds were prevalent there, and because whatever depravity there was in the entire world converged there. In this city, says St. Peter, a congregation has been gathered. These people are Christians. They send you their greetings. But I am willing to give everyone freedom here to interpret this verse as he chooses, for it is not vital.

And so does my son Mark.

It is said here that St. Peter means the evangelist Mark, whom he calls his spiritual son, not his physical son, just as Paul calls Timothy and Titus his sons (1 Tim. 1:2; 2 Tim. 1:2; Titus 1:4) and tells the Corinthians that he became their father in Christ (1 Cor. 4:14-15; 2 Cor. 6:13).

14. *Greet one another with the kiss of love.*

This custom is no longer in vogue today. In the Gospel we read clearly that Christ greeted His disciples with a kiss (cf. Matt. 26:49). This was customary in those countries. St. Paul, too, often speaks of kissing (cf. Rom. 16:16).

---

[6] Cf. Eusebius, *Ecclesiastical History*, Book II, ch. 15, par. 2.

[7] For other speculation about Babylon cf. *Luther's Works*, 2, pp. 199–200.

Peace to all of you that are in Christ.

That is, those who believe in Christ. This is the word of farewell with which he commends them to Christ. Thus we have the first epistle. May God grant us grace to understand and retain it. Amen.

SERMONS
ON THE SECOND EPISTLE
OF ST. PETER

Translated by
MARTIN H. BERTRAM

FOREWORD

St. Peter wrote this epistle because he saw that the true and pure doctrine of faith would be adulterated, obscured, and suppressed. It was his purpose to disprove two errors that result from a misconception of the doctrine of faith, namely, the error which ascribes to works the power, which faith alone has, to render a person pious and acceptable to God and, on the other hand, the mistaken notion that faith can exist without good works. For when preachers declare that faith justifies and saves without any assistance from works, people say that one need not do any works. We encounter this every day. On the other hand, when works are resorted to and stressed, faith must languish. Thus where there are no upright preachers, it is difficult to stay on a middle course.

Now we have always taught that everything must be credited to faith and that it alone justifies and sanctifies us before God, but that then, when faith is present, good works should and must result from faith, since it is also impossible for us to go through life in complete idleness and not to do a single work. This is what St. Peter will teach in this epistle. Furthermore, he will take issue with those who may have misunderstood his first letter to say that faith is enough even if one does not do a single work. The first chapter in particular is directed against those who have this notion. Here St. Peter teaches that believers should give an account of themselves by means of good works and become sure of their faith.

The second chapter is directed against those who emphasize works without further ado and suppress faith. Therefore the apostle warns against future false teachers who, as he says, will completely destroy faith with human doctrines. For he saw clearly what terrible seduction there would be in the world. In fact, this was already beginning at that time, as St. Paul says in 2 Thess. 2:7: "For the mystery of lawlessness is already at work." Hence this letter is written as a warning to us, in order that we may give evidence of our faith by means of good works, yet without relying on these works.

CHAPTER ONE

1. *Simon Peter, a servant and apostle of Jesus Christ, to those who have obtained a faith of equal standing with ours in the righteousness of our God and Savior Jesus Christ.*

This is the signature and the superscription of this epistle, in order that we may know who is writing and to whom he is writing, namely, to those who have heard the Word of God and now have faith. But what kind of faith is it? "In the righteousness of our God," says the apostle. Here he ascribes righteousness to faith alone, as St. Paul also does in Rom. 1:17: "For in the Gospel the righteousness of God is revealed through faith for faith, as it is written: 'He who through faith is righteous shall live'" (Hab. 2:4). In this way St. Peter wants to exhort them to be armed and not to let the doctrine which they have taken hold of and know well to be carried away.

And by adding the words "the righteousness of our God" he excludes all human righteousness. For we are made righteous before God solely through faith. Therefore faith is also called a "righteousness of God." For before the world it has no validity. Indeed, it is even condemned.

2. *May grace and peace be multiplied to you in the knowledge of God and of Jesus our Lord.*

This is the greeting commonly used to preface the letters. It means: Instead of my service, I wish that you may increase in grace and peace, and become richer and richer. This grace comes from the knowledge of God and of the Lord Christ, which means that it is something only he who has knowledge of God and Jesus Christ can have.

The apostles and also the prophets constantly refer to this knowledge of God in Scripture. Thus we read in Is. 11:9: "They shall not hurt or destroy in all My holy mountain; for the earth shall be full of the knowledge of the Lord as the waters cover the sea." That is, the knowledge of God will burst forth as exuberantly as when a body of water gushes forth, rushes out, and inundates a whole country. From this such peace will result that no one will harm or injure his neighbor.

But the fact that you, like the Turks, the Jews, and the devil, believe that God created all things — this is not the knowledge of God. Nor is this knowledge your belief that Christ was born from a virgin, suffered, died, and rose again. No, you have the true knowledge of God when you believe and know that God and Christ are your God and your Christ. This the devil and the false Christians cannot believe. Thus this knowledge is nothing else than the true Christian faith; for when you know God and Christ in this way, you will rely on Him with all your heart and trust in Him in good fortune and misfortune, in life and death. Evil consciences cannot have such trust, for they know no more about God than that He is a God of St. Peter and all the saints in heaven. But they do not know Him as their God; they regard Him as a jailer and an angry judge.

To have God is to have all grace, all mercy, and everything one can call good. To have Christ is to have the Savior and Mediator who brought us to the point that God belongs to us, and who acquired for us all mercy from Him. You must weave this together in such a way that Christ becomes yours and you become His. Then you have a true knowledge. An unmarried woman can say, of course: "This is a man." But she cannot say that he is her man. Thus we can all say, of course, that this is a god; but we cannot all say that He is our God. For we cannot all trust in Him and take comfort in Him. To this knowledge also belongs what Scripture calls the *facies et vultus Domini,* that is, the countenance of the Lord about which the prophets have much to say. He who does not behold the face of God does not know Him but sees only His back, that is, an angry and cruel God.[1]

Here you see that St. Peter does not propose to write particularly about faith at this time, since he did this adequately in the first epistle. No, he wants to exhort believers to give evidence of their

---

[1] It is evident that here Luther is using the terms "face" and "back" in a way different from his more familiar distinction; cf. *Luther's Works,* 22, p. 157, note 125; 4, p. 371.

faith by means of good works. For he does not want faith without good works or works without faith. But he wants faith first and good works in addition to and flowing from faith. Therefore he now says:

3. *His divine power has granted to us all things that pertain to life and godliness.*

This is the first part. Here Peter begins to write about the kind of blessings we have received from God through faith, namely, that—since we have learned to know God through faith—divine power has been granted to us. But what kind of power? It is the kind of power that pertains to life and godliness. That is, when we believe, we receive so much that God gives us His power of every kind, which dwells with and in us in such a way that what we say and do is not said or done by us but is said and done by God Himself. God is strong, powerful, and almighty in us even though we suffer, die, and are weak before the world. Accordingly, we have no power or ability if we do not have this divine power.

But St. Peter does not want this divine power in us to be understood in such a way that we also have the ability to create heaven and earth and should work miracles, as God does. For how would this help us? No, we have divine power with us to the degree that it is useful and necessary for us. Therefore the apostle adds the words "that pertain to life and godliness." That is, we have the kind of divine power with which we are abundantly blessed to do good and to live eternally.

Through the knowledge of Him who called us.

Such divine power and great grace come from nothing else than this knowledge of God. For if you regard Him as a god, He will also deal with you as a god. Thus St. Paul also declares in 1 Cor. 1: 5-7: "That in every way you were enriched in Him with all speech and all knowledge—even as the testimony of Christ was confirmed among you—so that you are not lacking in any spiritual gift." This is the greatest, noblest, and most necessary gift God can give us— a gift we should not exchange for everything heaven and earth contain. For what would it profit you to be able to go even through fire and water and to perform all kinds of miracles, if you did not have it? In fact, many people who perform such wonders are damned. But the greatest miracle of all is the tact that God gives us the kind of power through which all our sins are remitted and eradicated, and death, the devil, and hell are vanquished and devoured, so that we have an undaunted conscience and a cheerful heart, and fear nothing.

To His own glory and excellence.

How did it happen that we were called by God? God let the holy Gospel go out into the world and be proclaimed. No man worked for this beforehand. Nor did anyone implore and beg Him to do so. But before anyone thought of it, He offered us such grace, presented it, and poured it out richly and beyond measure, in order that He alone might have the glory and the honor resulting from it, and that we might ascribe to Him alone the ability and the power. For this is not our work; it is His alone. Therefore since we did not do the calling, we should not boast, as though we had done it; but we should extol and thank Him for giving us the Gospel and in this way bestowing strength and power against the devil, death, and all adversity.

4. *By which He has granted us His precious and very great promises.*

St. Peter adds these words in order to explain the nature and character of faith. If we know Him as God, then, through faith, we have eternal life and the divine power with which we overcome death and the devil. But we do not see and feel this. Nevertheless, it has been promised to us. To be sure, all this is ours; but it is not yet manifest. On the Last Day, however, we shall see it revealed. Here it has its beginning in faith, but we do not have it in perfection. Yet we have the promise that we shall live here in divine power and later in eternal bliss. Now he who believes this has it; he who does not believe this does not have it and must be lost eternally. Peter now explains further how great and precious this is. He says:

That through these you may escape from the corruption that is in the world because of passion, and become partakers of the divine nature.

[W, XIV, 18-20]

Through the power of faith, he says, we partake of and have association or communion with the divine nature. This is a verse without a parallel in the New and the Old Testament, even though unbelievers regard it as a trivial matter that we partake of the divine nature itself. But what is the divine nature? It is eternal truth, righteousness, wisdom, everlasting life, peace, joy, happiness, and whatever can be called good. Now he who becomes a partaker of the divine nature receives all this, so that he lives eternally and has everlasting peace, joy, and happiness, and is pure, clean, righteous, and almighty against the devil, sin, and death. Therefore this is what Peter wants to say: Just as God cannot be deprived of being eternal life and eternal truth, so you cannot be deprived of this. If anything is done to you, it must be done to God; for he who wants to oppress a Christian must oppress God.

All this is included in the term "divine nature," and St. Peter has used it for the very purpose of including all this. It is surely something great when one believes it. But, as I have stated above,[2] with all these instructions he does not lay a foundation for faith but emphasizes what great and rich blessings we receive through faith. For this reason he says: You will have all this if you live in such a way that you give evidence of your faith by shunning worldly lusts. Now he continues:

5. *For this very reason make every effort to supplement your faith with virtue.*

Here St. Peter admonishes them to give evidence of their faith with good works. Since such a great blessing has been given to you through faith that you truly have everything that is God, he wants to say, add to this, be diligent, do not be lazy, supplement your faith with virtue; that is, let your faith break forth before the people, in order that it may be helpful, busy, powerful, and active, and may do many works and not remain sluggish and sterile. You have a good inheritance and a good field. But see to it that you do not let thistles or weeds grow in it.

And virtue with knowledge.

In the first place, understanding, or knowledge, means to lead

[2] Cf. p. 3.

one's outward life and practice the virtue of faith in a sensible manner. For one should restrain and curb the body, in order that it may remain sober, alert, and fit for what is good. One should not hurt it too much and slay it, as some mad saints do. For even though God loathes the sins that remain in the flesh, yet He does not want you to slay your body on this account. You should check its wickedness and wantonness, but this does not mean that you should destroy or injure it. You must give it food and necessities, in order that it may remain healthy and alive.

In the second place, understanding also means to lead a fine, sensible life and to act judiciously in external matters, in matters of diet and the like. One should not do anything imprudently, and one should not give offense to one's neighbor.

6. *And knowledge with self-control.*

Self-control applies not only to eating and drinking; it is moderation in all circumstances of life, in words, deeds, and bearing. One should not live extravagantly. Excess in adornment and dress should be avoided, and no one should make himself conspicuous by being haughty and arrogant. But St. Peter refrains from fixing a rule, a standard or aim, pertaining to this, as the orders have made bold to do. They undertake to formulate rules for all this and have added commandments that apply to everything. In Christendom it will not do to issue laws, so that there is a general rule pertaining to self-control. For people are not alike. One is strong, another is weak by nature, and no one is always as fit in every respect as the other person is. Therefore everyone should learn to know himself, what he can do and what he can stand.

And self-control with steadfastness.

This is what St. Peter wants to say: If you lead a temperate and sensible life, you should not suppose that you will live without trials and persecution. For if you believe and lead a good, Christian life, the world will not let you alone. It must persecute you and be your enemy. You must bear this with patience, which is a fruit of faith.

And steadfastness with godliness.

This means that in our whole outward life, in what we do or

suffer, we should conduct ourselves in such a way that we serve
God and do not seek our own glory and advantage. It means that
God alone must be praised by what we do and that we must act in
such a way that one can see that we do everything for God's sake.

7. *And godliness with brotherly affection.*

With these words St. Peter obligates us all to help one another
like brothers. One person must look after the other person. No one
should be an enemy of the other person. Nor should he despise or
harm him. This is also an evidence of faith. In this way we show
that we have the godliness of which the apostle has spoken.

And brotherly affection with love.

This love extends to both friends and enemies, also to those who
do not act in a friendly and brotherly way toward us. Thus here
St. Peter has expressed in a few words what belongs to a Christian
life and what the works and the fruits of faith are, namely, knowledge, self-control, patience, a God-fearing life, brotherly affection,
and kindness to everybody. Therefore he continues:

8. *For if these things are yours and abound, they keep you from being ineffective or unfruitful in the knowledge of our Lord Jesus Christ.*

That is, if you do works of this kind, you are on the right path and
have a true faith, and the knowledge of Christ is active and fruitful
in you. Therefore see to it that you do not make light of this. Hold
your body in subjection, and do for your neighbor as you know that
Christ has done for you.

9. *For whoever lacks these things is blind and shortsighted and has forgotten that he was cleansed from his old sins.*

He who does not have such a supply of the fruits of faith gropes
about like a blind person and lives in such a way that he does not
know what his plight is. He does not have the true faith, and his
knowledge of Christ does not exceed his ability to say how he
heard it. Therefore he goes along and fumbles in uncertainty, like
a blind man on the road. He forgets that he has been baptized and
that his sins have been forgiven. He becomes ungrateful and a lazy

and careless person who takes nothing to heart and neither takes hold of nor tastes such great grace and blessings.

With this exhortation St. Peter wants to incite and urge us who believe to do the works with which we should prove that we really have faith. He always insists that faith alone justifies. For where there is this faith, the works must follow. What now follows will pertain to the strengthening of faith.

10. *Therefore, brethren, be the more zealous to confirm your call and election.*

Indeed, the election and God's eternal foreordination is firm enough in itself and requires no confirmation. The call is also strong and firm. For he who hears the Gospel, believes in it, and is baptized is called and will be saved. Now since we, too, are called, we must be zealous, says Peter, to confirm this call and election for ourselves, not only for God.

Now this is a way of speaking employed in Scripture, just as St. Paul says in Eph. 2:12: "You were strangers to the covenants of promise, having no hope and without God in the world." Although there is no man, whether good or evil, over whom God is not lord, since all creatures are His, yet Paul declares that he who does not know God, does not love Him, and does not trust in Him has no God, even though God remains God so far as He Himself is concerned. Thus here, too, although the call and election is firm enough in itself, yet it is not strong and firm enough for you, since you are not yet certain that it pertains to you. Therefore Peter wants us to confirm this call and election for ourselves with good works.

Thus you see what this apostle attributes to the fruits of faith. Although they apply to our neighbor, in order that he may be served with them, yet the fruit does not fail to strengthen faith and to cause it constantly to do more and more good works. Thus this strength is far different from physical strength, which decreases and is consumed if one uses and does something too much. But this spiritual strength increases the more one makes use of and applies it. It decreases when one does not apply it. Therefore with the battle of faith God first led, drove, and disciplined Christendom this way in shame, death, and bloodshed, in order that it might become truly strong and powerful. The more it was oppressed, the more it flourished. Now St. Peter means that one should not let faith rest and

lie still, for it is so constituted that through application and practice it becomes stronger and stronger until it is sure of the call and
election and cannot be wanting.

Here bounds are fixed with regard to how one should deal with
election. There are many frivolous spirits who have not felt faith
deeply. They rush in, attack the matter at the top, and concern
themselves with it for the first time. They want to ascertain with
their reason whether they are elected, in order that they may be
sure of where they stand. But desist from this quickly. It is not the
proper method. But if you want to be sure, you must adopt the
method St. Peter suggests here. If you choose another way, you
have already failed. Your own experience must teach you this.[3]
If your faith is well exercised and applied, you will finally gain
assurance, and this will keep you from failing, as is clear from what
follows:

For if you do this, you will never fall.

That is, you will stand firm and not stumble or sin; but you will
proceed properly and confidently, and everything will turn out
well. Otherwise, if you undertake to accomplish this with your own
notions, the devil will soon cast you into despair and into hatred
of God.

11. *So there will be richly provided for you an entrance into the
eternal kingdom of our Lord and Savior Jesus Christ.*

This is the road by which one enters the kingdom of heaven.
Therefore no one should get the thought that he will enter by
means of the kind of dream and ideas of faith he has devised in
his own heart. It must be a faith that is alive — a faith well exercised
and applied. So help me God, how our seducers have written and
taught contrary to this text! They have said that he who has even
the slightest degree and only a little spark of faith in the hour of
death will be saved.[4] If you want to postpone matters until that
time and expect to acquire such faith suddenly and quickly, you

---

[3] Luther is, of course, giving an account of his own struggles over the problem
of divine election.

[4] On the basis of Is. 42:3 it was argued that even the spark of a "weak and feeble
faith and hope . . . in cross and conflict" (cf. *Luther's Works*, 27, p. 27) was enough.

will have waited too long. Yet mark well that even those who are strong have enough to take care of, even though one should not despair of those who are weak. For it can well happen that they will enter the kingdom of heaven. But this will be difficult and arduous, and it will cost much toil. He, however, whose manner of living shows that his faith is accompanied by good works and thus becomes strong will have an entrance richly provided for him, and he will enter yonder life cheerfully and confidently. Thus he dies courageously, despises life, departs with pride, as it were, and leaps into the eternal kingdom. But if the others enter at all, they will not go so joyfully. The door will not be open so wide for them. They will not have such a richly provided entrance; but it will be narrow and difficult for them, so that they struggle and prefer a lifetime of weakness to the thought that eventually they will have to die.

12. *Therefore I intend always to remind you of these things, though you know them and are established in the truth that you have.*

This is what we, too, have often stated,[5] namely, that although God has now let such a great light shine through the revelation of the Gospel, so that we know what genuine Christian life and doctrine are and see how all Scripture insists on this, we must not desist but should teach it daily, not for the sake of the doctrine but in order to keep it in mind. For there is a twofold office in Christendom, as St. Paul declares in Rom. 12:7-8: "He who teaches, in his teaching; he who exhorts, in his exhortation." One teaches when the foundation of faith is laid and proclaimed to those who know nothing about it. To exhort, however, or, as Peter says here, "to remind," is to preach to those who already know and have heard it, to persist, and to rouse them not to lose sight of it but to continue and to make progress. We are all burdened with that old rotten sack,[6] with our flesh and blood. It always chooses the wrong path and constantly pulls us down to its own level, so that it is easy for the soul to go to sleep. Therefore it is necessary to drive constantly and to persevere, just as the master of a household drives his

[5] See, for example, p. 41.
[6] Cf. *Luther's Works*, 13, p. 412, note 25.

domestics, lest they get lazy, even though they are well aware of what they should do. For since it is necessary to do this for the sake of temporal sustenance, it is much more necessary to do it in spiritual matters.

13. *I think it right, as long as I am in this tent, to arouse you by way of reminder.*

Here St. Peter calls his body a tent in which the soul dwells. This expression is similar to the one he used in his first epistle (cf. 3:7), where he calls a female body a vessel or tool. Thus Saint Paul also says in 2 Cor. 5:1-2, 4: "For we know that if the earthly tent we live in is destroyed, we have a building from God, a house not made with hands, eternal in the heavens. Here indeed we groan, and long to put on our heavenly dwelling. . . . For while we are still in this tent we sigh with anxiety, etc." Likewise (vv. 6, 8): "So we are always of good courage; we know that while we are at home in the body, we are away from the Lord. . . . We would rather be away from the body and at home with the Lord." Here the apostle Paul also calls the body a house and designates two homes and two pilgrimages. Thus here Peter calls the body a tent in which the soul rests. He speaks disparagingly enough of this and does not want to call it a house; he calls it a hut and a barn such as is used by shepherds. The treasure is great, but the box in which it lies and dwells is small.

14. *Since I know that the putting off of my body will be soon, as our Lord Jesus Christ showed me.*

15. *And I will see to it that after my departure you may be able at any time to recall these things.*

Here St. Peter testifies concerning himself that he is sure of eternal life and that God has revealed to him beforehand when he will have to die. But this was done for our sakes and for the sake of our faith. For there had to be some people who knew for sure that they were elected, who should lay the foundation of faith, in order that it might be known that they were proclaiming God's Word, not human doctrines. But before they came to this assurance, God undoubtedly tested and purged them.

Now this is what Peter says: I will remind you not only viva voce but also in writing, and I will command you through others always to remember this while I am alive and after my death, and not to forget it. Note here how greatly concerned the apostle is about souls. Unfortunately, however, this did not help.

16. *For we did not follow cleverly devised myths when we made known to you the power and coming of our Lord Jesus Christ, but we were eyewitnesses of His majesty.*

17. *For when He received honor and glory from God the Father and the voice was borne to Him by the Majestic Glory, This is My beloved Son, with whom I am well pleased,*

18. *we heard this voice borne from heaven, for we were with Him on the holy mountain.*

Here St. Peter refers to an account in the Gospel of Matthew, chapter 17:1-9, where we read that Jesus took with Him three of His disciples, Peter, James, and John, "and led them up a high mountain apart. And He was transfigured before them, and His face shone like the sun, and His garments became white as light. And behold, there appeared to them Moses and Elijah, talking with Him. . . . A bright cloud overshadowed them, and a voice from the cloud said: 'This is My beloved Son, with whom I am well pleased; listen to Him.' When the disciples heard this, they fell on their faces and were filled with awe. But Jesus came and touched them, saying: 'Rise, and have no fear.' . . . And as they were coming down the mountain, Jesus commanded them to tell no one the vision until He was raised from the dead."

Now this is what St. Peter wants to say: What I preach to you about Christ and His coming, the Gospel we proclaim, has not been made up or invented by us. Nor has it been taken from clever writers of myths, who know how to speak splendidly about everything (as the Greeks did in that day). For these are purely fables, fairy tales, and idle talk, which they cleverly fabricate and in which they try to be wise. We did not listen to such people. Nor did we follow them; that is, we do not teach trumpery of men, but we are certain that our message is from God. We saw it with our eyes and heard it with our ears, namely, when we were on the mountain with Christ and beheld and heard His glory. But His glory was evident when His face shone like the sun and His garments were as white as snow. Furthermore, we heard a voice from the Most Sublime Majesty say: "This is My beloved Son; listen to Him."

Now every preacher should be so sure of having and preaching God's Word that he would even stake his life on this, since it is a matter of life for us. He should not be in doubt. Now no man is so holy that he would dare die on the strength of the doctrine he himself has taught. Therefore it is established here that the apostles were assured by God that their Gospel was God's Word. And here it is also shown that the Gospel is nothing else than a sermon about Christ. Accordingly, one should listen to no other sermon; for the Father wants no other sermon. "This is My beloved Son," He says; "listen to Him. He is your Teacher." It is as if He were saying: "If you listen to Him, you have listened to Me." Therefore Peter now says: We have proclaimed and made known to you that Christ is a Lord, that He rules over all things, that all power belongs to Him, and that he who believes in Him also has all this power. We have not invented this ourselves; but we have seen and heard it through the revelation of God, who has commanded us to listen to this Christ.

But why does Peter distinguish between the power and the coming of Christ? As we heard above,[7] Christ's power consists in the fact that He is sovereign over all things, that everything must lie at His feet. It will endure as long as the world stands. Christ's kingdom will flourish as long as we are flesh and blood and live on earth. It will do so until the Last Day. Afterwards a new era will begin. Then Christ will hand over the kingdom to God the Father. St. Paul speaks of this in 1 Cor. 15:23-24: "Christ the first fruits, then at His coming those who belong to Christ. Then comes the end, when He delivers the kingdom to God the Father, etc." And then (v. 28) he says: "When all things are subjected to Him, then the Son Himself will also be subjected to Him who put all things under Him."

What? Does the kingdom not belong to God the Father now? Is not everything subject to Him? Answer: St. Paul interprets himself in the same place by adding the words "that God may be everything to everyone" (v. 28). This means that God will be everything that everyone will need and should have, that we will "become partakers of the divine nature," as St. Peter stated above (v. 4).

[7] See pp. 6-7

Therefore we shall also have all that God has, and in Him we shall have all that is necessary for us: wisdom, righteousness, strength, and life. All this we now believe. We grasp it only with our ears and have it in the Word of God. But then the Word will cease. Then our soul will open and behold and feel that all this is actually there. Now St. Paul and St. Peter mean that the power of Christ's kingdom is in operation at the present time. Today He employs the Word, and with it He reigns through His humanity over devil, sin, death, and all things. But on the Last Day this will become manifest. Therefore although God rules constantly, yet this is not manifest to us. To be sure, He sees us; but we do not see Him. Accordingly, Christ must deliver the kingdom to Him in order that we, too, may see it. Then we shall be brothers of Christ and children of God. Thus Christ received honor and glory from God, St. Peter states here, when the Father subjected all things to Him, made Him Lord, and glorified Him through this voice, when He said: "This is My beloved Son, in whom I am well pleased" (Matt. 17:5).

With these words St. Peter wants to confirm His teaching and preaching, in order that we may know what its source is. But here no more happened to him than that he heard this and was able to preach about it. In addition, however, the Holy Spirit had to come and strengthen him, so that he believed in it and confidently preached and confessed it. The former pertains solely to the office of the ministry, not to the soul; the latter, however, pertains to the Spirit.

19. *And we have a sure prophetic Word. You will do well to pay attention to this as to a lamp shining in a dark place, until the day dawns and the morning star rises in your hearts.*

Here St. Peter goes to the core of the matter and wants to say: The whole purpose of my preaching is to make your conscience sure and to give your heart a firm footing from which it should not permit itself to be torn, in order that both you and I may be certain that we have God's Word. For the Gospel is a serious business. It must be grasped and retained in all purity, without any addition or false doctrine. For this reason St. Peter now begins to write against human doctrines.

But why does he say: "We have a sure prophetic Word"?

Answer: I believe indeed that henceforth we shall not have prophets like those the Jews had in times past in the Old Testament. But a prophet must really be one who preaches about Jesus Christ. Therefore although many prophets in the Old Testament foretold future things, they really came, and were sent by God, to proclaim the Christ. Now those who believe in Christ are all prophets; for they have the real and chief qualification prophets should have, even though they do not all have the gift of foretelling the future. For just as through faith we are brothers of the Lord Christ, kings, and priests, so we are also all prophets through Christ. For we can all state what pertains to salvation, God's glory, and a Christian life. In addition, we can also talk about future events insofar as it is necessary for us to know about them. For example, we can say that the Last Day will come and that we will rise from the dead. Furthermore, we understand all Scripture. Paul also speaks about this in 1 Cor. 14:31: "For you can all prophesy one by one."

Thus Peter now says: We have a prophetic Word that is sure in itself. Just see to it that it is sure for you. "You will do well to pay attention to this." It is as if he were saying: It will be necessary for you to hold fast to it. For the Gospel does the very thing that happens when one is caught in a house in the middle of the night when it is pitch-dark. Then it would be necessary to provide a light until daybreak, so that he could see. Thus the Gospel is really in the midst of night and darkness. For all human reason is sheer error and blindness. Thus the world, too, is nothing else than a realm of darkness. In this darkness God has now ignited a light, namely, the Gospel. In this light we can see and walk as long as we dwell on earth, until the dawn comes and the day breaks.

Thus this text also vigorously assails all human doctrine. For since the Word of God is the light in a pitch-dark place, it is established that everything else is darkness. For if there were a light apart from the Word, St. Peter would not speak this way. Therefore pay no regard to the intelligence of people who teach something else, no matter how impressive they pretend that it is. Where you are not aware of God's Word, do not doubt that this is sheer darkness. Do not be troubled by their statement that they have the Holy Spirit. How can they have God's Spirit if they do not have God's Word? Therefore they do nothing else than call darkness light and "put darkness for light," as Is. 5:20 states. It is God's Word, the Gospel, that we have been redeemed from death, sin, and hell through Christ. He who hears this has lighted the light and the lamp in our hearts to enable us to see. The Gospel illumines us and teaches what we should know. But where it is missing, we rush in and want to find the road to heaven with a self-invented way of life and self-invented works. Concerning this you cannot judge and see by means of your light that it is darkness. Consequently, since they do not want to have or accept the light, they must remain in darkness and blindness; for the light teaches us everything we should know and everything that is necessary for our salvation. This the world does not recognize by means of its wisdom and reason. And we must have the light and cling to it until the Last Day. Then we shall no longer need the Word, just as artificial [8] light is extinguished when the day dawns.

20. *First of all you must understand this, that no prophecy of Scripture is a matter of one's own interpretation,*

21. *because no prophecy ever came by the impulse of man, but men moved by the Holy Spirit spoke from God.*

Here St. Peter attacks false doctrine. Since you know that we have God's Word, he says, cling to this knowledge, and do not be misled by other false teachers, even though they come with the allegation that they, too, have the Holy Spirit. For "first of all you must understand this" — he will state the rest later — "that no prophecy of Scripture is a matter of one's own interpretation." Be governed by this, and do not think that you can interpret Scripture with your own reason and wisdom.

With these words all the fathers who interpret Scripture in their own way are refuted, and their interpretation is invalidated. It is forbidden to rely on such interpretation. If Jerome or Augustine or anyone of the fathers has given his own interpretation, we want none of it. Peter has stated the prohibition: You shall not give your own interpretation. The Holy Spirit Himself must expound Scripture. Otherwise it must remain unexpounded. Now if anyone of the saintly fathers can show that his interpretation is based on Scripture, and if Scripture proves that this is the way it should be interpreted, then the interpretation is right. If this is not the case, I must not believe him.

[8] Although Luther uses the word *naturlich*, it is evident that "artificial" light is meant.

Thus Peter attacks even the most estimable and competent teachers. Therefore we dare not believe anyone who presents his own explanation and interpretation of Scripture. For no correct understanding can be arrived at by means of one's own interpretation. Here all teachers and fathers, as many as there are who have interpreted Scripture, have stumbled, as when they refer Christ's statement in Matt. 16:18 – "You are Peter, and on this rock will I build My church" – to the pope. This is a human, self-invented interpretation. Therefore one should not believe it, for they cannot prove from Scripture that Peter is ever called the pope. But we can prove that Christ and faith are the Rock, as St. Paul declares.[9] This explanation is correct, for we are sure that it has not been devised by man but has been drawn from God's Word. Now what is written and proclaimed in the prophets, says Peter, has not been invented or devised by man; but the pious and holy men have said it as they were moved by the Holy Spirit.

Now this is the first chapter. In it St. Peter has taught, in the first place, what the genuinely good works are with which we should show our faith. In the second place, he has taught that nothing but God's Word alone should be preached in Christendom. The reason for this is no other, as we have said, than this, that a Word must be proclaimed that remains eternally – a Word through which souls may be saved and may live forever. Now a faithful admonition follows – an admonition which Christ, Paul, and all the apostles have given, namely, that we should beware of and be on our guard against false preachers. It is especially necessary for us to understand this well, lest we permit the right and the power shared by all Christians to pass judgment on all doctrine to be wrested from us, and lest we let it come to the point that we must wait until the councils decide what we are to believe and must follow them. This we shall now consider.

---

[9] Cf. *Luther the Expositor*, pp. 113–116, on the interpretation of Matt. 16:18.

CHAPTER TWO

1. *But false prophets also arose among the people, just as there will be false teachers among you.*

This is what St. Peter wants to say: Just as all prophecy has emanated from the Holy Spirit since the beginning of the world, so this must be true until the end of the world, in order that nothing but God's Word may be preached. Yet it has always happened that there have been false teachers alongside the true prophets and God's Word. And so it will remain. Therefore since you now have God's Word, you must expect to have false teachers too. This is sufficient warning. Nor can it fail to happen that where God's Word is correctly proclaimed, false preachers will arise hard by. The reason is that not everybody lays hold of the Word and believes in it, even though it is preached to all. Those who believe it follow and retain it. But the majority, who do not believe, get a false understanding of it, and this gives rise to false teachers. Unfortunately, however, we paid no attention to this. Nor did we heed this warning. Instead, we ran along and did what was preached. Here we lost our heads; we fell into and went along in the delusion that the pope, together with his priests and monks, could not err. And those who should have arrested this error were the first to instil it in us. Therefore we are not excused if we believe falsely and follow false teachers. The fact that we did not know better will not help us, since we were warned in advance. Furthermore, God gave us the command that everyone should judge, and be accountable for, the message of this or of that preacher. If we do not do this, we are lost. Thus the salvation of everyone's soul depends on knowing what God's Word and false teachings are.

Many more such warnings are found here and there in Scripture. In Acts 20:29-30 St. Paul also adds such an admonition at the end of his sermon in which he blessed the Ephesians and took leave of them. This is what he says: "I know that after my departure fierce wolves will come in among you, not sparing the flock; and from among your own selves will arise men speaking perverse things, to draw away the disciples after them." Christ also announces this in Matt. 24:23-24:[1] "Then if anyone says to you: 'Lo, here is the Christ!' or 'There He is!' do not believe it. For false Christs and false prophets will arise and show great signs and wonders, so as to lead astray, if possible, even the elect." And Paul declares again in 1 Tim. 4:1-2: "Now the Spirit expressly says that in later times some will depart from the faith by giving heed to deceitful spirits and doctrines of demons, through the pretensions of liars, etc." Now as forceful as these warnings were, we should surely have been wise. Yet it did not help. The warnings were ignored. Thus we always went along and let ourselves be misled.

Now let us see who the false teachers are about whom Peter is speaking here. I believe that God's arrangement to have our teachers called *doctores* was based on a special decision.[2] The purpose was to let us see whom Peter has in mind. For he used the very same word here: *falsi doctores,* "false teachers." He does not say "false prophets" or "false apostles." In this way he hits the schools of higher learning, where such people are turned out. From these schools come all the preachers in the world, so that under the papacy there is no city that does not have teachers of this kind who are turned out in the schools of higher learning. For the whole world thinks that these schools should be the springs from which those who are to teach the people should flow. This is a dreadful error, and nothing more horrible has ever happened on earth than what has come out of the schools of higher learning. Therefore Peter says that such utterly false teachers will arise. But what will they do? We read on:

Who will secretly bring in destructive sects.

The apostle calls them "destructive sects," or estates and orders, since he who gets into them is already lost. These, he says, they bring in secretly, not that they will preach as if the Gospel and Holy Scripture were false—for this would be in complete op-

[1] The original has "Matt. 20."

[2] On the importance which Luther attached to this cf. *Luther the Expositor,* pp. 46–47.

position – but they will retain the terms "God," "Christ," "faith," "church," "Baptism," "Sacrament" and let them remain. Under these terms, however, they will proceed to establish something different. Accordingly, there is a great difference if I say: "This man preaches against this" or "He preaches along with this." When I ·proclaim: "Christ is God's Son and true man, and he who believes in Him will be saved," this is proper preaching and the true Gospel. Now if someone preaches: "Christ is neither God's Son nor true man. Faith does not save," this is saying the very opposite. St. Peter is not speaking about this – for our schools of higher learning, priests, and monks do not do this – but he is speaking about the doctrine they introduce alongside the true doctrine. It is as if I were to say: "It is true that Christ is true God and man, that He died for our sin, and that no one who does not believe in Him can be saved. All this, however, pertains only to the rank and file. But we desire to establish something more perfect, namely, that one should vow chastity, poverty, and obedience, so many fasts, foundations, etc. He who does this will go straight to heaven."[3] Now where such things are proclaimed and heard, namely, that nothing is better and more blissful than virginity and obedience, that monks and priests are in a higher and more perfect estate than the common man, there nothing is said directly against the pure Christian doctrine. Nor are faith, Baptism, etc., and the fact that Christ is the Savior denied. Nevertheless, something different is brought in secretly, and it leads people away from the right course, so that they rely on their own way of life and works and believe no more about Christ than these words: "We believe that Christ is God's Son and man, that He died and rose again, that He saves the world, etc." But they do not place their reliance wholly on Him; for if they did this, they would not persevere in their way of life for a single hour.

In this way they also preached among the laity and said: "To be sure, you are Christians; but this is not enough. In addition, you must perform such and such works, erect churches and cloisters, and found Masses and vigils." And the common people plumped in and thought this was right. In this way Christendom was divided and split into almost as many sects as there are cities and people.

[3] The Weimar editors have suggested that the phrase *von mund auff* here reflects the medieval idea that the soul forsakes the body through the mouth.

They should have preached and taught as follows: "You are already Christians just as well as those who are more than 100 miles away. You all have one Christ, one Baptism, one faith, one Spirit, one Word, one God. Therefore no work one can do helps make a Christian." In this way the people would be kept in one common faith, and there would be no difference before God; but one person would be like the other. This unity they have rent asunder by saying: "You are a Christian, but you must perform works in order to be saved." They lead us away from faith to works. Therefore St. Peter—if one wants to interpret his words aright—says nothing else than this: Schools of higher learning and *doctores*, priests, and all the people will arise. They will introduce destructive sects and orders, and they will mislead the world with false doctrines. These are the very people he has in mind, for they all think that their positions and orders save, and they bring it about that reliance and trust are placed on these. For if they did not think so, they would surely remain out of them.

Even denying the Master who bought them.

"Oh," they say, "we by no means deny the Lord!" Then if one says: "If you are redeemed through Christ, and if His blood wipes out your sin, then what do you propose to wipe out with your way of life?" they reply: "Ah, faith alone does not do this; the works must contribute to it!" In this way, to be sure, they confess the Lord Christ with their lips, but with their hearts they deny Him completely.

Behold, what powerful words St. Peter uses! He says: "They deny the Master who bought them." They should be under Him as under a Master who owns them. But now, even though they believe that He is a Lord who has ransomed all the world with His blood, yet they do not believe that they are ransomed and that He is their Master. They say that although He ransomed and redeemed them, this is not enough; one must first make amends and render satisfaction for sin with works. Then we say: "If you take away your sin yourself and wipe it out, what, then has Christ done? You surely cannot make two Christs who take away sin. He should, and wants to, be the only One who puts sin aside. If this is true, I cannot make bold to wipe out sin myself. But if I do this, I cannot say or believe that Christ takes it away." This amounts to a denial of Christ. For even if they regard Christ as a Lord, yet they deny that

He redeemed them. To be sure, they believe that He sits up there in heaven and is a Lord; but that it is His real work to take away sin, this they take from Him and ascribe to their own works. Thus they leave Him no more than the name and the title. But they want to have His work, His power, and His office themselves. Therefore Christ speaks truly (Matt. 24:5): "Many will come in My name, saying: 'I am the Christ,' and they will lead many astray." For they really do not say: "My name is Christ." No, they say: "I am Christ." For they arrogate to themselves the very office that belongs to Christ and thus push Him from the throne and sit on it themselves. This is so apparent that no one can deny it. Therefore St. Peter calls them damned or destructive sects, for they are all running straight to hell. Consequently, I think that among a thousand scarcely one is saved. For he who wants to be saved must say: "My obedience, my chastity, etc., do not save me; my works remove no sin from me." But how many there are who have this notion and remain in such a damnable estate!

Bringing upon themselves swift destruction.

This means that their destruction will soon overtake them. Even though it seems that God tarries a long time, yet He will come soon enough. But this does not happen physically, so that one can see it with one's eyes; but it takes place as Ps. 55:23 states: "They shall not live out half their days"; that is, death will seize them before they are aware of it, so that they say with Hezekiah in Is. 38:10: "I said: 'In the noontide of my days I must depart; I am consigned to the gates of Sheol for the rest of my years.'" It is as if they were saying: "Lord God, is death already here?" For those people who do not live in faith never weary of life. The longer they live, the longer they want to live; and the saintlier they seem, the more terrible death will be to them, especially to those who have tender consciences and cruelly drive and torment themselves with works. For it is impossible to vanquish death with human powers. Where faith is lacking, the conscience must flounder and despair. Where faith is strong, death comes too slowly. On the other hand, it always comes too soon for the unbeliever; for there the fond desire to live never ceases.

Now this is what St. Peter means here: The people who establish these sects and thus deny Christ will have to die with great reluctance. They will have to flounder and despair, for the only way they can think is this: "Who knows whether God is gracious to me and wants to forgive my sin?" They remain constantly in such despair. "Who knows? Who knows?" And their conscience never becomes cheerful. The longer they remain in this condition, the more terrifying death will be to them. For death cannot be conquered before sin and the evil conscience are removed. Thus their destruction will come upon them swiftly, and they will have to remain in death eternally.

2. *And many will follow their destruction.*

It is now apparent that things have gone exactly as St. Peter predicted. There was no father and no mother who did not want their child to become a priest, a monk, or a nun. Thus one fool led to the other; for when people saw the misfortune and the misery in the estate of matrimony and did not know what a blessed estate this is, they wanted to help their children, in order that these might have good days and be spared such unhappiness. Therefore Peter has proclaimed nothing else here than that the world will be full of priests, monks, and nuns. The youth and the best in the world flocked in this direction to the devil, so that St. Peter unfortunately says all too truthfully that many would follow their destruction.

And because of them the way of truth will be reviled.

This is also something one sees. To revile means to rebuke, condemn, and curse, as when the Christian estate is condemned as error and heresy. Now when it is preached and stated that their way is in opposition to the Gospel because they lead people away from faith to works, they proceed to cry out: "You are accursed; you are misleading the world!" And they revile even more by distorting Christ's statements and saying no to them (cf. Matt. 5:20 ff.), as when they make mere suggestions out of Christ's commands, when they forbid where Christ accords liberty and make sin out of what Christ does not make sin, and, in addition, condemn and burn at the stake him who preaches against this. The way of truth is an upright life and conduct free from sham and hypocrisy. It is the faith in which all Christians walk. This way they cannot bear; they revile and condemn it in order to praise and protect their own way of life and their sects.

3. *And in their greed they will exploit you with false words.*

It is really characteristic of all false teachers to preach about greed in order to fill their bellies. Thus we see that not one of them has observed a Mass or a vigil for nothing, that no cloister or charitable foundation has ever been built for which interest in plenty did not have to come in, and that there is no cloister in the world which serves the world for the sake of God. It is all a matter of money alone. But when faith is preached in the proper manner, this does not bring in much money; for then all pilgrimages, letters of indulgence, cloisters, and foundations suffer a loss of revenue. For these more than half of all the world's goods has been applied and given, and only priests and monks have had any benefit from it.

But what do they do to get money? "They will exploit you with false words," says Peter. For they have chosen words with a view to defrauding the people of their money, as when they say: "If you give so many hundred guldens to Our Dear Lady or to this or that saint, you are doing a great and excellent good work, are earning so much indulgence and forgiveness of sin, and are redeeming so many souls from purgatory, etc." These and similar statements are nothing but false words chosen for the sole purpose of wheedling money from us. For here there surely is no merit and no grace or wiping out of sin. Yet they use all these noble words for the purpose of getting money in a fraudulent manner. Thus even the holy Sacrament, which is rich in grace, has become nothing else than a business; for they use it for no other purpose than to butter up the people and relieve them of their money. Now see whether St. Peter has not put his finger on our clergy with good reason and portrayed them properly.

From of old their condemnation has not been idle, and their destruction has not been asleep.

St. Peter wants to say: They will not carry on like this indefinitely. When worse comes to worst, their judgment and condemnation will come upon them. This is already happening. They will not escape it. Thus St. Paul, too, says in 2 Tim. 3:9: "They will not get very far, for their folly will be plain to all," in order that they may be put to shame. May God grant that they repent and turn from their evil life when they hear and experience this! For although there are a few who are not misled in this way of life, yet the way of life in itself is nothing more than destructive sects.

Thus St. Peter has begun to describe the shameful and ungodly life that would follow the true doctrine of the Gospel which the apostles preached. Now he continues and presents to us three terrible examples: of the angels, of the entire world, and of Sodom — how God condemned them. He says:

4. *For if God did not spare the angels when they sinned, but cast them into hell and committed them to pits of nether gloom to be kept until the judgment.*

With these words St. Peter frightens those who go through life impudently and smugly, as we see those do who adhere to what the pope has established. They are arrogant and brazen, as though they wanted to tread everybody underfoot. Therefore the apostle wants to say: Is it not great presumptuousness on their part to go along so boldly and to insist on having their own way, as though God had to give way to them and spare them, even though He did not spare the angels? It is as if he were saying: It stands to reason that even the saints should be frightened when they see such a serious judgment, namely, that God did not spare the high spirits and noble creatures, who are much smarter and wiser than we, but cast them into chains of darkness. This is the stern judgment and the damnation to which He sentenced them, in which they are held captive and bound. They cannot escape the hands of God; they are to be hurled into outer darkness, as Christ says in the Gospel (Matt. 22:13).

And here St. Peter also points out that the devils do not yet have their final punishment but go along in their unrepenting and evil way of life and expect their judgment every moment, just as a man who is condemned to death becomes desperately hardened and ever more evil. But their punishment has not yet come upon them; now they are only bound and kept for it. This is the first example. The second follows:

5. *If He did not spare the ancient world, but preserved Noah, a herald of righteousness, with seven other persons, when He brought a flood upon the world of the ungodly.*

This, too, is a terrifying example. No harsher example is found in Scripture. Even one who is strong in faith would almost despair.

For if such statements and God's judgment go to man's heart, and if man is not well prepared when death approaches, he must tremble and quail at the thought that among so many only eight were preserved. But why did they deserve such a severe sentence from God that He drowned the whole world at one time — man and woman, master and servant, young and old, beast and bird? Because they led such an evil life. Noah was a pious man and a preacher of righteousness. He had lived for 500 years before the Flood when God ordered him to build an ark. This occupied him for 100 years, and he always led a truly godly life. You can imagine what a cross this pious man bore and what trouble and anxiety he suffered when he had to testify with words and deeds that he was a Christian. For it is impossible for faith to conceal itself and not to become evident before the people because of preaching and deeds of kindness. Thus perhaps this man alone administered the office of preaching the Word of God — not at one place but throughout many lands — long before God ordered him to build the ark. In consequence, he must have endured much bitter persecution and, as Peter states, was especially preserved and saved by God. Otherwise he would soon have perished and been slain. For by doing what he did he incurred much envy and hatred, and antagonized even many eminent, wise, and saintly people. But what he did was to no avail, for the world disdained God's Word and only grew ever more evil. Now after they had gone along in their wickedness for a long time, God said: "My spirit shall not abide in man forever, for he is flesh; but his days shall be a hundred and twenty years" (Gen. 6:3). Likewise: "I will blot out man whom I have created from the face of the ground, man and beast and creeping things and birds of the air" (v. 7). Noah proclaimed and inculcated these words daily, and he began to build the ark, as he had been ordered. This took 100 years. The people laughed at him, however, and became more stubborn and unrepentant. But the sin because of which God destroyed the world is mentioned in Gen. 6:2, where we read: "The sons of God" — that is, those who were descended from the saintly fathers and had been instructed and brought up in faith and in the knowledge of God — "saw that the daughters of men were fair; and they took to wife such of them as they chose." These became "mighty men" (v. 4) who, in their wantonness, did what they pleased. Therefore God punished the world and destroyed it with the Flood.

6. *If by turning the cities of Sodom and Gomorrah to ashes He condemned them to extinction.*

This is the third example, how the five cities were destroyed, as is told in Gen. 19:24-25. The prophet Ezekiel also speaks about this to the city of Jerusalem in chapter 16:49-50: "Behold, this was the guilt of your sister Sodom: she and her daughters had pride, surfeit of food, and prosperous ease, but did not aid the poor and needy. They were haughty, and did abominable things before Me; therefore I removed them when I saw it." Moses says that Sodom was "like the garden of the Lord" (Gen. 13:10), a fruitful land dripping with precious oil and wine and everything, so that everyone thought that God dwelt there. Therefore the inhabitants were smug and led the kind of shameful life Moses describes. No particular person introduced this sin; it was prevalent because of the pert manner in which the people prided themselves on having an abundance of food and drink. Besides, they were lazy. As we still see, the richer cities are, the more shameful is the life that is lived there. But where hunger and sorrow reign, there sins are fewer. Therefore God lets those who are His work hard for a living in order that they may remain pious as they do so.

These are the three terrible examples with which St. Peter threatens the ungodly. Now since he impresses this on them, we must conclude that the same conditions prevail here. And this really applies to the spiritual estate: the pope, the cardinals, the bishops, the priests, the monks, the nuns, and all who adhere to them. Like the angels in the stead of the apostles, these are appointed to preach and proclaim God's Word; for an *angelus* is a messenger or an ambassador who brings his message orally. Therefore Scripture calls preachers *angeli*, that is, messengers of God.[4] Our clergy should be such angels. But just as those angels fell away from God, exalted themselves above God, and wanted to be their own lords, so these do the same thing and retain no more than the name "messengers," as those alone are called angels. Thus these, too, since they have fallen away from God, are now held in bonds of darkness and kept for damnation. St. Peter said above (v. 3) that "their condemnation has not been idle, and their destruction has not been asleep," even though the punishment has not yet come upon them.

[4] Luther is thinking of passages such as Gal. 4:14 and Rev. 1:20.

In the second place, they are like the ancient world, which, although it had the prophets and the Word of God, nevertheless reviled and defamed this Word, and, as Moses writes (Gen. 6:2, 4), took to wife those whom they chose and became mighty tyrants. Now see whether everything Moses wrote about them is not happening today. These are the bigwigs. They live a riotous life and oppress the world with their tyranny. No one has the courage to take them to task. They have the audacity to take the wife and daughter from any man they please in spite of complaints; for even if someone complains about this, they themselves are the judges, and no one can do anything against them. What they contrive to acquire by means of swindling and taxing, this they also do. And if anyone wants to attack them, they reply: "This is the spiritual property of the church. It is exempt. Therefore one dare not touch it." And those who preach God's Word, reproach them for their conduct, and proclaim God's judgment upon them, they ridicule. They refuse to listen to this, and they persecute these preachers of righteousness and remain great and mighty lords. They want to retain the name "clergy," just as the others want to be known as children of God. They rule with full power and in a completely arbitrary way. Yet ultimately they will perish and be destroyed. But the others, who preach God's Word, will be preserved and saved.

In the third place, just as the land in which the cities Sodom and Gomorrah were situated was a land of plenty and had enough of everything the earth could bring forth, from which the people lived a life of idleness, ate and guzzled themselves full and did not help the poor, so matters stand in our clerical estate. Everywhere they have the best land, the best castles and cities, the highest rentals and interest rates, and also enough to eat and guzzle. There are no lazier people on earth; they live without care and work, and they support themselves solely from the sweat of the poor. But the fruit of their indolence is apparent. The pope forbids them to marry. But if they keep whores and have children, they must pay the bishop money for each child. In this way they want to remedy the situation and to check the sins. I do not want to speak here of other secret sins which are unmentionable.

In brief, you see here that St. Peter regards the clerical estate as no different from Sodom and Gomorrah. For they are all people from whom no one can benefit and who lend no one a helping hand but grab everything under the pretext that what is given to them is given to God; and they let no one who is in need be helped. Therefore just as the inhabitants of Sodom and Gomorrah were overturned and reduced to ashes, so these, too, will be destroyed on the Last Day.

7. *And if He rescued righteous Lot, greatly distressed by the licentiousness of the wicked.*

Was it not a great abomination that they not only whored and committed adultery but also committed such an unspeakable sin openly and brazenly, and did not spare even the angels who came to Lot? And both young and old in all corners of the city were addicted to this sin. Pious Lot preached against this daily and reproved the people. But this did not help. Lot was drowned out by them, so that he had to stand still and was unable to correct the evil. This is what is happening to us today, for there is no longer any hope that the abominable way of life to which the world is addicted can be corrected or remedied.

8. *For by what that righteous man saw and heard as he lived among them, he was vexed in his righteous soul day after day with their lawless deeds.*

Here Peter describes the cross the saintly man had to bear because he preached to the people, brought up his daughters in the faith, and thus was saved by God together with them. Now St. Peter concludes by telling how the ungodly are kept "under punishment until the Day of Judgment."

9. *Then the Lord knows how to rescue the godly from trial, and to keep the unrighteous under punishment until the Day of Judgment,*

10. *and especially those who indulge in the lust of defiling passion.*

This betokens great wrath and earnestness on the part of the apostle. If God did not spare the young and new world, he says, how much harder and more severely He will punish the world after the Gospel has been revealed and preached, and no light so great has ever before dawned! Thus Christ also proclaims in Matt.

11:23-24: "And you, Capernaum, will you be exalted to heaven? You shall be brought down to Hades. For if the mighty works done in you had been done in Sodom, it would have remained until this day. But I tell you that it shall be more tolerable on the Day of Judgment for the land of Sodom than for you." Yet such threats are to no avail; the ungodly pay no attention to them.

"To indulge in the lust of defiling passion" is to live like an irrational beast according to one's own notion and all lust. Thus in the pope's law's everything has been laid down as it pleased him. Everything had to serve their arbitrariness and tyranny. They bent and interpreted everything as they desired, and then they declared that the Holy See in Rome cannot err. Not one of them has preached anything about faith or about love, but they have taught only their own fabrications.

They despise authority. Bold and willful, they are not afraid to revile the glorious ones,

11. *whereas angels, though greater in might and power, do not pronounce a reviling judgment upon them before the Lord.*

He calls kings, princes, lords, and all worldly government, not the popes and the bishops, "authority," for the latter were not to be lords, since Christ appointed only servants in the New Testament. One Christian was to serve and honor the other Christian. Therefore Peter means that they should be subject and obedient to the secular overlords, in order that the sword, which is instituted by God's arrangement, might be feared. But they do the very opposite; they have excluded themselves and say that they are not subject to the secular government. Yes, they have not only excluded themselves; but they have also subjected the secular government to themselves and have trodden it underfoot. Brazenly they let themselves be called lords even by kings and princes, just as the pope writes about himself that he is lord of heaven and earth, that he has both the spiritual and the secular sword in his hand, and that everyone is obliged to fall down before him.[5]

Furthermore, St. Peter says that "they are not afraid to revile

---

[5] Luther seems to be paraphrasing the claims of the bull of Boniface VIII, *Unam sanctam* (November 18, 1302), which restated the doctrine of the two swords.

the glorious ones." For it has been a trifling and simple matter for the pope to excommunicate kings and princes, to anathematize them, and to depose them, likewise to bring about such misfortune among them and to set the princes against one another. Those who opposed this he soon silenced and subdued, not because they acted contrary to faith and love, but solely because they refused to be subject to the Roman See or to kiss the pope's feet; for the power of the popes is as much greater than that of the secular lords as the sun is superior to the moon and as high as heaven is from the earth, as they blaspheme and lie.[6] Yet they should be subject and obedient to, bless, and pray for, the secular lords, just as the Lord Christ was subject to Pilate and gave the tribute money to the emperor.[7] They should tremble at the thought of reviling the majesties. Yet they are unafraid. Besides, they are insolent, and they revile them in a completely outrageous and arrogant manner, though even the most powerful angels cannot bear the Lord's adverse judgment. Still they are unrepentant, and they revile and curse the judgment they cannot escape. How, then, do these wretched people hope to be able to bear it?

12. *But these, like irrational animals, creatures of instinct, born to be caught and killed, reviling in matters of which they are ignorant, will be destroyed in the same destruction with them,*

13. *suffering wrong for their wrongdoing.*

Peter calls them "irrational animals," since they do not have in them even a tiny spark that reflects the spirit and do not administer a spiritual office, which should be their duty, but live like sows and are completely absorbed in their carnal way of life. But the apostle's statement that they are "born to be caught and killed" can be understood in two ways. In the first place, they are people who catch and kill, like wolves, lions, bears, sparrow hawks, and eagles, since they scrape and tear from the people everything they can, property and honor. In the second place, these words can be understood to mean that they are to be caught and killed for the judgment on the Last Day.

[6] Cf. *Luther's Works*, 2, p. 152, note 40; 31, p. 385.

[7] Luther seems to be thinking of Matt. 22:17-21 (which does not, however, say that Jesus paid the tax) or of Matt. 17:24-27 (which describes a tribute paid for the support of the Jewish temple).

They count it pleasure to revel in the daytime.

Behold, how angry St. Peter is! I would not have the courage to revile the junkers in such a cruel manner. They suppose that they have enough of everything and that all is well so long as they devote themselves to pleasure and have good days. This is very noticeable in their ecclesiastical law, where they say that he who touches their property or their bellies is of the devil.[8] They themselves cannot deny that their whole regimen is adjusted to affording them days of indolence, leisure, and enough of everything. They refuse to burden themselves with toil and labor. Instead, everyone must provide enough for them, while they pretend that they have to go to church and pray. God commanded all men to eat their bread in the sweat of their faces, and He imposed misfortune and heartache on everybody. Now these junkers want to pull their heads out of the noose and sit on their cushions. But it is the greatest blindness on their part to be so unrepentant and to consider such a disgraceful life proper and praiseworthy.

They are blots and blemishes.

They are convinced that they adorn Christendom as the sun and the moon adorn the heavens, and that they are the noblest and best treasures, like gold and precious stones. But St. Peter calls them "blots and blemishes." The truly Christian life goes along in faith, serves everybody through love, and bears the holy cross. This is the true color, adornment, treasure, and honor of the Christian Church. But these people have substituted sensual pleasure and a life of ease for the cross. Instead of love for their neighbor they seek their own advantage. They seize everything for themselves and let nothing of theirs benefit another person. Moreover, they are totally ignorant of faith. Therefore they are nothing else than "blots and blemishes," and Christendom has to suffer disgrace and mockery on their account. This, I think, is adequate rebuke for our spiritual lords.

Reveling in their dissipation, carousing with you.

What has been given out of Christian love in the first instance to maintain a common treasury for widows, orphans, and other poor

---

[8] See, for example, the passage cited in *Luther's Works*, 13, p. 42, note 1.

people, lest anyone among the Christians suffer want or have to beg—all such property has now been devoted to foundations and cloisters. From this our clerics fatten their bellies. They live in the utmost luxury and squander everything on good times. Furthermore, they say that they are entitled to this and that no one should reproach them for it. The Holy Spirit does not want to tolerate a state of affairs where the servant of the church lives a life of luxury at the expense of other people's labor, for in any case it is impossible for craftsmen and the common man with wife and child to do this.

14. *They have eyes full of adultery.*

This is the inevitable consequence when, as stated above, the body has enough to eat and guzzle and is idle. But why does St. Peter not say that they are adulterers instead of saying: "They have eyes full of adultery"? He wants to say that they think constantly of whoring and that they can never curb their knavery or become sated with and weary of it. Hence they constantly carouse and live in luxury. They want to continue this mode of life freely, with impunity, and unhampered. This we see from what follows.

Insatiable for sin.

The pope has forbidden any prince or secular government to punish the clerics, and if they make bold to do so, he excommunicates them.[9] The authority to punish he has delegated to the bishops. But since these men themselves are rascals, they are lenient. Thus they have excluded themselves from the secular government and sword. Consequently, no one has the courage to check their wantonness, and, like the people before the Flood, they live just as they please.

They entice unsteady souls.

With such a great appearance of saintliness, which they feign while leading a rascally life—for example, with the reading of Masses, praying, singing, etc.—they entice and lure frivolous and

[9] Luther is referring to the medieval principle of "benefit of clergy," under which a priest accused of a felony under civil law was nevertheless to be tried before an ecclesiastical tribunal, not before a secular court.

fickle souls that are without faith, so that everybody wants to enter the church and is brought up for this estate. For it is thought that in this estate everybody has a life of abundance and ease, and, in addition, that everybody goes to heaven. Yet it is all a matter of filling the belly and our lazy sack.

They have hearts trained in greed.

Among the clergy this vice is so gross and open that even the common man has complained about it. But the apostle does not say that they are greedy; he says: "They have hearts trained in greed." This is evident from the innumerable cunning and clever schemes they have devised for the purpose of appropriating the property of the whole world. Everything these people do and practice is greed pure and simple; everything must be lucrative. They also prove most pointedly how adept and well prepared in every way they are in defrauding the people of their money, lest St. Peter ever turn out to be a liar.

Accursed children!

This is a Hebrew way of saying that they are damned people under the curse of God, that before God they have neither happiness nor salvation and only become worse from day to day, and constantly blaspheme God all the more, in order that they may bring the wrath of God and His terrible judgment upon themselves in abundance. This is surely a statement that is harsh and terrible enough. In view of this it is high time for him who can to flee and hasten out of this accursed estate. It is surely terrible to have such a title; for when the Sublime Majesty rebukes, curses, and condemns in this way, who will bear it?

15. *Forsaking the right way, they have gone astray.*

They should have taught the right way: how one must cling to Christ and come to God through faith and through love for one's neighbor, and then bear the holy cross and suffer whatever befalls us on this account. But all their preaching amounts to no more than saying: "Run hither and thither! Become a monk and a priest! Endow churches, Masses, etc.!" In this way they lead people away from faith and direct them to their works, which, after all, are of no benefit to their neighbor.

They have followed the way of Balaam, the son of Beor, who loved gain from wrongdoing

16. *but was rebuked for his own transgressions; a dumb ass spoke with human voice and restrained the prophet's madness.*

Here he introduces an illustration from Num. 22, 23, and 24. When the Children of Israel had departed from Egypt and came into the land of the Moabites, King Balak sent messengers to a prophet in Syria, named Balaam, and asked him to come and curse the Jewish people, in order that they might become weak and he could defeat them. Then God came to Balaam and forbade him to curse the people. Therefore the prophet refused to go with the messengers. Then the king sent messengers to the prophet again and promised to reward him richly; and God permitted him to go to him, but He ordered him not to say anything except what He would tell him.

Then Balaam set out and rode on an ass. Now the angel of God appeared on the road and stood before him "with a drawn sword in his hand." The ass saw this "and turned aside out of the road." Then Balaam struck the ass to turn her into the road. At this juncture the angel stood in a narrow place in the road, where the ass could not turn aside. She pressed against the wall and bruised the prophet's foot, and she had to fall on her knees under Balaam. This made Balaam angry, so that in his rage he struck her with his staff. Then God opened the beast's mouth, so that she spoke with a human voice and said: "What have I done to you that you strike me this way?" Then Balaam said: "I wish I had a sword in my hand, for then I would kill you." The ass answered and said: "Am I not your ass, upon which you have ridden all your lifelong to this day? Was I ever accustomed to do so to you?" Then the prophet's eyes were opened, and he saw the angel with the drawn sword. He became frightened and wanted to go back. The angel commanded Balaam to proceed. At the same time, however, he ordered Balaam not to say anything else than what he would tell him.

When the prophet came to the king, the latter took him up to a mountaintop from which he could see all the people of Israel. Then the prophet ordered seven altars to be built and an offering to be placed on each altar, and he went and asked the Lord what he should say. Then God put the words into His mouth, and Balaam began to bless and praise the people of Israel with beautiful words. This he did three times in succession. At this juncture the king became angry and said: "Did I not call you to curse my enemies, and yet you have blessed them three times? I intended to honor you, but the Lord has held you back from honor." Balaam replied: "Did I not tell you in advance that even if you gave me your house filled with silver and gold, I could not say anything else than what God would tell me?"

Later, however, the prophet advised the king how he should deal with the people. He did so because he was not able to curse them and to persuade them by force to sin against God. Then the king erected an idol called Baal of Peor, and brought it about that the women of the Moabites, the daughters of lords and princes, invited the people to the sacrifice to their idols; and when the people came to where they were, they worshiped the idol, ate, drank, and sinned with the women. Then God became angry, gave orders that the chiefs of the people be hanged on the gallows, and let 24,000 men perish on one day. This prophet Balaam did this for the sake of money.

When St. Peter speaks here about this, he wants to say that our clerics are really the children and disciples of Balaam. For just as Balaam gave the evil advice to erect an idol, so that the Children of Israel were induced to sin, made God angry, and were smitten, so our bishops have also erected an idol in God's name, namely, their human doctrine of their own works. They abandon faith and seize the Christian souls. These they ravish, and in this way they arouse God's anger, so that He has punished the world with blindness and impenitence. We can thank our spiritual junkers for all this.

Thus Peter actually compares these false teachers to the prophet Balaam; for, like Balaam, they establish such idolatry and destroy souls. Furthermore, his real name is fitting; for in Hebrew Bileam or Balaam denotes one who devours or who squanders on drink, one who opens his jaws and devours and consumes everything. Balaam bore this disgraceful name because he caused so many people to sin, so that they were slain and perished. Our bishops and clergy are Balaamites of this kind. They are the devil's jaws with which he seizes and devours innumerable souls. But this prophet's surname was *filius Bosor*, which means "flesh" or as

Moses says *filius Beor,* that is, "of a fool." His father is a fool. Thus these, too, are blind, mad, and foolish people. They themselves need to be ruled. The flesh gives birth to such people, for the spirit produces people who are different. Thus God has given them their real name in Scripture and has portrayed them in this way in order that we may know what to think of them.

Now the dumb beast of burden, the ass, stands for the people, who permit themselves to be tamed and ridden, and who go blindly as they are led. Just as the ass was urged on and hit hard when it turned aside on the narrow path and had to return to the road until it could no longer evade the angel or turn aside and had to fall down, so the seducers have driven the people. Then the people found this unbearable and realized that the treatment they received was not right. They wanted to turn aside. But the might with which the people were oppressed was too great. Finally God opened our mouths and put words into them so that even the children talk about it. In this way their folly was revealed, and they had to be ashamed. With this one should confront them when they come along and say that it is not proper for the laity to read Scripture and talk about it, but that one should listen to what the councils decree. Then you can answer: "Did not God speak even through an ass? Be satisfied with our admission that you preached God's Word in times past. But now that you have become fools and are in the grip of greed, why is it surprising that now the common people are being awakened by God and are beginning to speak the truth, which was burdened and weighed down by you like a dumb beast of burden?" This is the comparison to the prophet Balaam. Now St. Peter continues on the subject of the false prophets.

17. *These are waterless springs and mists driven by a storm.*

This is a comparison made by Solomon in Prov. 25:14, where he says: "Like clouds and wind without rain is a man who boasts of a gift he does not give." Thus Peter says here: "These are waterless springs and mists driven by a storm"; that is, they make a big show, but there is nothing behind it. They are like dry, disfigured, and waterless springs, even though they are reputed to be and are called true springs. For Scripture calls teachers springs,[10] since from them should spring the salutary doctrine through which souls

[10] Luther may be thinking of such passages as Is. 49:10; Is. 58:11; Ps. 84:6.

should be refreshed. For this office they are smeared and anointed. But what do they do? Nothing at all. Here there is nothing more than the mere name, just as they are called shepherds in spite of the fact that they are wolves.

Furthermore, they are "mists driven by a storm." They are not like the thick, black, and murky clouds, which commonly bring rain. No, they are like the wispy and light clouds, which float and fly in the air and which the wind drives where it pleases. These clouds cannot bring rain. Thus our teachers, like the clouds in the heavens, also float on high and conduct themselves in an overweening manner in Christendom. They let themselves be driven whereever the devil pleases and are ready to do his every bidding. But they do not preach God's Word, as is done by the true preachers and teachers, who are called clouds in Scripture—in Is. 5:6, for example—just as in Scripture everything that supplies water represents preachers.

For them the nether gloom of darkness has been reserved.

To be sure, they live well now and fare as they themselves desire; but an eternal darkness will come upon them, even though they do not believe or feel this.

18. *For, uttering loud boasts of folly.*

Do you ask how they can be called waterless springs and clouds without rain, even though they fill the whole world with their preaching? St. Peter replies: Unfortunately, they rain and preach far too much. But they speak nothing but vain, bombastic, and inflated words. With these they fill the ears of the poor crowd, so that one thinks it is something precious, even though there is nothing behind it. Thus the monks boast of their obedience, poverty, and chastity with high-sounding words, so that one thinks they are saintly people, even though this is nothing but sheer fraud devoid of any vestige of faith or love. The same thing is true of their allegation that the episcopal estate is a perfect estate,[11] even though the bishops do nothing else than show off, ride handsome stallions, and at times consecrate churches and altars and baptize bells. The entire ecclesiastical law of the pope is filled through and through with such inflated and bombastic words.

---

[11] Cf. Thomas Aquinas, *Summa Theologica*, I, Q. 108, Art. 2.

They entice with licentious passions of the flesh men who have barely escaped from those who live in error.

This is what these springs and teachers do. Consequently, those who had barely escaped must fall into the snare of the rogue and be enmeshed more than ever. When a child that has been baptized and has escaped from all sins and from the devil, and has been taken out of Adam and put into Christ, begins to reason, it is soon caught in a snare and led into error. One should teach people about faith, love, and the holy cross. But our clerics come along and boast of their works. Because of this, people fall back into error, even if they have escaped. But how does this take place? Because they are enticed with licentious passions of the flesh. The greatest enticement is their statement that priests, monks, and nuns should not marry, and that they obligate themselves to lead a life of chastity. In this way they only entice to unchastity. As a result, the wretched people must perish in evil lusts and are beyond help.

But here you see clearly that Peter is speaking of no others than the teachers who rule in Christendom, where there are baptized and believing people. For among Turks and heathen no one escapes in this way. This happens among the Christians, where they have the opportunity to seduce souls and to bring into the devil's snare.

19. *They promise them freedom, but they themselves are slaves of corruption; for whatever overcomes a man, to that he is enslaved.*

They set up estates through which one should merit salvation. Thus Thomas, the Dominican monk, wrote unashamedly that when a person enters an order, this is just like coming directly from Baptism.[12] There they promise freedom and the remission of sins through one's own works. One has to listen to such blasphemy. They equate their human dreams and jugglery, which is without faith, with faith and Baptism, which God instituted and which are really His work. Who can tolerate this and be silent in the face of it? Such statements have been drawn up by the monks and driven into the young people, and such teachers have been declared to be saints. But the other, true saints have been burned to ashes.

---

[12] On the understanding of profession in Thomas Aquinas cf., *inter alia*, *Summa Theologica*, II-II, Q. 88, whose articles discuss the theology of profession at length.

20. *For if, after they have escaped the defilements of the world
through the knowledge of our Lord and Savior Jesus Christ,
they are again entangled in them and overpowered, the last
state has become worse for them than the first.*

Here St. Peter shows why they are servants of perdition. "The
knowledge of our Lord Jesus Christ" means knowing what He is,
namely, our Savior, who forgives us our sin out of pure grace.
Through this knowledge we escape wickedness and the defile-
ment of the world. But when they have escaped this in Baptism,
they are later thrown back into it again. Then they give up their
faith and return to their own deeds. For where there is no faith,
there is no spirit; but where there is no spirit, there is nothing but
sheer flesh. Consequently, nothing that is pure can be there either.
This is what has happened so far in Christendom. First Rome heard
the Gospel in its purity; but later it departed from this and clung to
works, until every abomination arose there. Therefore "the last
state has become worse for them than the first." The result is that
now they are worse heathen than they ever were before they heard
the Word of God.

21. *For it would have been better for them never to have known the
way of righteousness than after knowing it to turn back from
the holy commandment delivered to them.*

22. *It has happened to them according to the true proverb, The
dog turns back to his own vomit, and the sow is washed only
to wallow in the mire.*

St. Peter took this saying from Prov. 26:11, where we read:
"Like a dog that returns to his vomit is a fool that repeats his folly."
Through Baptism these people threw out unbelief, had their unclean way of life washed away, and entered into a pure life of
faith and love. Now they fall away into unbelief and their own
works, and they soil themselves again in filth. Therefore this verse
should not be applied to works; for little is accomplished if after
confession one says and commands: "Henceforth you must be
chaste, gentle, patient, etc." But if you want to become pious, you
must ask God to give you a genuine faith, and you must begin to
desist from unbelief. When you receive faith, then good works will
come automatically, and you will lead a pure and chaste life.

Otherwise you will preserve yourself by no other means. And even if you are able to conceal the knave in your heart for a while, yet he will finally emerge.

This is the second chapter of this epistle. Here the apostle has foretold that we would be deceived so deplorably by our teachers. To be sure, we have been warned sufficiently. But we paid no attention to this. Therefore it is our fault that we have not taken hold of the Gospel and that we have deserved such wrath of God because of our way of life. As a rule, we are all glad to hear the pope, together with priests and monks, attacked and censured. But no one is willing to be reformed as a result of this. It is not such a trifling matter that one has to laugh. No, it is so serious that the heart should fear and tremble. Therefore we should tackle it earnestly and ask God to turn His anger and such a plague away from us. For this misery did not come upon us unexpectedly; it was inflicted on us by God as a punishment, as Paul declares in 2 Thess. 2:10-11: "Because they refused to love the truth and so be saved. Therefore God sends upon them a strong delusion, to make them believe what is false, etc." For if the punishment had been extended only to the destruction of the false teachers, it would still be slight when compared with the fact that they have had the rule and have led the whole world to hell with them. Therefore the only remedy for this evil is this, that we attack the matter in a God-fearing and humble way, confess our guilt, and pray God to take the punishment from us. With this prayer we must assail the false teachers. Otherwise one cannot get the better of the devil. He continues:

CHAPTER THREE

1. *This is now the second letter that I have written to you, beloved, and in both of them I have aroused your sincere mind by way of reminder,*

2. *that you should remember the predictions of the holy prophets and the commandment of the Lord and Savior through your apostles.*

Here St. Peter now comes to us again and warns us in this epistle to be prepared and to expect the Last Day every moment. In the first place he states that he has not written this epistle for the purpose of laying the foundation of faith. This he did previously. No, here it is his purpose to arouse the people, to remind them, and to urge and impel them not to neglect their faith and to remain in their sincere mind and in their understanding of what a true Christian life is. For, as we have often said, the office of preachers is not confined to teaching. In addition to this, they must always exhort and urge. For since our flesh and blood always clings to us, the Word of God must be awake in us, lest we give way to the flesh instead of fighting against it and being more than a match for it.

3. *First of all, you must understand this, that scoffers will come in the last days with scoffing, following their own passions*

4. *and saying: Where is the promise of His coming? For ever since the fathers fell asleep, all things have continued as they were from the beginning of creation.*

People are still being guided by a book about the Antichrist in which it is written that before the Last Day they will fall into such error that they will deny the existence of God and ridicule everything that is preached about Christ and the Last Day.[1] This is true, no matter what its source may be. But one should not understand this to mean that the whole world will say and believe such things. The majority, however, will do so. For today this is already evident, and it will gain more ground when the Gospel is more widely disseminated among the people. Then the people will bestir themselves well, and many hearts that are now concealed and are not evident will become more vocal. Furthermore, the number of those who do not believe that the Last Day will come has always been rather large.

Here St. Peter warns against these scoffers and tells us beforehand that they will come, risk all, and live as they please. Indeed, in Rome and in Italy this statement has long since been fulfilled, and those who come out of Rome and Italy also bring this delusion out with them. Therefore just as they have taught this for a long time in Rome and in Italy, so the people on the outside must also teach it. Furthermore, now that the Last Day is at the door, such people must come forth, in order that Christ's words in Matt. 24: 37-39 may be fulfilled. "As were the days of Noah," He says, "so will be the coming of the Son of Man. For as in those days before the Flood they were eating and drinking, marrying and giving in marriage, until the day when Noah entered the ark, and they did not know until the Flood came and swept them all away, so will be the coming of the Son of Man." Likewise: "The Son of Man is coming at an hour you do not expect" (v. 44). Likewise in Luke 21: 34-35: "That Day will come like a snare upon all who dwell upon the face of the whole earth." And in Luke 17:24 we read: "As the lightning flashes and lights up the sky from one side to the other, so will the Son of Man be in His Day." That is, He will appear swiftly, unexpectedly, and suddenly, when the world will be living in the greatest smugness and will be making light of God's Word.

Therefore the nearness of the Last Day will be betokened when people live just as they please, following all their passions, and when questions like "Where is the promise of His coming?" will be heard among them. The world has been standing for such a long

---

[1] The later Middle Ages were a time when books on Antichrist became extremely popular, and it is not clear which of these Luther has in mind here. Shortly before this commentary he had edited *The Passion of Christ and of Antichrist* (W, IX, 701-715).

time and has always remained. Now shall things finally change? Thus Peter warns us, to keep us from worrying and to give us a sure sign that the Day will come soon. He continues:

5. *They deliberately ignore this fact, that by the Word of God heavens existed long ago, and an earth formed out of water and by means of water,*

6. *through which the world that then existed was deluged with water and perished.*

He says that such people do not go to the trouble of reading Scripture and deliberately refuse to consider and realize that the same thing happened long ago. When Noah built the ark, the earth, "formed out of water and by means of water," was destroyed by water. Indeed, the people were so smug and sure that they thought there was no urgency at all. Nevertheless, they were all destroyed by water. It is as if he were saying: If God destroyed the world with water at that time, and proved with an example that He is able to sink it, how much more likely He is to do so today, since He has made this promise!

Here St. Peter speaks quite sagaciously about creation. In times past heaven and earth were also firm; they were formed out of water and existed in water through the Word of God. Heaven and earth have a beginning. They have not had an eternal existence. Heaven is formed out of water and has been water above and below. But the earth has been formed in water and has existed in water, as Moses describes it. Here St. Peter refers to Moses. All this is preserved through the Word of God, just as it was also formed through the Word of God. For it is not the nature of heaven and earth to exist in this way. Therefore if God did not keep it this way, everything would soon collapse and perish in the water. For God spoke a powerful word when He said (Gen. 1:9): "Let the waters under the heavens be gathered into one place, and let the dry land appear"; that is, the waters must move aside and make way, in order that the earth, on which one can dwell, may come forth. Otherwise the water would naturally flood the earth. Therefore this is one of the greatest miracles God still does today.

Thus St. Peter now wants to say that the scoffers are so wanton and hardened that they refuse to honor the Holy Spirit by reading how God preserves the earth in the water. From this they would become aware that everything rests in the hand of God. Consequently, since God drowned the earth at that time, He will do this for us again. For that example should surely persuade us that since He did not lie then, He will not lie today either.

7. *But by the same Word the heavens and earth that now exist have been stored up for fire, being kept until the Day of judgment and destruction of ungodly men.*

At that time, when God destroyed the world with the Flood, the water came down from above, up from below, and from all sides. Consequently, nothing but water was visible; and the earth, in conformity with its nature, had to be submerged in the water. But now God has promised that He will never again destroy the world with water, and as a sign of this He placed the rainbow in the heavens. Now, therefore, God will let the world be consumed and perish only by fire, so that there will be nothing but fire, just as at that time there was nothing but water. St. Paul also speaks of this in 2 Thess. 1:7f.:[2] "When the Lord Jesus is revealed from heaven with His mighty angels in flaming fire, etc." Likewise in 1 Cor. 3:13: "Each man's work will become manisfest; for the Day of the Lord will disclose it, because it will be revealed with fire." Thus when the Last Day breaks all of a sudden, in one moment there will be nothing but fire. Everything in heaven and on earth will be reduced to powder and ashes. Everything must be changed by fire, just as the water changed everything at the time of the Flood. Because God let what took place at that time be a sign, therefore the fire shall be the sign that He will not lie.

8. *But do not ignore this one fact, beloved, that with the Lord one day is as a thousand years, and a thousand years as one day.*

9. *The Lord is not slow about His promise as some count slowness, but is forbearing toward you, not wishing that any should perish, but that all should reach repentance.*

10. *But the Day of the Lord will come like a thief, and then the heavens will pass away with a loud noise, and the elements will be dissolved with fire, and the earth and the works that are upon it will be burned up.*

[2] The original has "1 Thess. 1."

With these words St. Peter confronts those about whom he has just spoken and who say: "The apostles have stated repeatedly that the Last Day will come soon. Yet everything is as it was before, even though such a long time has now elapsed." St. Peter took this verse from Ps. 90:4, where Moses says: "For a thousand years in Thy sight are but as yesterday when it is past." This comes about in the following way: There are two ways of looking at things: God's way and the way of the world. Thus this life and the life to come are of two kinds. This life cannot be the same as the life to come, since no one can enter the life to come except through death, that is, through the cessation of this life. Now this life amounts to eating, drinking, sleeping, digesting, begetting children, etc. Here everything goes by number: hours, days, and years in succession. Now when you want to look at the life to come, you must erase the course of this life from your mind. You dare not think that you can measure it as this life is measured. There everything will be one day, one hour, one moment.

Now since before God there is no reckoning of time, before Him a thousand years must be as one day. Therefore Adam, the first man, is just as close to Him as the man who will be born last before the Last Day. For God does not see time longitudinally; He sees it transversely, as if you were looking transversely at a tall tree lying before you. Then you can see both ends at the same time.[3] This you cannot do if you look at it longitudinally. With our reason we cannot look at time in any other way than longitudinally. Beginning with Adam, we must count one year after the other until the Last Day. But in God's sight everything is in one heap. What is long for us is short for Him and vice versa. Here there is neither measure nor number. Thus man dies. His body is interred and decays. It lies in the ground and knows nothing. But when the first man arises on the Last Day, he will think that he has been lying there barely an hour. Then he will look about and discover that many people were born before[4] him and came after him. About this he knew nothing. Now, therefore, St. Peter declares here that the Lord is not slow about His promise, as some scoffers think, but that He is long-suffering. Therefore you should be prepared for the Last Day, for it will come soon enough for everyone

---

[3] See also Luther's comments, p. 114.

[4] The Weimar text has *von*, but we have read *vor*.

[W, XIV, 71, 72]

after his death. Then he will say: "Behold, I died only a short time ago!" But this Day will come all too quickly for the world. When people say: "There is peace, and all is well," the Day will break and come upon them, as St. Paul says in 1 Thess. 5:3. And, like a mighty thunderstorm, the Day will burst forth with such a great crash that everything will have to be consumed in one moment.

11. *Since all these things are thus to be dissolved, what sort of persons ought you to be in lives of holiness and godliness,*

12. *waiting for and hastening the coming of the Day of God,*

Since you know that everything must pass away, both heaven and earth, consider how completely you must be prepared with a saintly and godly life and conduct to meet this Day. Thus St. Peter describes this Day as imminent, in order that they may be ready for it, hope for it with joy, and hasten to meet it as the Day which delivers us from sin, death, and hell.

because of which the heavens will be kindled and dissolved, and the elements will melt with fire!

13. *But according to His promise, we wait for new heavens and a new earth in which righteousness dwells.*

Through the prophets God promised again and again that He would create new heavens and a new earth. Thus He says in Is. 65:17:[5] "Behold, I create new heavens and a new earth," in which you shall be happy, rejoice, and leap. Likewise in Is. 30:26: "The light of the moon will be as the light of the sun, and the light of the sun will be sevenfold, as the light of seven days." And in Matt. 13:43 Christ says: "Then the righteous will shine like the sun in the kingdom of their Father." How this will take place we do not know, except that it is promised that there will be the kind of heaven and earth in which there will be no sin, but that only righteousness and God's children will dwell there, just as St. Paul also says in Rom. 8[6] that there will be nothing but love, nothing but joy and pleasure, and nothing but the kingdom of God.

[5] The original has "Is. 64."
[6] This may be intended as a reference to Rom. 8:21.

Here one may be concerned about whether the blessed will live in heaven or on earth. Here the text gives the impression that they will dwell on earth, so that all heaven and earth will be a new Paradise, in which God resides. For God dwells not only in heaven but everywhere. Therefore the elect will be where He is.

14. *Therefore, beloved, since you wait for these, be zealous to be found by Him without spot or blemish, and at peace.*

Since you have escaped such misfortune and are coming to such great joys, he says, you should let this induce you willingly to despise everything on earth and gladly to suffer what you must. Therefore you should be zealous to live "without spot or blemish."

15. *And count the forbearance of our Lord as salvation.*

Count it as your gain that God is forbearing, delays, and does not judge at once. Indeed, He would have reason to be angry and punish; yet His grace prevents Him from doing so.

So also our beloved brother Paul wrote to you according to the wisdom given him,

16. *speaking of this as he does in all his letters. There are some things in them hard to understand, which the ignorant and unstable twist to their own destruction.*

Here St. Peter bears witness of his teaching to the apostle Paul, which is ample proof that this epistle was written long after Saint Paul's epistles. This is one of the verses which might induce someone to believe that St. Peter is not the author of this letter.[7] And earlier in this chapter there is a verse in which he says: "The Lord does not wish that any should perish, but that all should reach repentance" (3:9). For he descends a little below the apostolic spirit. Yet it is credible that this is nonetheless the apostle's letter. For since here he is not writing about faith but is writing about love, he also descends. It is the nature of love to descend toward one's neighbor, just as faith moves upward.

He saw that many frivolous spirits were jumbling and twisting

---

[7] Cf. Eusebius, *Ecclesiastical History,* Book III, ch. 3, par. 1.

[W, XIV, 73, 74]
St. Paul's words and teaching, because some things in the latter's epistles are difficult to understand, as, for example, when he says that "man is justified by faith apart from works" (Rom. 3:28), that "the Law came in to increase the trespass," that "where sin increased, grace abounded all the more" (Rom. 5:20), and when he makes other similar statements. For when people hear this, they say: "If this is true, we will be idle, do no good work, and thus become pious," just as it is also said today that we forbid good works. For if St. Paul's words have been twisted, is it surprising that our words are also twisted?

17. *You therefore, beloved, knowing this beforehand, beware lest you be carried away with the error of lawless men and lose your own stability.*

18. *But grow in the grace and knowledge of our Lord and Savior Jesus Christ. To Him be the glory both now and to the day of eternity. Amen.*

Since you know everything that has been stated above, he says, and since you see that many false teachers who seduce the world must come, and that there will be scoffers who twist Scripture and do not want to understand it, be on your guard, lest you fall away from faith because of false doctrine. And grow, in order that you may become stronger from day to day by constantly occupying yourselves with and proclaiming God's Word. Behold, how greatly concerned the apostle is about those who have come to faith! This concern also impelled him to write the two epistles, which contain in rich abundance everything a Christian should know and also what is still to come. May God give His grace that we, too, may grasp and retain this! Amen.

SERMONS ON
THE EPISTLE OF ST. JUDE

Translated by
MARTIN H. BERTRAM

CHAPTER ONE

1. *Jude, a servant of Jesus Christ and brother of James, to those who are called, beloved in God the Father and kept for Jesus Christ:*

2. *May mercy, peace, and love be multiplied to you.*

This epistle is ascribed to the holy apostle St. Jude, the brother of the two apostles James the Less and Simon, the sons of the sister of the mother of Christ who is called Mary the wife of James or Cleophas, as we read in Mark 6:3. But this letter does not seem to have been written by the real apostle, for in it Jude refers to himself as a much later disciple of the apostles. Nor does it contain anything special beyond pointing to the Second Epistle of Saint Peter, from which it has borrowed nearly all the words.[1] It is nothing more than an epistle directed against our clerics—bishops, priests, and monks.

3. *Beloved, being very eager to write to you of our common salvation, I found it necessary to write, appealing to you to contend for the faith which was once for all delivered to the saints.*

That is to say: I also find it necessary to write to you, in order to remind and exhort you to persevere and forge ahead in the faith once preached to you. It is as though he were saying: It is necessary for me to admonish you to be careful to remain on the right course. But he tells why this is necessary.

4. *For admission has been secretly gained by some who long ago were designated for this condemnation.*

Therefore I want to remind you to remain in the faith which you have heard, for preachers who are introducing another teaching

[1] Cf. also *Luther's Works*, 35, pp. 397–398.

alongside the faith are already beginning to come. This is leading
people deliberately and unawares from the right course. Thus
St. Peter also stated in his epistle (2 Peter 2:1): "There will be false
teachers among you who will secretly bring in destructive heresies,
etc." These, says Jude, "were long ago designated for this condemnation." This we understand well now, since we know that no one
becomes pious and righteous by reason of his own works but solely
through faith in Christ, in reliance on Christ's work as his chief
treasure. Then, when faith is present, all the works man does
should redound to the welfare of his neighbor; and one should
beware of all works that are not done with the service of one's
neighbor in mind, as is the case nowadays among priests and
monks. Hence if from such estates and works someone introduces
anything else alongside the doctrine of faith, he misleads the
people, so that they are damned with him.

> *Ungodly persons who pervert the grace of our God into licen-
> tiousness.*

The message which has been given to us concerning the grace
of God and which holds Christ before us, how He, together with
everything He has, has been offered and presented to us, so that
we are delivered from sin, death, and all adversity – this grace
and gift, offered through the Gospel, they misuse and pervert into
licentiousness. To be sure, they call themselves Christians and put
the Gospel on display; but at the same time they live in an estate
in which they are completely wanton in eating, drinking, and
rascally living. Boastfully they say: "We are not in a worldly estate;
we are in an estate that is spiritual." Under this name and semblance they have grabbed all property, honor, and sensual pleasure.
This is already beginning, says Jude. For we read that 1,000 years
ago the bishops began to desire to be lords and to be held in
higher esteem than the common Christians, as is also to be seen in
the epistles of St. Jerome.[2]

> *And deny God, the only Master, and our Lord, Jesus Christ.*

St. Peter also said this in his epistle. As we have heard, the act
of denial is not perpetrated with the mouth; for with the mouth they

---

[2] Luther may be referring to the well-known letter of Jerome to Evangelus,
Epistolae, CXLVI, *Patrologia, Series Latina*, XXII, 1192 – 1195.

confess that God is a Lord.[3] But they deny the Lord Christ with deeds and with works. They regard themselves, not Him, as their Lord. When they proclaim that fasting, pilgrimages, founding churches, chastity, obedience, poverty, etc., are the way to salvation, they direct people to their works and keep silence about Christ. This is tantamount to saying: "Christ is of no use to you; His works do not help you. But you must merit salvation with your own works." In this way, as Peter says, they deny the Lord, who has ransomed us with His blood.

5. *Now I desire to remind you, though you were once for all fully informed, that He who saved a people out of the land of Egypt afterward destroyed those who did not believe.*

6. *And the angels that did not keep their own position but left their proper dwelling have been kept by Him in eternal chains in the nether gloom until the judgment of the great Day,*

7. *just as Sodom and Gomorrah and the surrounding cities, which likewise acted immorally and indulged in unnatural lust, serve as an example by undergoing a punishment of eternal fire.*

Here St. Jude cites three examples, just as St. Peter did in his epistle. But he adds an example, namely, how God let the Children of Israel, whom He had led out of Egypt with many miraculous signs, perish and be slain when they did not believe, so that only two survived, even though all those who had departed and were 20 years of age and older exceeded 600,000 men in number. Jude now mentions these examples as a terrifying warning. It is as if he were saying: May those who are called Christians and under this name "pervert the grace of God into licentiousness" beware, lest they share the fate of those people! Indeed, since the rise of the papacy and the suppression of the Gospel in the whole world God has punished the unbelievers and hurled them into the jaws of the devil with one plague after the other.

8. *Yet in like manner these men in their dreamings defile the flesh.*

He calls these teachers dreamers. For in a dream a person concerns himself with images and thinks that they are real; but when

---

[3] Cf. p. 171.

he awakens, nothing is there. Then he sees that it was a dream,
and he pays no attention to it. Thus what these people say is nothing else than a mere dream. But once their eyes are opened, they
will see that it amounts to nothing. Thus when they say that their
tonsures and cowls, their obedience, poverty, and chastity please
God, they look at this; but before God this is nothing but a mere
dream. Thus our text has given them a truly excellent name by
saying that they occupy themselves with dreams with which they
deceive themselves and the world.

But the particular vice with which the apostles charge the
spiritual estate is this, that they lead an unchaste life. God proclaimed long ago that they would not have wives. Now it is impossible for God to perform as many miracles as there are persons in
this estate. Therefore they cannot be chaste. Thus the prophet
Daniel said about the pope's rule in chapter 11:37: "He shall give
no heed to wives." This is an external characteristic, just as the
fact that they are dreamers is internal.

Reject authority, and revile the glorious ones.

The third characteristic is their refusal to be obedient to secular
authority. We have taught that as long as we sojourn on earth, we
must be subject and obedient to the government; for the Christian
faith does not do away with the secular rule. Therefore no one can
withdraw from it. Consequently, the pope's decree with regard to
the liberties of the church is nothing but the law of the devil.

9. *But when the archangel Michael, contending with the devil,
   disputed about the body of Moses, he did not presume to pronounce a reviling judgment upon him but said: The Lord rebuke
   you.*

This is one reason why this letter was rejected in times past;[4]
for it refers to an example not recorded in Scripture, namely, how
the angel Michael and the devil disputed about the body of Moses.
It is said that this came about because so much is written about
Moses in Deut. 34:6, namely, that God buried him and that no man
knows the place of his burial to this day, and because Scripture
bears witness that "there has not arisen a prophet since in Israel

---

[4] The basis of this report seems to be Jerome, *De viris illustribus*, ch. 4, *Patrologia, Series Latina*, XXIII, 646.

like Moses, whom the Lord knew face to face" (Deut. 34:10). Concerning this text it is also stated that Moses' body remained hidden to prevent the Jews from using it for the purpose of establishing idolatry, and that for this reason the angel Michael is said to have resisted the devil, who wanted the body to be revealed in order that it might be worshiped by the Jews.[5] And although Michael was an archangel, says Jude, he was not so bold as to curse the devil himself. These blasphemers trample underfoot the authority ordained by God and curse it into the seventh, eighth, and ninth generation, even though they are men, and even though this archangel did not venture to curse the exceedingly wicked devil, who is already condemned, but only said: "May the Lord restrain and punish you!"

10. *But these men revile whatever they do not understand, and by those things that they know by instinct as irrational animals do, they are destroyed.*

These people are such blasphemers that they can do nothing else than excommunicate, curse, and consign to the devil not only kings and majesties but also God and the saints, as is to be seen in the bull *In Coena Domini*.[6] They do not know that our salvation rests on faith and love. They cannot bear our rejection and condemnation of their works. Nor can they bear our proclamation that Christ alone must help us with His works. Therefore they ban and revile all Christian doctrine, which they do not know. But what they do know through natural knowledge, namely, that the endowing of Masses and the like brings money and property, this they stress with a vengeance, and in this way they destroy themselves and everybody.

11. *Woe to them! For they walk in the way of Cain.*

Cain slew his brother for no other reason than that the latter was more righteous than he was. For his brother's sacrifice was pleasing to God, whereas his own was not (Gen. 4:4, 8). Thus to walk in the way of Cain means to depend on one's own works and to revile

---

[5] See *Luther's Works*, 9, p. 310.

[6] The title *In Coena Domini* was borne by a series of bulls of excommunication, which by Luther's time were issued on Maundy Thursday; in 1522 Luther had published an attack on the practice (W, VIII, 691–720).

true works, to kill and murder those who walk in the right way, as these people also do.

And abandon themselves for the sake of gain to Balaam's error.

Inwardly they should remain confident of God's grace; but they go forth and allow themselves to be diverted in all directions by many kinds of external works only for the sake of money, in order that they, like the prophet Balaam, may fill their bellies, as we have heard in Peter's epistle (2 Peter 2:15).

And perish in Korah's rebellion.

In Num. 16:1 ff. we read about Korah's rebellion and how he, together with his company, perished. Moses had been summoned and called by God to lead the people out of Egypt, and his brother Aaron had been appointed chief priest by God. Now Korah belonged to the same family and their circle of friends. He, too, wanted to be prominent and to be singled out. He attached to himself 250 of the best and foremost men and stirred up such a rebellion and uproar that Moses and Aaron had to flee. Moses fell on his face and prayed God not to respect their offering. He ordered the congregation to separate themselves from them and said (Num. 16:28 ff.): "'Hereby you shall know that the Lord has sent me to do all these works. If these men die the common death of all men, or if they are visited by the fate of all men, then the Lord has not sent me. But if the Lord creates something new, and the ground opens its mouth, and swallows them up, and they go down alive into Sheol, then you shall know that these men have despised the Lord.' And as he finished speaking all these words, the ground under them split asunder; and the earth opened its mouth and swallowed them up, with their households and all the men that belonged to Korah and all their goods. So they and all that belonged to them went down alive into Sheol." And the fire consumed the other 250 men who had sided with him.

Jude now applies this example to these revilers who accuse us of stirring up rebellion when we preach against them, even though they themselves are really responsible for all the misery. For Christ is our Aaron and our Chief Priest. We should let Him alone reign. But the pope and the bishops refused to tolerate this. They set *themselves* up. They want to rule by force, and they rebelled against Christ. God punished them, and the earth swallowed and covered them, so that they are submerged and swallowed in worldly life and pleasure and are nothing but world pure and simple.

12. *These are blemishes on your love feasts, as they boldly carouse together, looking after themselves; waterless clouds, carried along by winds; fruitless trees in late autumn, twice dead, uprooted;*

13. *wild waves of the sea, casting up the foam of their own shame; wandering stars for whom the nether gloom of darkness has been reserved forever.*

This we have heard often enough in St. Peter's letter. All the world has brought up its children to become clerics and to have good days, not to have to support themselves with the labors of their hands or to preach but to live without a care in revelry and to have good cheer from the property which poor people acquire with their sweat. One thinks that they should be the best part and treasure in Christendom, yet they are nothing but blemishes and abominations. They live well. "What is good belongs in the bellies of the priests," as the saying goes. They live without care and fear. They think that the devil cannot overthrow them. They do not feed the sheep, but they themselves are wolves who devour the sheep. They are the clouds that soar on high in the air. They sit in high places in the church as those who should preach. Yet they do not preach. No, they let themselves be driven hither and thither by the devil.

They are "fruitless trees in late autumn," he says. They have neither fruit nor leaves. They just stand there like other trees and let themselves be regarded as Christian bishops. Neither a word nor works are there; but everything, together with the root, is dead. Furthermore, they are like "wild waves of the sea"; that is, just as the wind raises and drives the waves and billows on the water, so they go as the devil leads them. They cast up "the foam of their own shame" like a boiling pot. They are so full of villainy that they overflow and cannot retain anything. Everything has to come out. They are "wandering stars," as one calls the planets that recede and do not follow a fixed and straight course. Thus they do not have a true course either. Their life and teaching are nothing but error, with which they deceive themselves and all who follow them. Therefore for them "the nether gloom of darkness has been reserved forever."

In this way Jude has now appraised and portrayed our spiritual lords who introduce all manner of knavery under the name of Christ and Christianity, appropriate all the world's goods to themselves, and forcibly subject everyone to themselves. Now he continues:

14. *It was of these also that Enoch in the seventh generation from Adam prophesied, saying: Behold, the Lord came with His holy myriads,*

15. *to execute judgment on all.*

This statement, which is attributed to Enoch, is not found anywhere in Scripture. Consequently, some fathers did not accept this epistle, although this is not sufficient reason for rejecting a book.[7] For in 2 Tim. 3:8 St. Paul also mentions two opponents of Moses, Jannes and Jambres, whose names are not found in Scripture either. But be that as it may, we shall let it pass. Nevertheless, it is true that from the beginning of the world God always let His Word—which promises believers His grace and their salvation but threatens unbelievers with judgment and damnation—be proclaimed until after Christ's ascension. Now it is preached publicly in all the world. But before the birth of Christ God took for Himself only a line from Adam to Abraham and from then on to David up to the time of Mary, the mother of Christ. This line had God's Word. Thus the Gospel has always been preached in the world, but never so publicly as now in the last times.

Thus also this father, Enoch, devoted himself to the Word of God, which he had undoubtedly learned from his father Adam and had received from the Holy Spirit. For in Gen. 5:24 Scripture says about him that he "walked with God" and for this reason was taken by God and was seen no more. This gave rise to the saying that he would return before the Last Day. But this should not be expected, unless one wants to understand it to mean that he will come spiritually, namely, in such a way that his preaching is linked with the Last Day, just as in this verse he speaks with such certainty of the Last Day, as though he were already seeing it. He says: "Behold, the Lord came with His holy myriads," that is, with an innumerable

[7] See p. 206 note 4.

host. This can refer only to the Last Day, on which God will come with all the saints to sit in judgment. For previously He did not come to the world with many thousands of saints. No, He came alone, not to judge but to dispense grace.

And to convict all the ungodly of all their deeds of ungodliness which they have committed in such an ungodly way.

It is by no means out of order for Jude to quote this statement as speaking about false teachers who will come before the Last Day. It also points out that when the Lord comes, He will destroy the pope along with his rule. There is no other help; for, since things cannot become worse, as long as the world stands, there can be no end or improvement. Thus this statement cannot be understood to mean anyone else than our clerics, who have miserably misled the whole world. Since things cannot become any worse – and even if things were to become worse – yet the name of Christ would have to be retained, and all misery would be caused under His name. Thus Jude undoubtedly refers this statement to the Last Judgment and names those whom the judgment will hit. Therefore we conclude that our clerical junkers have to wait for the Last Day, whether the time is long or short.

And of all the harsh things which ungodly sinners have spoken against Him.

Here Jude hits both their life and their preaching. This is what he wants to say: They speak harshly and sharply against the Lord who will come. They are insolent and arrogant; and, as St. Peter has said, they mock and revile Him. He is not speaking about their sinful and shameful life; he is speaking about their godless nature. But he who lives without faith is godless, even though he may lead an outwardly honorable life. To be sure, external evil works are fruits of unbelief; but actually that nature is called godless which glitters beautifully on the outside, even though the heart is filled with unbelief. He says that the Lord will punish these ungodly sinners because of their impudent and stubborn preaching. For they are always strongheaded, do not let anyone guide them, are as hard as an anvil, and constantly condemn and revile. Thus in his statement Enoch has hit the very estate which would exist in the world before the Last Day, as is apparent today. Jude continues:

16. *These are grumblers, malcontents, following their own passions, loudmouthed boasters, flattering people to gain advantage.*

If one refuses to call what they do proper and reasonable, there
is nothing but grumbling and complaining. Thus when one does not
give a bishop his proper title, they cry out about disobedience.
They are people who cannot be restrained, for they pretend to
have jurisdiction over body and soul. They have usurped both the
secular and the spiritual sword. Consequently, one cannot curb
them. Nor dare one preach against them. They have exempted
themselves from all taxes, tribute, and revenue. One dare not touch
their property. Furthermore, no one dare preach a word without
first getting their permission. And even if one attacks them with
Scripture, they say that they alone must be permitted to interpret
Scripture. Thus they live everywhere as they please, according to
their lusts. For they are not able to apply this to us, no matter how
much they would like to, since we have submitted ourselves both
to the Gospel and to the secular sword. But they want to be free
from and unrestrained by both. Over and above this, their entire
law and standard of justice is nothing but an abundance of high-
sounding, arrogant, and inflated words without any meaning.

Flattering people to gain advantage.

It is characteristic of them to judge everything according to
the person. In all the pope's laws from beginning to end you do not
find it stated a single time that a bishop should humble himself
under a priest. Nor do you find mention of any fruit of a Christian
life. No, the gist of everything is as follows: The chaplain must be
under the priest, the priest under the bishop, the bishop under the
archbishop, the archbishop under the patriarch, and the patriarch
under the pope. And then there are regulations regarding attire,
tonsures, and cowls, and the number of churches and benefices
one is to have. Thus they have reduced everything to externals.
This is the kind of child's play and tomfoolery they have practiced.
And they have regarded any violation of these regulations as a
grave sin. Therefore Jude says very pertinently that they concen-
trate all their attention on masks. No one knows anything about
faith, love, or the cross. The common man lets himself be tricked
and fooled by this and devotes all his goods to it, as though it were

the true service of God; that is, they are governed by appearances for the sake of gain.

17. *But you must remember, beloved, the predictions of the apostles of our Lord Jesus Christ;*

18. *they said to you: In the last time there will be scoffers, following their own ungodly passions.*

This verse probably also indicates that this epistle was not written by the apostle Jude, for the writer does not number and reckon himself among the other apostles but speaks of them as men who preached long before him. Therefore one may well assume that another pious man wrote this epistle, a man who read St. Peter's epistle and took these verses from it. We have mentioned above[8] who the scoffers are, likewise those who follow their own passions, not only their carnal passions but also those of their ungodly life. We have said that they do everything as they please, that they respect neither the secular power nor the Word of God, that they are neither in the external nor in the internal rule, neither in the divine nor in the human rule; they hover in the air between heaven and earth as the devil leads them.

19. *It is these who set up divisions, worldly people, devoid of the Spirit.*

Here the author's words coincide with those written by Peter, namely, that they bring in destructive heresies (2 Peter 2:1). For they are the ones who have set themselves apart and destroy unity in faith. They are not satisfied with the common Christian estate, in which one serves the other; but they set up other estates and pretend to serve God by doing so. Moreover, they are sensual or beastly people with no more spirit and understanding than a horse or an ass has. They go along in their natural understanding and carnal mind. They have no Word of God by which they can be guided or live.

20. *But you, beloved, build yourselves up on your most holy faith; pray in the Holy Spirit;*

[8] Cf. p. 193.

21. *keep yourselves in the love of God.*

Here he summarizes in a few words what a completely Christian way of life is. Faith is the foundation on which one should build. But to build up means to increase from day to day in the knowledge of God and Jesus Christ. This is done through the Holy Spirit. Now when we are built up in this way, we should not do a single work in order to merit anything by it or to be saved; but everything must be done for the benefit of our neighbor. Here we must be concerned to remain in love and not to fall from it like the fools who set up special works and a special way of life and thus divert people from love.

Wait for the mercy of our Lord Jesus Christ unto eternal life.

This is the hope; here the holy cross begins. Our life should be arranged in such a way that it is nothing else than a constant longing and waiting for the future life. Yet this waiting must be directed toward the mercy of Christ, so that we call upon Him in order that He may help us from this life into the life to come out of pure mercy, not through any work or merit.

22. *And have compassion on these, and set them apart;*

23. *but save those, and snatch them out of the fire.*

I have not expressed this well in German. But Jude wants to say: Have compassion on some; save some; that is, devote your life to showing mercy to those who are wretched, blind, and hardened. Do not take pleasure or delight in their condition. But let them go, depart from them, and have nothing to do with them. The others, however, whom you can snatch away, save with fear. Deal in a friendly and gentle way with them, just as God has dealt with you. Do not use force, and do not be impetuous; but treat them as people lying in the fire. You must pull them out and rescue them with all care, reason, and diligence. If they refuse to be snatched from the fire, one should let them go and have compassion on them, not burn them with fire and kill them, as the pope and the grand inquisitors do.

Hating even the garment spotted by the flesh.

To be sure, we have received the Holy Spirit through faith, and we have become clean; but as long as we live here, that old sack, our flesh and blood, still clings to us; it does not cease from its wantonness. This is the spotted garment which we must put aside and take off as long as we live.

24. *Now to Him who is able to keep you from falling and to present you without blemish before the presence of His glory with rejoicing,*

25. *to the only God, our Savior through Jesus Christ our Lord, be glory, majesty, dominion, and authority, before all time and now and forever. Amen.*

This is the conclusion of this epistle. When the apostles have written, taught, exhorted, and prophesied, they pray, wish, and give thanks. Thus we have seen in these epistles both what constitutes true Christian doctrine and life and what constitutes false and unchristian doctrine and life.

LECTURES ON
THE FIRST EPISTLE
OF ST. JOHN

Translated by
WALTER A. HANSEN

FOREWORD

Since I see that the devil is assailing us on all sides and that we do not have peace anywhere, we should bear in mind that God wants to keep us in His church, in which He has given us His Word. And we should understand that this Word of His is more powerful than all devils. For it is God's practice to join the cross and persecution to His Word, etc.

This is an outstanding epistle. It can buoy up afflicted hearts. Furthermore, it has John's style and manner of expression, so beautifully and gently does it picture Christ to us. It came to be written because at that time heretics and sluggish Christians had rushed in, which invariably happens when the Word has been revived. Then the devil harries us constantly and seeks in every way to cast us down, in order that we may give up preaching and good works. In John's time there were the Cerinthians, who denied the divinity of Christ; and there were sluggish Christians, who thought that they had heard Christ's Word enough and that it was not necessary to forsake the world and to do good to their neighbors. Here the apostle attacks both evils and urges us to guard the Word and to love one another. Thus we shall never learn so much and be so perfect that need for the Word of God will not remain. For the devil never rests. Thus exhortation and the use of God's Word are needed everywhere. It is a living and powerful Word. But we snore and are lazy. It is the Word of life. But we are in death every day. And because we are never without sins and the danger of death, we should never cease to ruminate on the Word. And this epistle is in the nature of an exhortation. In short, in this epistle the apostle wants to teach faith in opposition to the heretics, and true love in opposition to those who are wicked.

CHAPTER ONE

1. *That which was from the beginning.*

You see the simplicity of John's way of speaking. The language is elliptical and must be completed as follows: We preach to you about the Word of life, which was from the beginning. In other respects the language is altogether childlike; it stammers rather than speaks, and the greatest majesty is combined with the greatest simplicity of expression. We want to hear the Spirit stammer. He wants to make an announcement concerning the Word of life – the Word that did not come into existence recently but was from the beginning. Accordingly, John smites Cerinthus, who was denying the divinity of the nature of Christ.[1] "I am speaking of Christ," he says, "who did not have His beginning from Mary but was from the beginning. This is a discussion concerning the eternal Word of life. This Word put on flesh."

Which we have heard.

John says that Christ was true man and God. His divinity could be neither heard nor seen. Therefore He was true man.

Which we have looked upon.

This is an amplification.[2] We have looked carefully. We have not been deceived, but we are sure that it was not a phantom. He says this because he wants to make his hearers sure. Thus Peter too, says in 2 Peter 1:16:[3] "We were eyewitnesses of His majesty."

---

[1] Although Cerinthus is not mentioned by name in any of the Johannine writings, Irenaeus says that "John, the disciple of the Lord . . . seeks, by the proclamation of the Gospel, to remove that error which by Cerinthus had been disseminated among men," *Against Heresies*, Book III, ch. 11; see also *Luther's Works*, 22, p. 7.

[2] Cf. Aristotle, *Rhetoric*, Book I, ch. 9, on this device.

[3] The original has "1 Peter 1."

[W, XX, 602–604]

Our hands have handled.

Have no doubt whatever concerning what we are saying. The heretics are beginning to argue about the communication of properties, how His attributes must be assigned to each nature.[4] Thus they are falling into new errors. Be on your guard here. Accustom yourselves to speak about the Lord Jesus as Scripture does. Do not invent new words. In John 14:9 Jesus says: "Philip, he who has seen Me has seen the Father." Philip was forming an image of the Father from the humanity of Christ. These fluttery thoughts could easily have separated him from Christ. But Christ calls him away from those fluttery thoughts. "Have I been with you so long," He says, "and yet you do not know Me, Philip? He who sees Me has seen the Father" (John 14:9). We believe that Jesus Christ is one Person, made up, to be sure, of two natures. Whatever is stated now about the person is stated about the whole Person. But what the fanatics say, namely, that Christ suffered according to His humanity, is false. Scripture says that those two natures are in one Person. Indeed, Scripture says—see Rom. 8:3—that the Jews crucified the Son of God, not His humanity. And in 1 Cor. 2:8 it is stated that if they had understood this, they would never have crucified the Lord of glory. Paul does not say that they would never have crucified His humanity. Thus in Luke 1:35 we read: "The Child to be born of you will be called holy, the Son of God." Because of the oneness of the Person this passage does not say "humanity." Whatever is attributed to one, the same thing is also attributed to the rest. Indeed, it refers to the whole Person. Christ Himself, the Son of God Himself, was delivered for us. For the granting of eternal life an eternal and inestimable price had to be given. "He who gave His only Son for us," we read in Rom. 8:32. This indeed is true, that in His essence and so far as His essence is concerned the divinity is one thing and the humanity is another thing. In themselves, of course, they are distinct; but since they are presented as an object—a thing with which one must deal—the whole object is presented, the whole Christ. "Philip, he who sees Me" (cf. John 14:9) sees not only My humanity. The Person Itself, which was seen there, was true God and the Son of God. No one can touch or see these two natures from the outside as they are divided from

----

[4] Cf. *Luther's Works,* 37, p. 206, note 63.

the inside. He who believes in the Son of God believes not only in His humanity. "He who eats My flesh" (John 6:56), that is, he who believes that I am God. No one can drink the blood of the Son of God without drinking the whole Christ. The natures are distinct, but there is one Person. I am saying this in order that you may understand John's simple manner of speaking. John says that he saw and heard. Although he did not see the divinity, yet what he did see was the Son of God. Everything is referred to the Person. Some also imagine that Christ's humanity is at one place and that His divinity is everywhere.[5] But by the grace of God I have learned not to turn my eyes away from that Person who was born to Mary, and not to seek or acknowledge another god. One's eyes must be fixed on that Person who was born of the Virgin Mary. Where the Son of God is, there Christ is; where Christ is, there the Father is. I conclude that "in Him the whole fullness of the Godhead dwells," Col. 2:9. Thus everything in the Old Testament looks to the worship of Him who sits above the cherubim. They were always compelled to turn toward the mercy seat when they prayed. This was a figure. Christ says that He was concealed under that figure. John 14:6: "I am the Way, the Truth, and the Life." For it pleased the Father that all the fullness should dwell in Him, Col. 1:19.

Concerning the Word of life.

This is what we are discussing. We are speaking about life, but about that life which is no longer concealed before the world but has been made manifest, as John 1:4 states: "The life was the light of men." Here John says that he will proclaim the message of life in opposition to the death of the whole world, because the world does not have life. The devil, the prince of the world, has all men under his power. But the fact that the world not only does not have life but does not even acknowledge this is greater wretchedness.

2. The life was made manifest.

Previously it was not made manifest in the flesh. All those who were in the world—as so many kings, princes, self-righteous persons, and saints were—were in death and did not have life. But Christ, who gave His life for us, is the Word of life, and life itself.

---

[5] See, for example, *Luther's Works*, 37, pp. 46 – 49 and passim.

[W, XX, 607–609]

Christ Himself is such powerful life that He is more powerful than death and the prince of death.

We saw it, and we testify to it.

This life was made manifest when Christ rose again. Christ "was designated Son of God in power," Rom. 1:4. Therefore because we have seen this, because it has been revealed to us, we desire to reveal it to you too through the Word, in order that you, too, may believe. This the apostles do with all their strength, in order that they may lead all to the same knowledge. They are not content with knowing and having seen it themselves. Thus since all Christians believe, they say: "I believed. Therefore have I spoken," Ps. 116:10.

And proclaim to you the eternal life.

He explains what the nature of the life is, namely, that it no longer dies. The devil boasts of being able to slay, to multiply sins, yes, to make sin what is not sin and to frighten the hearts of men. He boasts of the power of death, likewise that one person falls into sin and another falls into blasphemy, because he is hurled down from faith, hope, etc. On the other hand, it is characteristic of a Christian always to be in the fear of God, always to pray that God may defend him and encamp round about those who fear Him (Ps. 34:7). The devil also encamps with his army, as Peter says in 1 Peter 5:8. If God withdraws His hand, we soon fall into every evil. In short, Christ has more weapons of righteousness than Satan has weapons of iniquity, more life than Satan has death.

And the life was made manifest.

It had been hidden in the Father in heaven before the creation of the world. This life we proclaim to you boldly. Just believe. But the fact that we proclaim with such boldness must be ascribed to our exceedingly great certainty.

3. *That which we have seen and heard.*

He repeats what he says above. We have not devised those arbitrary religions which have been brought forward by the will of men—religions which he himself has neither seen nor heard.

Therefore those religions should be abandoned and trodden underfoot. What is the devil, the author of death, going to care about your gray cowl? What is he going to care about your unclean virginity? Even under the rule of the Romans he had virgins.[6] For Satan has the wrath of God against you on his side. He knows that every sin displeases God. He strikes terror into our hearts and alarms us. Surely one must resist and do battle with other means than with those foolish sects and religions of ours. God defends us in Christ against Satan, since we are weak vessels. "We are not contending against flesh but against principalities and powers," Eph 6:12.

So that you may have fellowship with us.

I would be glad to share this great treasure with you but now I cannot do so in any other way than by means of the Word. He was seen and known by preordained witnesses (cf. Acts 10:41). Therefore if you are not able to hear and see Him as we did, nevertheless believe, and my treasure is being shown to you.

And that our fellowship may be with the Father.

This is inestimable love, surely great fellowship and participation. But we are by no means better than you, even though we have seen. You are by no means inferior to us, even though you have not seen. Just believe. Thus Peter says in 2 Peter 1:4 that we are partakers of the divine nature because we have all the good things God has. O wretched persons that we are, we who have neglected such holy things and seek other sects and mediators! Through the Word which is proclaimed we have fellowship with Christ. John portrays the Son distinctly, because in the epistle it is written that the Father and the Son have life, truth, and eternal salvation. On our side there are nothing but sins. We share His good things; He shares our wretchedness. I believe in Christ. Therefore my sin is in Christ.

4. *And we are writing this that your joy may be complete.*

This is how we satisfy you. Your joy had had its beginning in this knowledge. You have every right to rejoice in an inestimable blessing. Who would not rejoice in the fact that God has been

[6] Luther is referring to the Roman institution of the Vestal Virgins.

reconciled? Who would not rejoice in participation with God?

5. *This is the message.*

You see that the saintly man repeats and inculcates the same things with great emphasis. Accordingly, he stresses the words "we bear witness, we proclaim" in this way in order that he may keep us, who easily go astray, completely certain in the Word. For the saintly man sees our condition and Satan's adroitness. Therefore for us it is altogether necessary for him to repeat. Consequently, "This is the message" is a new repetition. He himself has instructed us to proclaim, in order that no one might be in doubt concerning the thing itself; for the thing that is proclaimed is important.

That God is light.

Thus in another place John says: "The light has come into the world and men loved darkness rather than light" (John 3:19). He opposes the light to the world, because all men, even saints and princes, are shut up in the universal darkness. Therefore John says: "We proclaim to you the light which we have heard; and if we do not proclaim it, you do not have it." The monks and the wise men of this world, who walk in their own ways, walk in darkness. Aristotle concludes as follows: "If God saw everything that is done here, He would never be at peace in His heart. Therefore He has no regard for our affairs."[7] But the subtler men are, the less regard they have for God. The monks, who want to follow reason, have chosen their own righteousness; they want to be changed for the better by means of their own works. The wiser they are, the more foolish they are. When a simple layman dies, he has the cross brought to him and keeps his mind on Christ. He prays, and he has better thoughts than those people have. Everything men invent in the cause of salvation turns out to be evil.

God is light.

What is not Christ is not light. As often as I hear "the fathers,

[7] Rörer's lecture notes refer to "12. Meth.," which is taken by the Weimar editors to be a reference to Aristotle's *Meteorologica*, often called *Libri metheororum*, which has, however, only four books. The idea however, is common in Aristotle, e. g., *Nicomachean Ethics*, Book X, ch. 8.

Augustine, Jerome, the councils," I ask: "Is there also a proclamation?" If not, I say: "Be off!"

God is light.

If the world and the flesh cannot grasp this, we do not care. We know that the Son of God put on flesh and was crucified for us. Our flesh laughs at this, and the world regards it as nothing. In short, the whole world should know that it is in darkness and should turn to this proclamation and acknowledge this light.

And in Him is no darkness at all.

We proclaim this light. Even if no one sees the light, yet it is proclaimed through the Word. And if we believe the Word, we surely come to that light. The Cerinthians want to destroy this light. One must be careful to understand what the source of the heresies is. They come from one's own reason, when the flesh begins to think: "This pleases and seems good to me. Therefore it will please God. The fathers said so. Therefore it is true." If you want to please God, listen to His words: believe in His Son, who died for you. This is not my reason; I am not inventing this color. But God Himself is the light. They want to smear darkness on our Lord God. They smear the cowl on God and paste the divine truth on their lies. This is putting darkness on the light. But there is no darkness in Him, not even the slightest.

6. *If we say we have fellowship.*

Forthwith he attacks the fanatics of his time. We see that they are bolder than those who are truly Christians and that they are boastful, as though they were sure of their fellowship with God. But they do not know their weakness. Christians speak with trepidation about their faith and their holy fellowship, and they desire to be strengthened. Christians say: "Lord, help! Lord, help!" Paul says that he has not yet apprehended, Phil. 3:13. Let us all remain in this light, John declares, and say: "This is indeed the true light, but we do not yet know it. Would that we might learn to know it more perfectly!"

While we walk in darkness.

If we do not abide in the proclamation, the Word is not in us.

No, then a lie and fallacious thinking are in us. The heretics walk in darkness and say that it is light. There are two evils: now to err, now to defend error. They do many things, but they smell of falsehoods; they lie with respect to faith, and with respect to works they do not devote themselves to the truth. Above all, one must see to it that the heart has this light. Then the works will follow. But if the light is impure – that is, if faith is mixed with the theories of men – we indeed do many works; but these works are in vain, since they are not the light. Christ is our true light. The angels see this light; we hear it.

7. . . . and the blood.

It is strange that although we preach about the blood and the suffering of Christ every year, yet we see so many sects bursting forth. Oh, the great darkness of the past! But if we cling to the Word that has been made known, we have this treasure, which is the blood of Christ. If we are beset by sins, no harm is done. The blood of Christ was not shed for the devil or the angels; it was shed for sinners. Accordingly, when I feel sin, why should I despair, and why should I not believe that it has been forgiven? For the blood of Christ washes sins away. The main thing is that we cling simply to the Word. Then there is no trouble. The apostles take heed most diligently that we retain the Word carefully and sincerely. If we remain in the light, we recognize what sin is; if we learn to know this, we have the blood of Christ, with which we are washed. The attacks of the devil have only one purpose: to snatch the light from us. Therefore nothing should give us more concern than the resolve to remain in that light.

8. If we say we have no sin.

This is a pleasing and comforting word. Augustine has commented: "To have sin is one thing; to sin is something else." [8] I approve of this, since Paul ascribes indwelling sin to those who have been justified, Rom. 7:7; Heb. 12:1. For although we have become a new creature, nevertheless the remnants of sin always remain in us. We still have sin, and the poison is still in us; and that sin incites us to the fruits of sin, as in the case of David, to

[8] Cf., for example, Augustine, *On Man's Perfection in Righteousness*, ch. 18, par. 39; ch. 21, par. 44.

[W, XX, 620 – 622]

whom inherent, encompassing, and indwelling sin said: "Slay Uriah" (cf. 2 Sam. 11:15). David consented and sinned. In this way Peter was incited when, after receiving the Spirit of the Gospel, he was compelling the Gentiles to live like Jews (cf. Gal. 2:11-14). Because of that sin Paul and Barnabas are stirred to anger. So are we – we who should by no means be placed on the same footing with the apostles. Although we are Christians sprinkled with the blood of Christ, yet we often err. Therefore the true knowledge of Christ causes a person to feel that he has sin. Furthermore, it causes us to lament this. The papists and those who are in despair are opposed to this. The former boast of their righteousnesses and their orders; they imagine that they are without sin. The scholastics teach that such things are possible, and Zwingli teaches that original sin is merely a defect.[9] Those who despair are those who feel sin, die in their consciences, and are tormented to such an extent on all sides that they are compelled to despair. Nevertheless, one should not despair because of sin or the fruits of sin. For even if we fall, we must rise again. Finally we should hold most firmly to this, that no one is or becomes righteous before God except through the blood of Jesus Christ. For God alone is righteous, truthful, and wise. Whatever we do out of faith, we should always say: "It is sin" and "We are unworthy servants," Luke 17:10. But we gain salvation solely because of the righteousness of God, and it is because of this righteousness that we are saved.

8. *If we say we have no sin, we deceive ourselves.*

This is said in opposition to those who are presumptuous. To be able to believe that the blood of Christ frees us from all sin is something that is necessary. But it is a gift of God. When we cling to our own righteousness, however, and boast of it, then we are not subjected to the divine righteousness. We learn from the example of Peter how difficult it is to give up the statutes of men. Look at the kind of righteousness into which he, by his example, compels the Gentiles to fall to their great destruction and damnation. Therefore to withdraw from the papacy, that is, from trust in one's own perfection, is a divine virtue. The flesh and blind reason always resist. The monks taught that their state was per-

[9] See *Luther's Works*, 37, p. 16, note 7.

fection.[10] We Christians boast of no perfection but always pray that we may grow in the knowledge of God and Christ, as Peter exhorts, 2 Peter 3:18. Nothing in our behavior justifies us, for we are justified gratis, Rom. 3:24. And this must be inculcated, lest we despair when we sin, no matter what kind of occasion may have led us to sin. But when the monks rely on the fathers, what are we going to say about them? I am wont to reply: "If the fathers have piled straw, hay, and wood on top of the foundation of Christ, what, pray, have they learned in death?" They have said: "I shall neither be justified because of these good works I have done, nor shall I be damned because of the evil works I have done. But I shall be preserved through the blood of Christ." Thus Bernard said: "What the monks have is uncertain; what we have is completely certain."[11]

And the truth is not in us.

Although they are completely sure that they have the truth when they condemn us and our teaching as heresy, they do not have the truth. No, they oppose the truth.

9. *If we confess our sins, He is faithful and just, and will forgive our sins.*

This is the second part. You should not despair. First he says: "I shall free you from presumption, then from despair, as if you had no sin. In order that you may be freed from the sin of Satan, just acknowledge and confess it before God, and give Him the glory, as David does when he says in Ps. 51:4: 'I have done that which is evil in Thy sight, so that Thou art justified and blameless in Thy judgment'; that is 'that Thy Word may be true, I confess that I am a sinner and that I have sinned against Thee only, since in Thy sight no one is clean. And enter not into judgment with me,'" Ps. 143:2. To our God belongs righteousness, but to us confusion, cf. Dan. 9:7. Those presumptuous people bring a sackful of prayers and alms. They trust in their own righteousness. They boast, saying: "I have done this; I have done that. Therefore I have become righteous in Thy sight." The cowl has been put on the laity

---

[10] The Weimar text has *perfectiorem*, but we have read *perfectionem* instead.

[11] From Rörer's lecture notes it appears that at this point Luther was thinking of his favorite words from Bernard: "I have wasted my time"; cf. p. 296, note 21.

[W, XX, 625 – 627]

because of trust in the good works which he to whom the cowl belonged had done.[12] But in this very way they had withdrawn from Christ, the Foundation, when they set up their works. "But cursed is the man who puts his trust in the flesh," Jer. 17:5.

9. *If we confess.*

Give only to God this honor: "To Thee, God, alone this righteousness, to Thee, God, alone this glory is due, that Thou art called just and justifiest him who believes."

He is faithful and just.

God is faithful because He keeps His promises. He is just when He gives righteousness to him who confesses that He is just. It is as if God were saying: "Because you say that I am just, which I am, for this reason I shall show you My justice and justify you." Therefore if you can say: "We have no righteousness," you should persuade yourself with certainty that God is faithful, clings to His promises that He wants to forgive sins because of Christ, and is just, since He gives to everyone that which belongs to him,[13] presents the righteousness acquired through the death of Christ to him who confesses his sins and believes, and in this way also makes him righteous. David confesses his sin, but Saul excuses his sin before Samuel and could not say: "I have sinned" in the way David did (1 Sam. 15). All he wanted was to be honored before the people. This is what we do when we defend our sins in order that we may not be shamed before men. It was Saul's wish that the prophet pray for him before the elders of Israel. For he certainly did not want to seem to have sinned against the Lord. But for this reason he, together with all our hypocrites, was shamed before God. Furthermore, this statement cannot be understood as referring to auricular confession, although I do not reject that confession either.[14] No, this statement must be understood as referring to confession before God by which we ourselves confess

---

[12] Cf. *Luther's Works*, 12, p. 71, note 25.

[13] An allusion to the first section of Book I of the *Institutes* of Justinian; cf. 36, p. 357, note 17.

[14] See, for example, Luther's statement of the previous year on private confession, *Luther's Works*, 36, pp. 359 – 360.

our sins as well as our faith. Thus God finally forgives sin and grants grace and a pacified conscience by taking away the sting and the bite of conscience.

10. *If we say we have not sinned.*

We not only have sin; but we also sin because of the weakness of our sinful flesh or as long as we are in our sinful flesh. And there is a perpetual conflict between the flesh and the spirit, as Rom. 7:8 states: "For nothing good dwells within me, that is, in my flesh. For I can will what is good, but I cannot do it." But not only is the desire of a man's flesh for a woman and, on the other hand, the desire of a woman's flesh for a man a sin, but in the legends of the saints many vices that have put on nothing more than a show of sanctity are regarded as good conduct. The fathers looked only at outward sins, not at that inner lust of the flesh, at envy, malevolence, an unfriendly heart, and the falling from faith and hope. And indeed we still have sin, which continues to bite and to urge us to sin, yet does not rule. But we and our sin have become like a bound man who is being led to death — a man from whom all weapons with which he could do harm have been taken. Still he is not yet dead. Therefore sin is still in our flesh. It boils and rages without ceasing. For we always love the things that are ours; we rely on our own strength without trusting in the Word and without believing God. Such things our flesh wants, nothing else. But the fathers and we, too, do not see things of this kind; we see the external works, such as fastings. The lust of the flesh is not cured by fasting; but the health of the body is more likely to be broken, which, as we see, happened in the case of Bernard.[15] But meditating on the Word of the Lord is the best remedy against sin. To be sure, the quenching of lust is helped by fasting; but it alone does not do or accomplish this. Something else that is better and more necessary is required.

10. *If we say we have not sinned.*

Others explain this as referring to sin committed in the past,[16] but I would be willing to explain it as referring to sin committed

---

[15] Cf. p 27, note 16.

[16] Augustine asserted that this referred "not only to past sins," *In epistolam Joannis ad Parthos*, Tractate I, par. 6, *Patrologia, Series Latina*, XXXV, 1982.

at the present time. For the Hebrew manner of speaking explains a verb in the past tense through a verb in the present tense. Indeed, it is my understanding that John himself often uses Hebraisms.[17] He wants to say: "We have sin, and we sin." In James 3:2 we read: "For we all make many mistakes." And Paul says in Rom. 7:14-15: "I am carnal, sold under sin. I do what I do not want; but what I hate, this I do." And thus the flesh does not do what the spirit wants. Sin is not so dead that it is not set in motion. Indeed, we have the lust of the flesh in us. But it does not rule. And a Christian differs from other people only in this respect that sin does not rule in him. Spiritual presumption itself is also sin, namely, when you consider what you have done today a good work, likewise when you are saddened, when you only despair, because you commit an act of unchastity. Accordingly, sin must be accused, and one must fight against it throughout one's life. Consequently, a Christian should not snore and sleep, as the monks do after reading Masses. Therefore a Christian man is a just, saintly, righteous, and blessed person and a child of God, namely, according to the spirit. According to the flesh, however, he still has sin. Nevertheless, because he is reborn through the Spirit and believes, sin is not imputed to him.

We make Him a liar.

These are the people who consider themselves saintly and righteous because of their exertions and works. For God shut up all under sin, in order that the whole world might become liable to punishment, Rom. 3:9 (cf. Gal. 3:22). He shut up all under unbelief, in order that He might have mercy on all, Rom. 11:32. God offers mercy to the godly as well as to the ungodly. Accordingly, all are under sin. For mercy is rendered to the unrighteous and not to the righteous. For in the sight of God no one is righteous (cf. Ps. 143:2). Consequently, mercy is necessarily offered to all. Since the time of the apostle John the heretical teaching which contends against the grace of God and wants to be without sin has come into being; it sets up its own norm of living, according to which they presumed to be saintly. Undoubtedly they were the preachers of circumcision from Judaism whom Paul commonly

---

[17] See, for example, Luther's observations on John 6:29, *Luther's Works*, 23, pp. 20–21.

calls "the circumcision party" (Titus 1:10). The saintly apostles oppose them, and here John, in particular, does so. A Christian always cries out: "Forgive us our sins!" He is always at war with those sins. Therefore though sins still cling to him, yet they are not imputed to him. For blasphemy is a great sin. But those who trust in their own righteousness blaspheme God. Our monks were people of this kind, and, provided that there were no gross sins, they lived in the greatest smugness, namely, by reason of their presumptuousness. Look also at others, who have sinned because of despair. Therefore it is a great gift of God to have His Word, to acknowledge sin on the basis of the Law, and to believe the Gospel. If one or the other is not there, God is charged with a lie and blasphemed.

CHAPTER TWO

1. *My little children I am writing this to you so that you may not sin.*

He who can make this text intelligible to us should be called a theologian. We sin in the world; we have sin. Who, like Peter at Antioch (Gal. 2:11), would not waver now and then in faith? Why does the apostle say "so that we may not sin"? The apostle wants us to be careful and to walk in the fear of the Lord. We should not say: "If this is the way the matter stands, I will sin." For John says: "The desire to sin should not reign in you. No, you should be watchful. But even if you fortify yourself to the utmost, yet sin remains, and you sin from day to day." Hence it is necessary to exercise foresight. For we must always be nourished by the Spirit, and we must also read the Psalms and Holy Scripture. This is our armor.

So that you may not sin.

You should wage war against sin and walk carefully. Do not be like the priests and the monks. No, you should fight against sin. I am saying this in order that a person may learn to know himself. For a contrite and humble heart does not displease God (cf. Ps. 51:17).

And if anyone does sin.

Who does not transgress now and then? I and everyone feel the need of praise. We should not despair of God's mercy. He who is presumptuous concerning his merits and is without confidence concerning God's mercy commits the same kind of sin. For God says in Ps. 86:5: "I am merciful to those who sin and call upon Me. No righteousness is so great that it pleases Me." Thus if someone errs and sins, he should not add the sin of despair. After sin the devil always alarms the heart and makes us tremble. For he hurls a person into sin in order that he may finally force him into despair. On the other hand, he lets some live smugly without temptation in order that they may think and believe that they are holy. And when somewhere he tears the Word out of one's heart, then he has conquered. This is his cunning. He wants to make saints sinners, and confident sinners saints. Do not despair after sin, but lift your eyes on high to where Christ intercedes for us. He is our Advocate. He intercedes for us and says: "Father, I have suffered for this person; I am looking after him." This prayer cannot be in vain. In Heb. 4:14 [1] we read: "We have a great High Priest." But even though we have had Christ as our High Priest, Advocate, Mediator, Reconciler, and Comforter, yet we have fled for refuge to the saints and have regarded Christ as a Judge. Accordingly, this text should be written with golden letters and should be painted in the heart. Therefore you should get understanding and say: "Christ,[2] I know Thee alone as the Advocate, the Comforter, and the Mediator; and I do not doubt that Thou art such a Person for me but cling firmly to this with my heart and believe." Christ is born for us, suffers, ascends into heaven for our sakes, sits at the right hand of the Father, and intercedes for us. Satan strives in every way to strike our hearts with blindness, lest they believe what the Holy Spirit says here through John. The condition of Christians is wonderful. For the same person is a sinner and is righteous — a sinner because of the infected flesh he bears, righteous because of the Spirit, who holds him in check. Reason can by no means understand that condition.

Jesus Christ the Righteous.

He is righteous and unstained. He is without sin. Whatever righteousness I have, this my Comforter has, He who cries out for me to the Father: "Spare him, and he has been spared! Forgive him! Help him!" The righteousness of Jesus Christ is standing on our side. For the righteousness of God in Him is ours.

2. And He is the expiation for our sins.

He does not sit at the right hand of the Father to terrify us,

[1] The original has "Heb. 5."
[2] The Weimar text has *Christi,* but we have read *Christe* instead.

[W, XX, 637–640]

but He is the expiation. Nevertheless, we seek other advocates, others to render satisfaction and make expiation for our sins. Our sins are too great. They cannot be atoned for with our works; this can be done only with Christ's bitter suffering and with the shedding of His precious blood. Sin causes heartache and depicts Christ for us differently from what He is; it shows Him to us through a colored glass. Even some teachers have done this, even the very saintly martyr Cyprian.[3] But these things must be proclaimed to those who have been terrified, not to those who are presumptuous. Christ, who does not spurn a contrite and humble heart, wants to be the Lord and Author of life, not of sin.

But also for the sins of the whole world.

It is certain that you are a part of the world. Do not let your heart deceive you by saying: "The Lord died for Peter and Paul; He rendered satisfaction for them, not for me." Therefore let everyone who has sin be summoned here, for He was made the expiation for the sins of the whole world and bore the sins of the whole world. For all the godless have been put together and called, but they refuse to accept. Hence it is stated in Is. 49:4: "I have labored in vain." Christ is so merciful and kind that if it were possible, He would weep for every sinner who is troubled. Of all men He is the mildest, of all the gentlest. With every member He feels more pity than Peter felt under the rod and the blows.[4] Take any man who is extraordinarily kind and gentle. Then you would know that Christ is much kinder to you. For just as He was on earth, so He is in heaven. Thus Christ has been appointed as the Bishop and Savior of our souls (cf. 1 Peter 2:25). But at His own time He will come as Judge. Since we see this, let us give no occasion to gratify lust.

3. *And by this we may be sure.*

The apostle is writing against two classes of people, as we have said at the outset, namely, against those who are presumptuous and rely on works and against those who are licentious or slothful.

---

[3] Luther seems to be thinking of such passages as Cyprian, *On the Lapsed*, ch. 17.

[4] Here Luther seems to be drawing on the *Legenda aurea*; cf. *Luther's Works*, 24, p. 147, note 83.

He wants to say: "If the true knowledge of Christ is present, it will not be without fruit or without works that are truly good." So far we have heard John mentioning the chief point of Christianity, that is, the true knowledge of God and of Christ Himself. Now he also gives the admonition that one must see to it that the knowledge itself is not false and counterfeit. This we see in many in whom it is not solid but is capricious and like foam on water. Although those people are better than those who persecute the Word, yet nothing results from this; nor are they regarded as true believers unless they prove their faith with good works. For the true knowledge does not consist in speculation but moves forward to performance.

That we know Him, if we keep His commandments.

He is speaking in general against all Christians, especially against those who are licentious, who remain in their previous life, in avarice, ambition, and whoredom. Therefore the knowledge of Christ has been handed down to us in order that we may fulfill the commandments of God. For the first part of Christianity is the Law; the second is love for one's brother. Rom. 13:8 says: "Owe no one anything, except to love one another." And in Matt. 7:12 we read: "Whatever you wish that men would do to you, do so to them." First we are freed from sin, and then we serve our neighbor with all our strength. And if you do not hate your brother, you learn in this way that the kingdom of God is in you. For even if you are angry at times, yet you must forgive; and you must bear in mind that you have done evil. If incitement of the lust to sin occurs, you must neither despair nor also desist from the battle. A Christian does battle against those who do not know Christ and against those who are not properly vigilant. These people must receive instruction in order that they may remain in the sound doctrine; and they must be diligently admonished, even though they are imperfect in both respects. Yet one should not desist from preaching, but false and negligent Christians must be warned and exhorted. Those, however, who are ignorant and in error should be instructed at every opportunity.

4. *He who says that he knows God and does not keep His commandments.*

He is speaking against boasters, who in everything they do seek nothing else than a name and glory. John is dealing with sons and daughters. Our fanatics are people of this kind. They confess that they know God and keep His commandments, even though they do not observe them and His Word or believe. To John these things are identical, as is pointed out later. But he who speaks differently from the way he feels is a liar.

And the truth is not in him.

This is what he stated above: "God is light, and in Him is no darkness" (1 John 1:5). In them there are the darkness of ignorance, errors, and heresies. Everyone devises for himself his own worship of God according to his own thoughts. They depict their God differently from what He is. John wants to say: "Everything you pretend is untrue, no matter what you say or do." And consider how in spite of this John distinguishes between saying that someone is a liar and the statement that the truth is not in a person. For the heretics, who spoke falsely about the saving faith, are beaten down. Indeed, they had not even come to the knowledge of the truth. The loathsome Donatists boasted much of their faith, life, and continence, also of suicide (αὐτοχειρία), of death inflicted either on themselves or on one another. For when two had met each other early in the morning, they immediately added the words "Kill me" to their greeting. If one had refused, the other hastened to take his own life.[5] Among them these were most splendid deeds. Yet the truth was not in them. For Augustine, who writes against them, says that a cause and a punishment are required for martyrdom.[6] He casts all their boasting aside.

5. But whoever keeps His Word.

This is a conclusion, since a dilemma has been presented in what has preceded and what has now been set forth next. It is my understanding that John is not speaking about the commandments, but that he is speaking about the Word of the Gospel, which he who knows God keeps. John 8:55 states: "I know Him, and I keep His Word."

---

    [5] Cf. Augustine, *The Correction of the Donatists*, ch. 3, par. 12.

    [6] Augustine, *The Correction of the Donatists*, ch. 2, par. 9.

In him truly love for God is perfected.

He has consolation in his heart, because he loves God and his neighbor.

By this we may be sure that we are in Him.

This is a way of speaking that is characteristic of John. Christ would say: "He who abides in Me, and I in him, he it is that bears much fruit," John 15:5. I, wretched Christian that I am, am protected by Christ, the eternal Righteousness, and I will not permit sin to reign in me. Therefore I hope, yes, I believe, that I am in Him.

By this we may be sure that we are in Him.

Here we have heard John urging us to bear witness of our faith with good works and the fruits of love. To love your brother it is not enough not to hate him; you must also do good to him.

6. *He who says he abides in Him.*

When John says: "He who says he," he always hits braggarts and false Christians hard. This should be the sign by which they should know whether they are true Christians or not. Where Christ dwells through faith, there He makes that person conform to Him; that is, He makes him humble, gentle, and ready to help his neighbor in any need.

7. *Beloved, I am writing you no new commandment.*

The saintly man is writing this proleptically. For John is writing against the new teachers. Then he hits them hard by saying: "Do not think that I am going to write new things to you. Indeed, you have more than enough of what is new. Wherever the light of truth arises, the devil is present and raises up new teachers. Indeed, brethren, I am writing this to preserve you in the doctrine you have received. (Thus Paul issues the same warning throughout his epistles. Thus we, too, should not spare any struggle to preserve the doctrine against the new teachers.) Brethren, do not think that I am going to teach anything that is new. My work has only one purpose: to keep you in the doctrine handed down previously. It

is my desire to keep you in simplicity against the new teachers.
Remain in simplicity and in the old doctrine you have received.
Above all, beware of boasting, of seeking glory. In the Holy Scriptures the desire to boast is a temptation of the devil. Therefore God
has ordered things in such a way that the Word of the Gospel should
be the Word of the cross. It is His purpose to suppress that empty
glory."

But an old commandment which you had from the beginning.

This is the commandment of the Gospel that has been proclaimed. From this passage one may gather that this epistle was
written toward the end of John's life, just as Peter's second letter
was written toward the end of Peter's life. During their lifetime
the apostles themselves were compelled to bear these new
teachers. It is by no means surprising if today, too, we are compelled to bear them.

8. *I am writing to you a new commandment, which is true in Him
and in you.*

It is truly a new doctrine. Indeed, it is the only doctrine. Again
John inveighs against the new teachers and the heretics. If they
want to have something that is new, let them accept this doctrine,
which certainly is new and has never been known to the world. It
is also new to those to whom it has been known, because from day
to day it renews those who accept it. It is a new commandment in
Christ, who has now been revealed. It is also new to us, whom it
illumines. Therefore keep this doctrine. The other doctrines will
be darkness, not light. In short, beware of new doctrine, as Paul
says in Eph. 4:14: "Do not be carried about with every wind of
doctrine."

*Because the darkness has passed away, and the Word is already
shining.*

Once more he condemns the adversaries, from whom the darkness had not yet departed. They had a false light, not the true light.
They transformed themselves into angels of light (2 Cor. 11:14) and
teachers. Thus the devil insinuates himself into our hearts, not as
one who is evil and false but as one who is good and the best, as

an angel of light (2 Cor. 11:14). His teachers, who call themselves "servants of Christ, ministers of Christ," do likewise. Under these titles they impose on the people. But the true light shines in Him and in us. By this we abide. In them, however, there is a false light.

9. *He who says he is in the light and hates his brother.*

The heretics cannot fail[7] to do this; for as the spirits are, so they bear fruit. We are obliged to hate their teachings and their exertions. "I hated them with perfect hatred; they are my enemies," as Ps. 139:22 says. I must hate them with all my heart. Or should I not hate them for the sake of Christ, because they distort Christ's words by saying that "is" means "signifies"?[8] When we do this, they hate us and cry out that we hold love in disdain. Although they make a pretense of modesty and love, inwardly they are full of hate. He who is not in the true light cannot love his brother. Indeed, he would want all love extinguished. The continuance of their teachings is their only concern. For this reason they conceal their hatred, persecutions, and tyrannical acts by saying that all this betokens devotion to the glory of God and glowing zeal for the truth. But he who does not abide in the true light does not abide in love. The fruits of the Spirit grow only in the Spirit. "A bad tree cannot bear good fruit," as Matt. 7:18[9] says.

9. *He who says he is in the light.*

This is what those sectarians have been saying up to the present time to give the appearance of a confession. They do not acknowledge this. Indeed, they say that they are in the light. But Christ and those who are His see that those people are in darkness because they obscure the light of the Gospel. Before the devil and the world they have the glory of possessing the Gospel. The apostles encountered this. It is not surprising that we, too, encounter it.

10. *He who loves his brother abides in the light.*

This is a contrast. Christians love. So do those people. But

---

[7] The Weimar text has *committere,* but we have followed Rörer's lecture notes and read *omittere* instead.

[8] Cf. *Luther's Works,* 37, p. 30.

[9] The original has "Matt. 8."

a Christian would not want them to perish. Indeed, he would want
to correct them, even though Christians have violent hatred for
their doctrine. Christ will judge whether the source is a holy and
good hatred.

And in it there is no cause for stumbling.

This is an ambiguous way of speaking. It can be understood as
being used in a passive or in an active sense. I would prefer to
take it as being used in a passive sense; that is, he walks in the
light and is not made to stumble by that semblance of light but
remains constantly in the light and is not disturbed by any cause
for stumbling. Ps. 119:165 says: "Great peace have those who love
Thy Law; nothing can make them stumble." Thus he causes no one
to stumble. But I do not believe that the apostle is speaking about
this weakness of the brethren. "Love is not irritable," we read in
1 Cor. 13:5, and again (v. 8) "love never ends." A true Christian is
by no means offended but is constant in the knowledge of that
light. He hears a new doctrine, but he is by no means disturbed.
He hears that there is persecution, but he turns a deaf ear to this.
On the other hand, the adversaries think evil, whether flattering
or harsh things are said to them. They turn our blandishments into
poison and fawning. Paul says in Titus 3:10: "As for a man who is
a heretic, after admonishing him once or twice, have nothing more
to do with him." And in Prov. 29:9 we read: "If a wise man has an
argument with a fool, the fool only rages and laughs; and there is
no quiet."

11. *But he who hates his brother is in the darkness and walks in
the darkness.*

To believe and think dark things is to be "in the darkness."
Whatever they do and suffer in this thinking of the heart is darkness. They think that they are going to the kingdom and to glory,
and they are on the way to hell. Here there is a close connection
with the metaphor taken from physical light.

Because the darkness has blinded his eyes.

The heretics boast of having the light, but what they have is
darkness pure and simple. And here there is a prolepsis, in order

that you may see what withdrawal from the true light is. We do not believe—but Christ knows—with what great zeal and snares Satan strives to eradicate this light from our hearts. He cares little about a beautiful life and beautiful conduct. "He prowls around, seeking someone to devour," as 1 Peter 5:8 says. Because he finds many who are not prepared, he overthrows many. It is the devil's great and stormy wind that seeks to extinguish our light.

Yesterday [10] we heard about the hatred of the godless saintlets. The new teachers are also heretics. They introduce destructive sects. Because their hatred is beautifully adorned with the finest semblance of sanctity and faith, it is not recognized by the flesh unless there is help from the Spirit. For what they strive to attain they call zeal for the glory of God. In other respects it concerns itself with hatred and grosser vices. For Scripture is wont to censure first those who sin with the semblance of sanctity, then those who sin more grossly. Therefore John proceeds at once to those who are negligent and lazy.

12. *I am writing to you, little children, because your sins are forgiven for His name's sake.*

This is a new exhortation to the godly. He exhorts them that since they have the sound doctrine, they should also bear fruit. The same procedure applies to all, except that he attributes knowledge to parents. As parents they should be wiser than the youth. John means that young people have a more fervid inclination to sin. A youth is inclined to lust, a man to avarice and fame. Thus there are spiritual vices for which one person is more fervidly eager than another. Thus David says in Ps. 25:7: "Remember not the sins of my youth, or my transgressions." Thus Job says in chapter 13:26: "Thou wilt consume me for the sins of my youth." Therefore John proclaims that the kingdom of Christ is a kingdom of the remission of sins, because those who have fallen have hope of remission. The godless teach the same thing, but they do not feel and understand the same thing. Accordingly, one must note this carefully, in order that all may know that the remission of sins is the chief point of the proclamation. If this is true, it follows that we are under sin and that we sin. For otherwise we would not say: "Forgive us our

[10] That is, on September 9; cf. Introduction, p. x

debts," Matt. 6:12, and "Clear Thou me from hidden faults," Ps. 19:13. The Lord's Prayer makes us answerable for sin and punishable for many sins. "Hallowed be Thy name" (Matt. 6:9). Therefore we do not hallow it. This life is nothing else than a profanation of God's name. As a result, the kingdom of Satan, which is full of thievery, robbery, adultery, and other offenses, is enlarged. Only the godly say: "Deliver us from this kingdom." The remission of sins has not been instituted in order that we may have permission to sin or that we may sin; it has been instituted in order that we may recognize sin and know that we are in sin, that we may fight against sin. A physician reveals an illness, not because he takes delight in the illness, but rather that the person who is sick may sigh and ask to be delivered from the illness. Indeed, the patient gets hope of health from his faith in the physician who gives him a promise. Thus in Baptism we, too, are translated from darkness into light and into the place where there is remission of sins. It would be a good thing if the books of Jerome and others had not come to light; for they give too many precepts about one's own efforts. The more the monks are in the clutches of sin, the more reason Jerome has given them to torture themselves. If they fast a great deal, they give relief to the gullet, it is true. Meanwhile, however, pride creeps in. One thing is removed; twice as much is introduced. Although such castigations have their use, yet sins are not purged away in this manner. Although the heart is prevented from bursting forth, yet it is not healed.

Because your sins are forgiven for His name's sake.

Sins are not forgiven because of application to works; they are forgiven when I call upon the name of the Lord Jesus Christ because I believe that He is the expiation for our sins. This is the truth. But the devil does not let us remain on this road. He immediately brings up our works. Therefore let no one cleave to his own works. It is our nature to say: "I have sinned with a deed. Therefore I shall make expiation with a deed." The devil, who strengthens our error, is present. One must attack this sin with the promise that sins are remitted for His name's sake, as Ps. 25:11 [11] says.

---

[11] The original has "Ps. 39."

13. *I am writing to you, fathers, because you know Him who is from the beginning.*

Do the Jews not also know Him, even though they do not have remission of sins? But they have not acknowledged His name, in which is our salvation, according to what is stated in Ps. 91:14: "I will protect him, because he knows My name." Nor do they know "Him who is from the beginning," that is, the eternal Son of God. But they know another god, a new god, contrary to the commandment of God in Ps. 81:8-9: "O Israel, there shall be no strange god among you; you shall not bow down to a foreign god." The new teachers have invented a new god. They go into the desert, observe fastings, erect monasteries, make vows, and say: "If you do this, you will please God." This is not the old God; it is a new god. For the old God does not have regard for me on account of my works. To make new gods is to invent new ways, new religions for the purpose of serving God. He who introduces a new doctrine introduces a new god; he denies the old God, who has been from the beginning. It is true idolatry to worship a new god, that is, Satan. Therefore what has been handed down to us in opposition to the Word is nothing but idolatry and godlessness. But for us, who have become accustomed to idolatry, it is difficult to believe this.

I am writing to you, young men.

John is writing to people of all classes. Therefore he has also wanted the youth to be partakers of grace. Undoubtedly he has an understanding of the age which must still be guided by parents. For it is most of all in need of instruction, and no age is more prone to sin.

Because you have overcome the evil one.

Young people are driven by passions; they do not have much judgment. In Christ we have victory over the devil and against the power of the devil. The power of the devil is death, sin, and an evil conscience. Through these he reigns. He also has shields and weapons. He terrifies hearts with death and inclines the will to sin wherever he desires. From all these we have not only been delivered, but we even have victory. He who has overcome the world has also overcome the devil. A youth who believes in Christ has victory over everything because of which Satan has power. Thus he has victory, not in such a way that sin, an evil conscience, and death are not felt, but because they are overcome. For Christ is greater. Although they have been overcome, they have not been destroyed. The sickness has begun to be cured, but it has not been completely removed.

I write to you, children, because you know the Father.

Because John makes distinctions here as he speaks, he finally mentions the children who are held in one's lap. It is as though he were saying: "Dear little children, you, too, have a heavenly Father." But I am not in agreement with the statement that children do not believe.[12] People say that they do not see faith in them. I reply: "Nor do they see it in old people." They counter by saying that adults know that they believe and that they profess their faith, but that children do not. I ask: "From what source is it certain that they are speaking the truth, since Simon Magus boasted of the same thing and yet was an impostor (cf. Acts 8:13)?" But just as sin has dominion over all, so grace has dominion through Christ; for just as a child becomes answerable because of the sin of another, so it becomes righteous because of the righteousness of another. Reason, you see, fights against faith. But the weaker it is in children, the more they believe. Here, just as elsewhere, Christ gives children a special invitation in Matt. 19:14: "Let the children come to Me." But He grants access to no one without faith.

14. *I write to you, fathers, because you know Him. I write to you, young men, because you are strong.*

He wants to comfort all and to exhort them to remain in the purity of the Word of God. After mentioning all the levels of age he addresses the fathers and the adolescents, or the young men, anew. But he gives to each age its own descriptive word and changes this into the spiritual sense. The fathers build, the youths fight for and defend the state, the children are preserved in it. All overcome the devil; but they do so with a new kind of warfare, namely, through the Word.

[12] Cf. also *Luther's Works,* 36, pp. 300–301, on the possibility of faith among young children.

15. *Do not love the world or the things in the world.*

We have heard the exhortation or commendation. John has commended the fathers, the young men, and the children. But he commends with respect to the faith that has been received, in order that they may remember what great grace it is to have come to and to know this faith. It is as if I were to say: "Sirs, you have the true knowledge; you have been called with a holy calling. Now see to it that you walk in a manner worthy of this calling (cf. Eph. 4:1), that you bear fruits worthy of repentance (Acts 26:20). Do not love the world." John is speaking in a simple manner to the little children, so that Erasmus seems to be offended by this simplicity.[13] But the Holy Spirit is a Teacher of those who are simple. Therefore He employs simplicity. Many do not know what the world is, as has been heard enough in Ecclesiastes,[14] where some understand the world to mean God's creatures themselves, as the Franciscan monks understand money and society. But they are in error, since every creature of God is good (cf. 1 Tim. 4:4), and Christ Himself used money and lived amid the society of men. Therefore in this passage the world is godlessness itself, man's state of mind deprived of the proper use of the creatures of God. This is true of those who do not understand the creatures of God in the right way and do not pursue the right end, who use the things of the world for their own pleasure and glory. Above all, the world is "subjected to futility" (Rom. 8:20). Man, who is futile himself, uses all these things in a futile manner. Therefore those people sin who "flee the world" by fleeing the society of men. And those who spurn the creatures of God, do not eat meat, do not wear clothing of a special kind—they use the creatures of God in such a way that they want to be saved through them. But this is a spiritual misuse of the world. Love for the world, however, turns its attention to a worldly state of mind. In the world you must be like a burning and shining lamp, in order that the others may be illuminated. To be in the world, to see the world, to be aware of the world, is different from loving the world, just as to have sin, to be aware of sin, is some-

---

[13] From Rörer's notes it is evident that at this point Luther said: "Here you see that John speaks simply, as Erasmus says in his anger: 'He crushes those who are merely pure.'"

[14] Luther is referring to the Preface of his *Notes on Ecclesiastes*, delivered in 1526 but not published until 1532 (W, XX, 7–8).

thing different from loving sin. To be sure, Abraham had property; but he did not love it, since he showed that he was a manager and knew that by God's will he had been appointed a steward of his goods. David was a mighty king. He did not insist on his own way (1 Cor. 13:5), but ruled in accordance with the will of God. For so far as he himself was concerned, he said in Ps. 39:12: "I am Thy passing guest, a sojourner, like all my fathers." He knew that he was one of the foreigners, that he was a guest. David ruled the kingdom according to the will of God and to glorify Him, not according to his own will and to glorify himself. Thus he did not love the world. But where someone afflicts the poor and uses the property of others as if it were his own, there the world is. This is wrong. Through Christ I have been placed in the midst of the world, namely, through Baptism, in order that others may be strengthened and buoyed up by my example. Therefore it is godless to flee the world, as those whom I have mentioned do. Christ says in John 16:8: "The Holy Spirit will convince the world of sin." Thus the world is nothing else than the people who have turned away from God, do not know God, and have turned to the creatures for their own advantage, for their own glory.

If anyone loves the world, love for the Father is not in him.

For love for God and love for the world are not compatible. There is only one thing with respect to which love for the world and love for God reveals itself. Jacob speaks in Gen. 33:5 of "the children whom God has graciously given Thy servant." He who loves them as a gift of God also loves God. But he who loves them as prospective children of the world and says: "Behold my child. I shall gather a treasure for him" [15] — he loves the world. He who loves his wife as a gift of God does not love the world; for God has given her to him, and children are a gift of God (cf. Ps. 127:3). He who does otherwise loves the world. Thus we do the right thing here when we just give our attention to the words "are a gift." James refers to this when he says in chapter 4:4: "Whoever wishes to be a friend of the world makes himself an enemy of God." The reason is to be found in the lust of the flesh and of the eyes. This is not of the Father but is simply of the world, as is set forth next.

---

[15] The Weimar text has *egi illis*, but we have read *ego illi* instead.

16. *The lust of the flesh is of the world.*

The lust of the flesh is that pleasure with which I desire to indulge my flesh, such as adultery, fornication, gluttony, ease, and sleep. The way of whoremongers and of spouses is not identical. The former despise the Word of God, indulge the flesh, and act as the madness of the flesh dictates; the latter have the word concerning the institution of marriage and know that they are living in an estate ordained by God. The former are of the world; the latter renounce worldly affections. It is madness to gratify the flesh for every enjoyment of pleasure. But if you contract a true and lawful marriage, that madness of the flesh disappears.

The lust of the eyes.

Many are the allurements of the eyes. I believe, however, that here avarice is meant most of all. For the eyes are satisfied with other things, but they are not satisfied with the accumulation of gold. No, they always lust for more, such as large numbers of estates, fields, and houses. Avarice is not content with the things it uses. No, it desires even the things it can never use. The riches of the godless are like the pleasure one takes in painted pictures.[16] I do not eat pictures, do not put them on, and do not lie down on them. Observe from this how those who separate themselves from the society of men, heap up riches, and erect palaces do not flee the world. Thus the cardinals, the bishops, and the abbots take pleasure in painted pictures and feast their eyes. For them this is nothing more than a feast for the eyes. Therefore are these people not of the world?

The pride of life.

This is a great stumbling block. The substance of life is one thing; pride of life is something else. A Christian is permitted to seek the former, as 1 John 3:17 says, but he should abhor the latter; for it is a misuse of sustenance and property, as we see in the case of the glutton in Luke 16:1ff. Therefore a Christian does not want to exalt himself but should be content with what he has. The world, however, is disposed otherwise. It always seeks things that are high. Everyone wants to be exalted. No one is content with his

---

[16] Horace, *Satires*, I, 1, 12.

lot in the matter of clothing, food, and other things. But such a person is not of the Father; he is of the world. Where there is love for the Father, there is no lust for the world and for things that are high. "If we have food and clothing, with these let us be content," 1 Tim. 6:8.

17. *And the world passes away, and the lust of it.*

The world appears to be great; but lusts are something greater, when we lust for things that are greater than those the world has. But they both pass away. It is really a pity. In barely an hour the lust of the world has passed away. Then they say: "If I had known that it would come to an end so soon, I would have stayed away from it." Thus foolish people build on sand.

He who does the will of God abides forever.

Thus in the end those people are wise who do the will of God, that is, believe in the name of the Son of God and love one another, as John states elsewhere, in 1 John 3:23. They do not love the world. No, they exercise themselves with the fruits of the love for God, and they do not pass away. For just as the will of God does not pass away, so those who do the will of God do not pass away either but abide forever. This doctrine is excellent with respect to the second part of what has just been stated: those who know God may be sure that they do not perish.

18. *Children, it is the last hour.*

Here John begins to reveal the reason for this epistle and to tell for whose sake he has written it. We have said that the false teachers, who were filling everything with false doctrines, have forced him to write this epistle. The Cerinthians and the Ebionites were expecting new revelations and a new world. These he now points out openly, calls them antichrists, and inculcates the apostolic teaching by saying: "Children, it is the last hour." For this is the way all the apostles speak. Agitated now and then by various reflections as to how this time could be called the last hour, even though the kingdom of Christ is eternal, I finally came to know that it is called the last hour, not because of the shortness of the time but because of the nature of the teaching. Thus because this teaching is the last or ultimate one, another kind of teaching should not be expected. A brilliant revelation follows this teaching. This cannot be said of the kingdom of Moses, because it was stated that there would still be another kingdom, namely, the kingdom of Christ. Therefore now that this has come to pass, we are compelled to conclude that this is the last hour. Furthermore, because the doctrine of the Gospel is being obscured and done away with through the Antichrist, for this reason it is the last hour. For this is how John shows that it is the last time. "Therefore we know that it is the last hour," he says.

And as you have heard that the Antichrist is coming.

This is an elliptical manner of speaking. One must supply the words "thus it has come to pass, thus it has happened." Just as the good teachers have foretold, so heretics are arising, like the Cerinthians, the Ebionites, and others, to whom they have given the excellent name "antichrists." Thus when Paul says in 2 Thess. 2:7: "The mystery of lawlessness is at work," he means that the true Antichrist will soon be here and is already making his heresies known. For one antichrist was contending against the Person of Christ, another against His humanity, another against His divinity. These are antichrists in part, as the fanatics are. Another opposes the whole Christ, and he is the head of all, as the papacy is. For the chief article of the Christian doctrine is this, that Christ is our Righteousness. He who is now attacking this is taking the whole Christ away from us and is the true Antichrist. The others are giving him assistance. A heretic opposed to the Person of Christ is not so great as one who is opposed to the merit of Christ.

There are two kinds of righteousness: mine and Christ's. The Gospel proclaims that we must be put into the righteousness of Christ and must be translated from our righteousness into the righteousness of Christ. Thus Paul says in Rom. 3:24 that we "are justified by His grace as a gift"; and in 1 Cor. 1:30 he says that Christ was made by God "our Wisdom, our Righteousness and Sanctification and Redemption." But the pope has instituted new kinds of life by which righteousness should be provided before God, namely, one's own deeds of satisfaction. If the pope taught that our righteousness is nothing and that we are saved solely because of the righteousness of Christ, then he would say: "Therefore the

Mass is nothing. Therefore the monastic life and one's own deeds of satisfaction profit nothing," and thus the whole kingdom of the pope would be overturned. To be sure, they say that Christ's merit saves us; but they mix in their own righteousness. Truly this amounts to repudiating Christ, yes, abolishing Christ and making the Son of God a mockery, as Heb. 6:6 calls it. To render satisfaction for sins is to absolve, to break the power of the devil and of hell. But, O wretched Carthusians, you who afflict yourselves so severely, what is your victory over hell? For if I say: "Indeed, I am a Christian and have been anointed. Nevertheless, I want to afflict myself in this or that way, to choose these and those works, in order that I may be saved and may render satisfaction for my sins," this would amount to saying: "Christ has not rendered satisfaction for me with His blood." "Then Christ died to no purpose," Gal. 2:21. Nature rushes in with full force; it wants to wipe out sin with its own strength, as we see in the case of Pelagius. He was the foundation and the cornerstone of all the papists. This is why there are monasteries, those bulwarks of the Antichrist. This is why justification through Christ has gradually come to be regarded as worthless and the Antichrist has appeared. Now he is sitting in the holy place (cf. 2 Thess. 2:4); and when Christ says: "Believe in Me," he says: "Believe in me." To be sure, he lets Christ be proclaimed, but in such a way that nothing is proclaimed in opposition to his own rules and traditions. I am afraid that most people die in such a way that they pray: "May God be willing to forgive them for having sinned against a rule, not for having sinned against the Word of the Gospel." Consequently, one must fear that they will be damned. The wretched people do not recognize the true Physician. When Moses lifted up the bronze serpent (Num. 21:9), no one could be healed by his own effort until he looked at that serpent. Thus if sin bites us, we cannot be freed either until we look at Christ crucified. Therefore you must cling to the wounds and the blood of Jesus Christ if you do not want to be lost forever.

And as you have heard that the Antichrist is coming.

Thus John concludes that because there are many antichrists, it is the last hour. How does this follow? Now that the doctrine is ceasing, Christ is withdrawing. Since Christ is withdrawing, what else can you expect than the darkness of ignorance and the works of darkness? Since the night is rushing on, it is the last hour.

19. *They went out from us, but they were not of us.*

This is deplorable and lamentable. Nevertheless, it is comforting. The wheat is not at fault when tares shoot forth. Nor is the truth the cause of so many evils. Today whatever evil arises in the world is ascribed to us, and as a result of this we suffer exceedingly grave reproach. If he had let the papacy alone, they say, perhaps so many heretics would not have arisen, and perhaps that rebellion of the peasants would not have occurred.[17] But whose fault is it? It is not the fault of the truth and the light. No, it is the fault of error and darkness. Not he who flees the darkness, but he who remains in it, is the Antichrist. When those people come forth, it never happens without a disturbance. Thomas Münzer was among us. But when he wanted to be wise and departed from us, he became the instigator of a rebellion, and his confederates came into this city and threw everything into confusion.[18] When the rascals come with a new gospel, such misfortune has to result. I see this evil and sob. And I have often reflected whether it would have been better to keep the papacy than to see so many disturbances. But it is better to rescue some from the jaws of the devil than for all to perish. The Day will reveal those who have been of us and have been born of the Gospel of truth, and vice versa. "For if they had been of us, they would have continued with us."

20. *But you have been anointed by the Holy One.*

Here John contrasts the anointing with the Antichrist and the heretics, who were expecting another Christ or anointed one and another anointing. From these he separates those who are his. "You have already been anointed, and you know everything that suffices for salvation," he says. Perhaps at this point his listeners would have said: "You are ascribing too much to us, John." But even if a teacher has a better understanding of the mysteries, yet perhaps there are in the group two or three who know everything about their salvation and have the Holy Spirit. For the sake of these

[17] Cf. Luther's defense against these charges, *Luther's Works*, 40, pp. 49–59.

[18] Luther seems to have met Thomas Münzer at the time of the Leipzig Debate in 1519, but Münzer came to Wittenberg in 1522 and disputed with Luther.

he must humble himself and think humbly about himself. "For you know the things that are necessary for godliness." The anointing of the Latins is one thing; that of the Christians is something else. For on the basis of this passage the pope calls his ordained clergy "anointed." [19] He does not understand that all Christians have been anointed in this way. This true anointing is nothing else than the Holy Spirit, who was poured out in the house on the day of Pentecost (Acts 2:1-4). With Him Christ, so far as His human nature was concerned, was anointed without measure. But His associates were anointed according to measure. Therefore it is stated in Ps. 45:8: "God, Thy God, has anointed Thee with the oil of gladness above Thy fellows." This spiritual anointing makes kings and priests. Just as that anointing makes Christ a King and a Priest, so it makes us, too, kings and priests in the sight of God, that is, believers and chosen ones. The Franciscans and the Dominicans have their names from the rules of men, but the Christian name comes from no work, only from Christ. For if perchance someone should inquire of me whether I am a Christian, I immediately answer this question satisfactorily by saying: "I am such a person not because of any work but only because of faith in Christ." Thus it has also been concluded that no one is to be saved except a Christian, that is, he who trusts in the works and merits of Christ. Therefore one is called a Christian because of this anointing. For Christ assigns everything that is His to those who are His — the same Spirit, the same righteousness, the same sanctity. As a result of this work of imputation and adoption, they are called Christians. For we receive everything through faith. The cowls of the Carthusians do not give it. Christ would have done an exceedingly foolish thing if one could have become a Christian by means of those things. Christ must be preached. Thus whenever Mechtilde was being hindered by the devil, she is said to have replied: "I am a Christian. For I believe." [20] He who says this from the depths of his heart is made certain that the devil will not prevail. For if I am a Christian, I now have the anointing and the Holy Spirit, and am now a warrior. But what strength will the devil have against this anointing? If you, too, were able to speak this way, the demon would have no strength at all. But we lack faith. The whole world

---

[19] The term *unctus* and *uncti* was used as a synonym for "clergy" because of the anointing at ordination.

[20] Probably a reference to Mechtild of Magdeburg (ca. 1210-ca. 1285).

reposes confidence in itself and desires to save itself by means of its own works. Hence the whole world has been filled with monasteries. To be sure, they sing: "Come, Holy Spirit, and anoint me";[21] but He will not come. But if you had a contrite and humble heart, He would come, just as He came when Peter was preaching in Acts 10:44. "Then the Holy Spirit fell on all who heard the Word," when they had been humbled. Therefore John reminds us here why we are called Christians, namely, because of the pious Christ. We become Christians through no work, but through faith. Although we can become saintly before the world through works, this is not possible before God. Paul says in Rom. 4:2: "If Abraham was justified by works, he has something to boast about, but not before God." He had to have the anointing, that is, the gift of faith, if he was to become pious. For through faith and because of no work we are made sharers of Christ. Why does he use the word "holy"? He distinguishes between the holy ones of the devil and the holy ones of God. The demon also has his holy ones. Indeed, they boast more of holiness than do the true holy ones. For the holy ones of God do not readily boast. But that spirit of demons makes some people 10 times worse and is a spirit of pride. Jer. 2:13 states: "My people have committed two evils." Thus it is a twofold sin to call righteousness that which is not righteousness and to abandon true righteousness. This is what all the monks do who give up faith and repose confidence in their own works. This is what John says here by antithesis: "to have the Spirit from that Holy One" and "not to have the Spirit from that Holy One."

And you know everything.

"To know everything" is the true mark of the church of the New Testament. For formerly, of course, they knew what sufficed for salvation; but today we know everything, and there is no need of more. Cerinthus was boasting of new revelations and greater knowledge. Hence he was leading many astray. But John tells us to avoid this man, for he was proclaiming a new gospel. You know this Gospel, but you also know everything that pertains to faith and to a Christian life.

---

[21] Luther seems to be referring, not to the *Veni, Sancte Spiritus*, but to the *Veni, Creator Spiritus*, which calls the Holy Spirit "the soul's anointing from above." *spiritalis unctio.*

21. *I have not written to you as to those who do not know the truth.*

Here John admits that they know the truth. But what truth? That Christ came into the flesh. For to him this is the principal truth of the Gospel – the truth on which all other wisdom depends.

And because no lie is of the truth.

It is a Hebraism to say that no lie is or comes from the truth. All this is said in opposition to the pretense of the false teachers who were denying the truth concerning the incarnation of Christ and for this reason were liars.

22. *Who is the liar but he who denies that Jesus is the Christ?*

Therefore those who have been born of the truth and confess Christ are not liars.

Who is the liar?

John applies that general statement of Ps. 116:11 that "all men are liars" to our wretchedness. Dear children, even though those people boast a great deal and deceive themselves, are we liars for this reason? Indeed, they, on the contrary, are liars. For we have the anointing; they are expecting it. We already know everything; they do not know the way of salvation.

But he who denies that Jesus is the Christ?

This is a reference to Cerinthus, who was the first to begin to deny that Christ is the Son of God, just as Pelagius was the first to deny the grace of God. What was begun by Pelagius, this the pope and his adherents have completed. What Cerinthus began, Arius finished. What Ebion[22] began, Mohammed continued. Thus all the throngs of heretics and sectarians, all nations and peoples, rise up against Christ. "They rage and speak vain things," as Ps. 2:1 says. But to John they are all liars.

[22] Luther is here repeating the idea of Pseudo-Tertullian, *Against All Heresies*, ch. 3, repeated by other fathers, that the Ebionite sect was founded by one Ebion; most scholars hold that the name refers to the Hebrew word for "poor," a title for the Christian congregation in Jerusalem (cf. Rom. 15:26; Gal. 2:10).

He who denies that Jesus is the Christ.

That man, of course, is Cerinthus. And there are more, those who follow in his footsteps. Christ is made up of the humanity and the divinity. Those who deny His humanity deny the whole Christ. Likewise those who deny His divinity. It is the will of the Father that all should honor the Son just as they honor the Father, as John 5:23 says. From this it follows that the Son is God. Everyone who denies the Son also denies the Father. He who confesses the Son also confesses the Father. If we have the Son, we also have the Father. But this is a great comfort for Christians. He, however, who denies Christ in one place denies Him everywhere. Thus those who say: "It is not Christ who has His body in the bread and His blood in the wine" do not have Christ. Indeed, they have an idol of their hearts. For they deny the chief attribute of the divinity, namely, the presence of Christ.

23. *No one who denies the Son has the Father.*

This has already been explained.

In spiritual matters we are kings over Satan, priests in spiritual things, because we call people to participate with us.[23] You see that it does not displease the apostles to repeat the same things, so great is the glory of not departing from them. Therefore Satan does not rest. It is his purpose to call us back from this Word. The fanatics depart from Christ and relinquish their posts. Day and night Satan does not cease to plot against us, in order that he may call us away from the knowledge of the Word. This is his verse in Ps. 2:3: "Let us burst Their bonds asunder and cast Their cords from us." There Satan is depicted. For this is how he roars; this is how he rages among the kings themselves. He seeks to burst us, who are a part of Christ, and the bond of that Word, with which Christ binds us, asunder. Therefore we should not cease to beware of his snares. Christianity is a continuous struggle, not against flesh and blood but against principalities and powers, against the world rulers of this darkness, as Eph. 6:12 says. One should not act smugly. The apostles inculcate the same things because they know these snares of Satan. We have been appointed kings and priests,

---

[23] We have followed the suggestion of the Weimar editor (cf. our Introduction, p. xi) and transposed to this place a paragraph that appears on p. 261.

but in such a way that we should make use of our office and wage war against the adversary. It is a great and arduous thing to be a priest in opposition to the prince of the world and the powers of the devil. Therefore John gives this warning. And we cannot be warned enough, so great is the malice of the devil. To be sure, the devil has the antichrists who have been mentioned before; but he is not content. The more he has, the more he wants to have. He has no rest as long as he sees one person who sincerely confesses the doctrine of Christ. Had Christ not established His kingdom, the devil would surely dash both the King and the kingdom to pieces.

24. *As for you, let that which you have heard from the beginning abide in you.*

Our nature is such that we always desire new things. We are not content with the doctrine that has been handed down and received. And because the devil knows that our nature is like this, he attacks it with his snares and introduces his light. He brings new sects and doctrines into being.

If that abides in you which you have heard from the beginning, you will also abide in the Son and in the Father.

It is as if he were saying: "If you admit antichrists or their followers, then you will surely deny the Father and the Son; for when no new article should be mixed with the doctrine, the previous doctrine must be so certain that no conflicting doctrine is admitted as proof." The devil orders me to doubt the truth of what I have believed. But if you should begin to be in doubt as to whether or not the Gospel is true, a fall is already threatening you, just as it threatened the first human beings. Therefore those who, as Erasmus does in his *Annotations*, ask whether it can be proved from Scripture that Christ is the Son of God must be reproved.[24] But if we accept this, see to it that we do not fall away from the true doctrine. Above all, it is necessary to stay with the bases of the first doctrine, in order that we may be convinced and certain. But

[24] Erasmus had attacked the use of proofs and disputations in theology, and in his letter to Abbot Paul Volz of the Benedictines, which became part of the introduction to his *Enchiridion*, he had stated: "Let this book lead to a theological life rather than to theological disputation."

when we are certain, then you must regard and despise as the hissing of Satan whatever has been added later. Christ died and was raised again for you. It is through Him that you must be saved. "But," says the devil, "what if the laws of the pope were also kept?" If you are attentive here and give ear to these thoughts, you will fall from your foundation and from the previous doctrine. Therefore James says properly in chapter 4:7: "Resist the devil, and he will flee from you." He does not say: "Argue with Satan and with a heretic." But resist by saying: "The Word of God is there. If you want to believe, fine. But if you do not want to believe, go to the Parisians and argue."[25] When you deal with heretics in another way and speak with them in a fawning manner, the devil assails you in order that he may remove the Word from your heart. Therefore avoid a heretic after admonishing him once or twice (cf. Titus 3:10). Accordingly, John admonishes us so carefully in order that we may bear in mind that we are not in peace and safety. When Dinah went out to visit the women of that land, as Gen. 34:1[26] describes, that is, when the church heard of those assaults of the devil and the heretics and was not content with our doctrine, Shechem, that is, the devil, the defiler of the truth, came and corrupted her virginity. Accordingly, it is a great thing to abide in the truth. There are many snares to prevent us from remaining in the ancient Word, but he who departs from it by even a fingerbreadth falls forthwith from fellowship with the Father and the Son. Therefore abide in the truth.

26. *These things I have written to you concerning those who lead you astray.*

I am writing to you who are being led astray. But I am not writing to those who are leading you astray. For, as we see, they do not return. Those who teach new doctrines rarely return. Thus Paul says in Titus 3:11: "I know that he who is a person of this kind and is found wanting is perverted, since he is self-condemned." One should not deal with the devil for the purpose of making him keep his mouth shut. These people are not silent, no matter how much you say and write. Let them go. The devil does not let anyone stop his mouth.

[25] Cf. Luther's edition of, and response to, the attack of the Parisian theologians, dated 1521 (W, VIII, 267–312; IX, 717–761).

[26] The original has "Gen. 36."

27. And the anointing which you received from Him.

We heard above about this word "anointing." [27] From it, namely, from the chrism, all Christians have their name. Now he repeats the same thing and points out how great this royal and priestly dignity is. We are kings because we have power over our misfortunes. "You will tread on the adder and the basilisk," says Ps. 91:13. We overcome the flesh, death, the devil, and hell, not with our own strength, merits, or efforts, but because Christ is the King and the Victor. Thus we, too, are victors. The other power is higher, because we have also been anointed to be priests. The duties of a priest are to prophesy, to be a mediator between God and men, to rule and direct in the things that pertain to God. All His saints have this glory. The fact that our word is the Word of salvation is a gift of God to us, because He has put that Word of His into our mouths, has put the Word of reconciliation into our midst. If you look at the judgment of the flesh, the Word is worthless. But a Christian, who teaches the Word of God, is like God in the world. Thus Moses was made as God to Pharaoh, as Ex. 7:1 [28] says. Therefore these duties — that we are able to be masters and teachers, to intercede and to reconcile — are priestly duties. This is our glory. No one can achieve it on the basis of reflections, even though it is easy to say what it is. Meanwhile this Word, which the devil fears, is great.

Abides in you.

That is, remain Christians. The emphasis [29] is on the word "abides." Many become Christians and receive the Word with joy (cf. Matt. 13:20). But they do not abide. Look at the Galatians, at how suddenly they were changed. Look at the fanatics. Hence they are all in ill repute, because they have fallen from the anointing, that is, from the revealed truth. Therefore when we have the Word, we must ask Christ to preserve us.

And you have no need that anyone should teach you.

The repetition is necessary because of the snares of Satan.

---

[27] See p. 254
[28] The original has "Ex. 8."
[29] Luther uses the technical term from Greek rhetoric and composition ἐπίτασις

For it is the custom of Scripture to state twice and three times that which is beautiful. But nothing is higher than this anointing, which is a pouring out of all spiritual gifts through the Word. For it "teaches you about everything." It also strengthens those who abide in it, "so that when He appears, we may have confidence and not shrink from Him in shame at His coming," as v. 28 says. Thus[30] when the Sacramentarians say that "is" means "signifies," this is not the Word; for the anointing does not teach this. Nor can their hearts establish that this is certain. Nor do they have confidence from this gloss. But they will shrink in shame at His coming, because they have not remained in the anointing as it has taught us. Indeed, we cannot have the certainty of faith from any other source. Satan, of course, can deceive in such a way that the allegorical sense seems to be certain. For just as he, conjurer that he is, can create an uproar in the eyes of the flesh in such a way that he seems to be present, so he can also ignite a light in the spiritual eyes—a light by which many are enveloped in fog but are not strengthened. The heretics are taken in by the false light, but they cannot be made certain by this light. Christians, however, feel in their hearts that what the anointing teaches is true; and they believe that this is how it is.

And just as it has taught you, abide in Him.

Everything is stated very simply, in order that he may keep you in the Word. But whether he tells you to remain in the Word or in Christ, this is one and the same thing. For if the Word which you heard from the beginning abides in you, then you, too, will abide in the Father and in the Son (v. 24). We have been placed in the midst of dangers. The devil besets us on all sides and lies in wait for us most where the matter is serious. Here steadfastness is needed, in order that we may abide in the Word. The greatest sagacity on our part is the knowledge that we have been placed amid the snares of the world and the devil. But it consists entirely in this, that we abide in the Word.

28. *And now, little children, abide in Him, so that when He appears, we may have confidence and not shrink from Him in shame at His coming.*

[30] The Weimar text has *Si*, but we have read *Sic* instead.

Again we see that he wants to impel us even by means of fright to abide in the doctrine of Christ, for at the coming of Christ the judgment cannot be borne unless we abide in the doctrine of Christ. For this is the source of confidence, so that we may remain firm at His coming. Why, then, should we traverse difficult paths and have innumerable orders devoted to works in spite of the fact that it is written that one should abide in Christ? Satan, of course, opposes this, and nature is inclined to render satisfaction for sins and to reconcile God. What should you do if the danger of death frightens you and your conscience troubles you? Abide in Christ. Believe that nothing can be accomplished with your works, but that only Christ's righteousness is effective. "This is the work of God, that you believe in Him whom He has sent," says John 6:29. Thus when Nathan had chided David and David confessed, Nathan added: "The Lord has put away your sins; you shall not die," 2 Sam. 12:13. David does nothing except to abide in the doctrine of grace. He gives no thought at all to rendering satisfaction with his works. "The Lord has put away your sins" was the true doctrine of grace, and David believed this. Thus Adam, too, when he sinned, contributed nothing at all to his restoration but was made alive through the well-known statement that the Seed of the woman would bruise the head of the serpent (Gen. 3:15). Since he believed in this Word, he was saved and justified regardless of all works. Nature resists stoutly, and an excellent semblance of righteousness deceives us. Therefore let us learn this, that whether we are attracted by a semblance of sanctity or are frightened by death or by the sight of sin, we should know no other way of being justified than through Christ. "We believe," says Peter in Acts 15:11, "that we are saved through the grace of the Lord Jesus Christ, just as they are." These people will not be abashed at the coming of Christ. For He wants to glorify His grace, in order that we may know that His grace devours death and hell. He could not do this without first convicting us all of sin. Therefore this is what John says: "Abide, in order that you may be able to stand and not be confounded." And he who does not abide in Him but strives to fortify himself with works will not pass muster—not even if he is a Carthusian. Here, therefore, there is the main exhortation to the Christian doctrine, which alone makes the tree good.

29. *If you know that He is righteous.*

[W, XX, 691, 692]

John proceeds to exhort to works and the fruits of grace, and he does so with various proofs, in order that he may arouse us to do good, yet in such a way that we do not put our confidence in these works. It is Christ's first aim that the tree be good, then that it bear fruit. What is the source of this goodness? It does not come from the fruits; it comes from the root. It does not come from sanctification; it comes from regeneration. For he who is born of Him is righteous (v. 29). Therefore it is John's desire that they become, not false Christians but Christians instructed in the true faith and thus please God and do good in the strength of God.

You may be sure that everyone who does right is born of Him.

He who boasts of knowing and having the true doctrine must show this faith and knowledge. He gets his proof from the accomplishment.[31] He who does right, shows this with fruits, and no longer sins against his neighbor is born of God. And he who does not do right to his neighbor is a false Christian, not a true one. God does not want those Christians who do not do right. God loves righteousness. Therefore those who are of God do right. Consequently, this is the first proof: He who boasts of being a Christian and does not do right is a false Christian. For the son must be like the father. He deduces the second proof from the fact that a Christian, who is born of God, is loved by God. And this is why in the following chapter he reminds us of the love of the Father.

[31] Cf. Aristotle, *Posterior Analytics*, Book II, chs. 16–17.

CHAPTER THREE

1. *Behold what manner of love the Father has bestowed upon us, that we should be called children of God; and such we are.*

Here we have that forge and furnace, namely, that Christ loved us in this way and rendered obedience to the Father, who gave us His Son to redeem us through Him. He who keeps this in mind cannot fail to bear fruit. For his heart says to itself: "What shall I render to the Lord for all His bounty to me?" as Ps. 116:12 states. Therefore see to it that you, too, are aroused to love.

What manner of love.

According to Luke 1:29, Mary considered what sort of greeting this might be, that is, how splendid it was. Thus here, too, John says: "What manner of love," that is "What splendid love." This is more forceful and emphatic than if he had used the word "grace." But he has spoken of the exceedingly great love shown by Him who was prompted to love by no merits or works but by love alone. Indeed, he has spoken of this love to us, who were enemies and persecutors of God and Christ.

The Father has bestowed upon us.

John calls God "the Father." With these words he wants to inflame Christians to know that they have a God who has been reconciled, and that they have Him as their Father.

That we should be called children of God.

It is not enough to say that we are friends. No, John says that we are called children of God. This love could not have been expressed more emphatically. Moreover, we are called children and brothers by God Himself. Ps. 22:22 says: "I will tell of Thy name to My brethren." Likewise Matt. 28:10: "Tell My brethren." And in

Rom. 8:17 we read: "And'if children, then heirs and fellow heirs with Christ." It is not enough that we become children of God, but because of this name we should also become renowned in the sight of God and the angels. But why do we have this name? Because of the love of God.

The reason why the world does not know us is that it did not know Him.

John deals with and impresses that proof more extensively because we should be inflamed as the result of love. For because we have the love of God, we are also called children of God. The world cannot understand that a man accustomed to sins and born in them has nevertheless been received by God into grace, so that he both is and is called a child of God. The flesh does not grasp this; the world does not accept it. But Scripture says in Ps. 2:12: "Kiss the Son." And the Son of God Himself calls us. "Come to Me, all," He says in Matt. 11:28. If we did not have this Word, nature, because of its faintheartedness, could not take hold of this. Therefore John says that one should not consider the judgment of the world, of the crowd, of the flesh, and of the monks. We speak the wisdom that is hidden in a mystery (1 Cor. 2:7) – the wisdom which the Father "has hidden from the wise and understanding," as Matt. 11:25 says. Therefore against this proof one cause for stumbling is this: Is it possbile that so many saintly men of learning could not have known this? This is how they speak. But do not be offended. The world does not know you; you know it, namely, that it is not capable of this fatherly love. Therefore the world does not know it. Nor do the universities and the fanatics, no matter how often they say: "I believe in God." The world does not know that the Father is such a One, even though it says that it knows God. For nature does not grasp it unless the anointing teaches us. If they believed that God would have given us love in order that through it we might become children of God, they would behave differently. They would abandon their own efforts and condemn all those blasphemies against Christ. Now, however, they show their teeth, defend their own efforts, and persecute us for teaching this. But the Father says: "I have given My Son in order that you might be saved through Him; I have consigned all men to sin and un-

[W, XX, 696–698]

belief that I might have mercy upon all," as Rom. 11:32[1] and Gal. 3:22 state. Therefore "whatever does not proceed from faith is sin" (Rom. 14:23). Accordingly, to know God is to know what He requires of us, what He does for us. But those people fashion another god for themselves. "Behold, whatever it is, I conclude it all under sin; it is only My grace that rules over you. If you want to be delivered from sin, learn to know the Son." Therefore to know that in this way the Father has mercy through the Son and saves all, this is the true wisdom of Christians.

2. *Beloved, we are God's children now, and it has not yet appeared what we shall be.*

Again John provides proof of this kind against faintheartedness. "God loves you," he says. John puts special emphasis on this proof and wants it to be impressed on our hearts. You must be a stumbling block and be called a child of God, even though you see that you are in flesh and blood, since you have a stumbling block not only in the world but also from yourself—you who do not yet feel and see that you are a child of God, since you are in flesh and blood and feel the flesh. Yet this should not disturb you. "It has not yet appeared what we shall be." John places the hidden Son of God before us. Formerly He revealed Himself under shadows but did not yet appear sufficiently. And God could not hide Himself more than He does. This means that our own flesh and blood prevents us from going about with a visible impression of His appearance. God does not withdraw Himself from us; but the world, the flesh, and the devil weaken us and thus prevent us from seeing God. The world is one covering, the flesh is the second, and the devil is the third. I must force my way through all these coverings with faith, which is acquired from the Word. Therefore we are children of God not by seeing God but through faith. Faith in the Word, however, promises us many things, what we shall be like; but as long as we are in the world, we are attracted by the allurements of the flesh and are led astray by the devil, and it does not appear what man's true bliss will be. "No eye has seen, nor ear heard; neither has it come into the heart of man what God has prepared for those who love Him," 1 Cor. 2:9.

---

[1] The original has "Rom. 13."

But we know that when He appears, we shall be like Him.

We shall be like Him but not identical with Him, as Pythagoras thought.[2] For God is infinite, but we are finite creatures. Moreover, the creature will never be the Creator. Yet we shall be like Him. God is life. Therefore we, too, shall live. God is righteous. Therefore we, too, shall be filled with righteousness. God is immortal and blessed. Therefore we, too, shall enjoy everlasting bliss, not as it is in God but the bliss that is suitable for us.

We shall see Him as He is.

Where there no longer will be a covering, there we shall see God "as He is." To be sure, we are handed over to death, and in the world we see nothing but the opposite; but it will surely happen that we shall see God and Christ. From what source does John teach this? Because we are already His children. Moreover, a child will not be shut off from the face of the Father but will see Him "face to face," 1 Cor. 13:12.

And everyone who has this hope in Him will purify himself.

John does not resort to flattery. No, he immediately urges me to bear fruit either through love — for we should love the brethren because the Father loves us — or through hope, because I hope to see God. Therefore I must be made clean, lest I be rejected from His sight, since without holiness no one can see God, as Heb. 12:14 states. Therefore he does not tolerate the hypocritical Christians who consider it sufficient for them to believe that they are Christians, remain in sins and filth, and are not changed. If they believed sincerely that they are children of God, they would not be polluted but would purify themselves. Thus Paul admonishes in 2 Cor. 12:20:[3] "I fear that perhaps I may find you not what I wish." But the emphasis is on the statement that "he purifies himself." For the Greek has ἁγνίζει ἑαυτόν, which means "he purifies himself." Yet it is translated properly into Latin with *sanctificat,* "sanctifies." For he who has this hope puts his flesh to death. "If by the Spirit you put to death the deeds of the flesh, you will

---

[2] Apparently Luther is referring to the Pythagorean idea of the kinship of all living beings, which underlay the Pythagorean theory of the transmigration of souls.

[3] The original has "1 Cor. 12."

live," Rom. 8:13 says. Against those who have received the doctrine one must resort to exhortations, in order that they may walk in a manner worthy of their calling.

4. *Everyone who commits sin commits lawlessness also; and sin is lawlessness.*

A difficult passage. For John distinguishes sharply between sin (ἁμαρτία) and lawlessness (ἀνομία). On the other hand, however, he uses the words interchangeably. Among the heathen and the heretics there was an infamous class of people who did not regard whoring, stealing, and other sins as sin and contrary to the Law of God. John reprimands these people and shows that sin of this kind is contrary to the Law of God. Otherwise "sin" is a word used simply and in general to refer to all vices. "Lawlessness," however, is that which goes so far that one's neighbor is made to stumble. We are all sinners, and now and then we fall into sin; but if a true Christian falls, he soon comes back, turns about, and fights against sin, lest it burst forth into a stumbling block for his neighbor. Although it is difficult to avoid being wounded in war, yet it is an honor to stand up. But it is a disgrace to yield. Thus even if a Christian is surrounded by sin, yet he fights against sin. There are Christians who think that they are Christians because they have been baptized. They relax the reins. They are not concerned about conquering sins, but they follow their lusts. To commit sin is to follow the impulse and the desire to sin. Many give free rein. They do not want to repent or to rise again. Today they commit adultery; tomorrow they want to purify themselves. It is impossible for them not to offend their neighbors, if not in a positive way, certainly in a negative way, by not giving their neighbor his due. For the other part of Christianity is love. But love does not insist on its own way (1 Cor. 13:5). Insisting on one's own way is not loving one's neighbor but following one's own desires. Therefore not to have love is to be guilty of lawlessness. He who does not purify himself, who does not battle against himself every day, yields to sin and is guilty of lawlessness. He who does not show fruit in his flesh does not show fruit toward his neighbor either. If I am not dead to myself, so that I do not give up the concern for pleasure, how can I seek the things of others? Therefore he who is guilty of lawlessness does not have love.

5. *And you know that He appeared to take our sins away.*

Where Scripture speaks about the coming of the Messiah, it does not easily keep silence about His merit, which consists in taking away sins, as Ps. 40:10f., Jer. 23:6, John 10:11, and 1 Tim. 1:15 show. First one must look at His merit, then at His example. Therefore do not deceive yourselves by boasting that you are Christians. He appeared in the flesh to take sins away, not to give license to sinning. With His blood Christ wanted to exhibit a holy church, not a church that is polluted (cf. Eph. 5:25-27).

The fact that everyone who commits sin fights against Christ is a new reason for John's exhortation. Therefore you may be sure that you are against Christ. "My name is blasphemed among the Gentiles because of you, because among you there is no concern for holiness," as Rom. 2:24 and Is. 52:5 put it. Thus today, too, those who hear the Gospel become more worthless, more unrighteous, and more avaricious. There is no one who considers what it means that Christ has taken away sins. For He took them away "to purify for Himself a people of His own who are zealous for good deeds," as Titus 2:14 says. This is an important and powerful reason for exhorting the Christians.

And in Him there is no sin.

There is sin in us; in Him there is absolutely no sin. For He did not seek the things that are His but did everything for us. And He who came to take away sin had to be altogether without sin.

6. *No one who abides in Him commits sin.*

All this is directed against the hypocrites. They say that they know God, but with their deeds they deny Him. In 1 Cor. 15:34 we read: "For some have no knowledge of God. I say this to your shame." He who is in Him, that is, in Christ, does not sin; for when Christ is present, sin is conquered. For, as Gal. 5:24 says, "Those who belong to Christ crucify the flesh with its passions and desires." Even if they sin, yet they do not permit sin to reign in their flesh to make them obey through its passions, as Rom. 6:12[4] says.

---

[4] The original has "Rom. 4."

No one who sins has either seen Him or known Him.

According to John's manner of speaking, to see and know is to believe. Everyone who sees the Son and believes in Him has eternal life, as John 6:40[5] says. John 17:3: "This is eternal life, that they know Thee, the only true God." Therefore he who sins does not believe in Him. For faith and sin have nothing in common. Although we can fall, we should not give way to sin. The kingdom of Christ is a kingdom of righteousness, not of sin.

7. Little children, let no one lead you astray.

This is what those do who make the liberty of the spirit the liberty of the flesh. We see that today we are freed from exactions and servitude. Yet we do nothing that is good. Therefore let everyone live in such a way that he serves others. To teach others out of a sincere heart is to be of service to one's neighbor. All that we have must be of service to our neighbor. When the heart is ready and prepared to look out for the welfare of the neighbors, God disposes it in such a manner that there is absolutely no station in life that serves itself. It is the duty of a wife to serve her husband; it is the duty of a husband to serve his wife. Thus it is the duty of the government to serve the state, to punish the guilty, and to defend the innocent. But he who seeks glory does not have love. The life that serves the other person—that, in the final analysis, is a man's life.

He who does right is righteous, as He is righteous.

Do not declare that anyone is a Christian unless you see that his works declare that he is such a person. Where you see anger, envy, avarice, pride, etc., do not call this person righteous; for he does not do right. But where you see the fruits of righteousness, you must declare that person to be righteous through the righteousness of faith; for he shows[6] righteousness and imitates Him who is righteous.

---

[5] The original has "John 5."

[6] We have followed the suggestion of the Weimar editors and read *exserit* for *exerit*.

8. He who commits sin is of the devil, because the devil sins from the beginning.

John makes it clear concerning what sin he has spoken of here. The devil sins in the way he sins from the beginning. He is not angry with himself. He does not repent. Indeed, he takes pains to sin. This is the way the hypocrites and the Epicureans sin. Those who are penitent do not sin in this way. A Christian can fall, but he soon feels this poison and is sorry. Therefore if this is the way it was in the church at the time of the apostles, this is the way we, too, shall fare. In those days there were people who deceived themselves by using the name "Christians." Therefore the preachers of the Word of God always had work to do and exhortations to deliver. To be sure, Christ lets those who are His fall; but He is quickly at hand and brings it about that they rise up from sin, as is true of Peter, for whom the Lord had regard, of Adam, of David, etc. He upheld them with His hand, so that they repented and rose up from sin. Thus David says in Ps. 73:14: "All the day long I have been stricken, and chastened every morning." If I wanted to forget it, Christ was soon there with the rod and said: "Did you do this?"

The reason the Son of God appeared was to destroy the works of the devil.

Here you have the fulfillment of the first sermon of the Gospel. The Seed of the woman had to be born to destroy the works of the devil (Gen. 3:15). Now He has appeared in the flesh and has destroyed them. For, as Col. 2:15 says, "He disarmed the principalities and powers and made a public example of them, triumphing over them through Himself." Thus Christ bore the sins of the world once. Yet He does not cease to bear them constantly in us through the battle of the spirit and the flesh. Those two princes drive each other out. Christ destroys the works of the devil; the devil destroys the works of Christ. Christ builds love, humility, chastity, etc., in us; the devil builds uncleanness, fornication, strife, and pride. Therefore if you realize that you are affected in such a way that you do not want to sin, to commit fornication; or if you feel this way and yet resist; or if you feel that you are inclined to have compassion, Christ already has His work in you. But if you feel the opposite, namely, an inclination to adultery, to fornication, etc.;

if you see that your brother is in need and do not want to come to his assistance if you are able to do so, the devil already has his work in you. Therefore one can easily know under whom you are. If you are under Christ, the works show this. But if you are under the devil, the works show this too. For "the works of the flesh are plain," as Gal. 5:19 says.

9. *Whoever is born of God.*

This has been stated above (2:29). He who believes is born of God and is not a false or counterfeit Christian.

Does not commit sin, because His seed abides in him.

This is a repetition and a reinforcement of the preceding. We who are Christians do not act hypocritically. To be born of God and to sprout sin are incompatible. For if the flesh wants to sin, our birth from God says: "Not so, not so! The seed of God abides in that man." Now the seed of God is the Word of God. Therefore Peter says in 1 Peter 1:23: "We have been born anew, not of perishable seed but of imperishable, namely, the Word of the living God." To be born of God, therefore, means to purge out sin. Then sin is impaled on the spit.

He cannot sin because he is born of God.

Nothing is easier than sinning. But to be born of God and to sin are incompatible. While the birth remains, and so long as the seed of God abides in a person who has been born again, he cannot sin. He can, of course, lose his birth and commit sin; but so long as the seed of God is in us, it does not permit that sin to be with it. For Christ is the expiation for sin. This seed remains in the heart, so that you do not descend into sin. When you have seen another man's wife or money, it says: "Brother, brother, desist from those desires. You are of God." Sin incites, murmurs, and desires to rule. But do not let it rule. Its desire must be subject to you. If you are stirred by anger, lust, envy, etc., retain the seed of the living God, and you will suppress those things. To walk about in smugness is to live in sin after Christ and the birth have been lost. May God protect us from this! Therefore if the works of the devil are in a person, Christ cannot be there. Just as the devil is not idle, so Christ is not idle either. "The devil prowls around like a roaring lion," as 1 Peter 5:8 says. Christ is not asleep either but is stronger than strong. 1 John 4:4: "Little children, He who is in you is greater than he who is in the world."

10. *By this the children of God and the children·of the devil are made known. Whoever does not do right is not of God. Nor does he do right who does not love his brother.*

This is just as if one wanted to state that whoever is not righteous is not of God, and that he who does not love his brother is not of God. Christianity is divided into two parts: faith and love. Faith is the covering, or rather the reconciliation, which covers the countless sins for which we are answerable before God. For all sins, even those that are hidden, are swallowed up by faith. But love checks manifest sins, although before God we are burdened with many sins. Yet John is speaking about the sin one strives to commit. Otherwise there is no one who does not sin. He is speaking about those smug spirits who, after hearing the Word of grace, do not serve their neighbor. Our works amount to nothing before God. But we have the remission of sins as a gift through Christ. The works of love are the evidences and seals of faith. By them we are proved to be children of God. To the promises of faith the promises of love and good works have been added to give proof of faith.

11. *For this is the message which you have heard from the beginning, that you should love one another.*

Above he urges us to believe; here he urges us to love. These are the two messages of the entire Gospel: the message of faith and the message of love—through faith before God, through love before or toward one's neighbor. Here, therefore, he will treat of two kinds of people who sin against love. In the first place, there are the hypocrites, who do the most harm by feigning love. Many seem to have love but do not have it. The fanatics are people of this kind. They wish, ask, and strive for the complete destruction of their opponents. Meanwhile, however, they preach love. Thus the greatest murderers are sometimes concealed under the guise of love and piety.

12. *Not like Cain, who murdered his brother.*

But this happened especially because of piety. Cain, Adam's first-born and priest, was very pious in appearance. Cain considers himself just as saintly as Abel. But God judges otherwise. Cain's countenance fell immediately when he saw that his brother's gifts were accepted, as Gen. 4:6 says. Look at our monks and priests. The saintlier they are, the more venomous they are. This is the result of a fictitious piety. Look at the Observantines.[7] When the Dominicans want to act in a superior manner, they develop a mortal hatred for the others. Therefore you would expect this from the Cainites, that is, from saintly persons who consider themselves righteous. Thus they persecute us because our opinion is true and sacred. As Ps. 109:4 says, "Instead of loving me, they slandered me." Moreover, their hatred is twofold. Some hate us because of money, but others hate us because of the truth. If we agreed with them and believed them, we would be their friends. This, therefore, is our consolation when their rage breaks forth. Therefore let us ask God to preserve us in the simplicity of the Word. If we are unable to understand the nature of Christ's being and how He comes into the flesh, this does not matter. Nevertheless, we shall abide with Christ. I cannot believe anything else than what Christ has taught. If He has deceived me, well and good, as Augustine says.[8]

13. *Do not be surprised, brethren, if the world hates you.*

John is still speaking about the first kind of people, that is, about the saints. It is not surprising that even the brethren persecute us. Cain persecutes Abel. Esau persecutes Jacob. And thus all false brethren persecute those who are born of God.

14. *For we know that we have been translated from death into life.*

This is what offends Satan, for he sees that we do not belong to the kingdom of death and darkness. Thus we would receive much praise today if we joined their crowd. But Paul has depicted their ways in 2 Cor. 10:12: "They measure themselves by one another,

[7] The Observantines arose in the latter part of the fourteenth century with the claim that they alone were completely strict in their observance of the Rule of St. Francis.

[8] A common idea in Augustine's writings; cf., for example, *Against the Academics*, Book III, par. 43.

but they are without understanding." Zwingli commends Oecolampadius. Oecolampadius commends Zwingli.[9] But Paul does not
commend himself in this way. "For it is not the man who commends himself that is accepted, but the man whom the Lord commends," as 2 Cor. 10:18 says.

That we have been translated.

The world hates us because we have been plucked up by the
roots from death and the power of Satan and have been translated
into life. Even though this translating is hidden from us, yet the
devil sees it well. Indeed, even we ourselves know that we have
been translated, because we love the brethren. Love for the brethren is the proof by which we know that we have been translated
into life. On the basis of this one proof I declare that I have been
translated into life if I love my brother, even though I still feel
other sins in my flesh.

15. *Everyone who hates his brother is a murderer.*

John directs his attention to the second kind of people — to those
who hate their brother out of open malevolence. Christ points
these out in Matt. 5:22, where He says: "Whoever says Raca to
his brother shall be liable to the council." Murder is a sign of
wrath. Therefore everyone who is angry with his brother from the
heart or hates him is also a murderer. Thus everyone who is en-
vious of his brother slays him. He wishes him every evil, and if
God were to grant him his wishes, his brother would be afflicted
with misfortunes of every kind. By this sign we detect the godless
and the children of wrath just as we do from the fruits. For the
godless have tails like those of scorpions, and there are stings
in their tails, as Rev. 9:10 says. Therefore if anyone says that he
loves and yet has a heart embittered against others and has that
sting on his tail, he is a scorpion. The heart certainly tells us
enough about that hatred, and when others do not see it, we recognize it from the signs.

And you know that no murderer has eternal life abiding in him.

This is the second class of people. They do not attract so much

---

[9] Cf. *Luther's Works,* 37, pp. 252–288.

attention. But they are manifest enemies, and John does not accuse them of hypocrisy; he accuses them of ferocity. To hate is characteristic of those who are not saintly. But although others hate too, yet they do not do this so violently. Therefore John attacks the false Christians everywhere, because he says that love is not the kind of thing that can be concealed; for love thinks and speaks well about the neighbor. If I teach, console, and pray for my brother, all this can be seen. Love is something that is manifest; it is not merely goodwill, as the sophists say.[10] For love goes to work. As 1 Cor. 13:4-6 says, "Love does not envy, is not pretentious, is not puffed up; it bears all things, endures all things." Therefore love is something that is most manifest. Just as Christ laid down His life for the brethren, so we, too, should lay down our lives in certain cases. Just as love is evident in Christ, so it should also be evident in us. And love for one's neighbor should not be neglected. A true Christian is good at all times and in all places.

16. *By this we know love, that He laid down His life for us; and we ought to lay down our lives for the brethren.*

It is altogether impossible to tell on what occasions we should lay down our lives for the brethren. But when we do lay down our lives for the sake of the Word, this is the greatest occasion. If a prince persecutes a preacher, the preacher should not flee, as Athanasius did.[11] When I see that faith is endangered in a brother, then I should instruct him, console him, and give up my life and everything for him. If I were to flee to a foreign land after being summoned to a council, this would amount to a desertion of the brethren.[12] To begin a new teaching and to give up the old one is to desert the brethren. Therefore the deliverance of the brethren is spoken of, namely, when their souls are in danger. For just as Christ laid down His life and the apostles laid down their lives, so we, too, should lay down our lives, namely, for the strengthening of the faith of the brethren. There are also other occasions, as,

[10] This is a common scholastic idea; cf., for example, Thomas Aquinas, *Summa Theologica*, II-II, Q. 44, Art. 7.

[11] In 357 Athanasius wrote an *Apology for His Flight, Athanasius' Werke*, ed. H. G. Opitz, II-1, 68–86. Luther seems to have known it only from excerpts in later writings.

[12] As early as March 15, 1520, there was a rumor that Luther had fled to Bohemia (W, *Briefe*, II, 67).

for example, when there is a pestilence. Then preachers should remain, in order that they may lay down their lives for the brethren.

17. *He who has the goods of this world and sees his brother in need.*

If one must die for the brethren, there is far greater reason to expend one's goods. If I have goods and do not expend them, do not give food, drink, clothing, etc.; that is, if I am greedy and niggardly, I am not a Christian. But today there is a great outcry that those who have learned to know Christ scrape together more money than others, so that God could now let His wrath be seen. Thus God is merciful. Yet He is not idle. He does not let sinners go unpunished. To the humble, who fear Him, He is merciful. It is foolish and godless on the part of some to have understood this as referring to extreme need. Furthermore, there are several degrees of love: an enemy must not be offended, a brother must be helped, a member of one's household must be supported. You know Christ's commandment concerning love for one's enemies. But you owe more to a brother who loves you in return. He who has nothing to live on should be aided. If he deceives us, what then? He must be aided again. But you owe most to those who are yours. "If anyone does not provide for his relatives, and especially for his own family, he has disowned the faith and is worse than an unbeliever," says 1 Tim. 5:8. It is a common rule that he who has goods and yet is not moved does not have love.

18. *Little children, let us not love in word, neither with the tongue.*

Here John concludes his exhortation concerning love. He goes back to where he began, in order to summarize the main points, namely, that we should love, not indeed in word or with the tongue, but that the whole man should love, as you have Christ's explanation in Matt. 22:37. There are many who feign love. But Rom. 12:9 says: "Let love be genuine."

But in deed and in truth.

"For the kingdom of God does not exist in talk but in power," 1 Cor. 4:20. Therefore John calls every Christian a brother, because there is a brotherhood among Christians. Moreover, brethren should share the same inheritance. But to love a brother who is

kind and pleasant in return – this is a trivial matter. This is the way
the world also loves. "The crowd judges friendships by their usefulness."[13] Accordingly, John does not say: "Let us love those who
are saintly, agreeable, and rich." No, he says: "Let us love the
brethren," in such a way that then nothing but the brotherhood is
loved and regarded; for a brother is loved out of a sense of duty,
not because of usefulness and not because of praise. All the gifts
we have should serve those who do not have them. For example,
he who is learned should serve him who is not learned; he who is
rich should serve him who is poor; he who is sensible should serve
him who is foolish, etc. It is easy to love Paul and other apostles.
They serve you even after their death. But to love those who are
weak, troublesome, and unlearned – this indeed is to love truly.
Otherwise there is no brotherhood, but there is carnality. In short,
it is the duty of Christians to serve, not for their own advantage but
for the advantage of the brethren.

19. *By this we know that we are of the truth.*

This is the evidence with which we assure ourselves of our
calling and by which it is established that we are standing in the
truth. If I am not moved by the weaknesses of my brother, I surely
do not love him. From the fruits of love we can learn that we have
love. Faith is established by its practice, its use, and its fruit.
For after one has devoted oneself to a life of idleness, it is difficult
to raise the heart up to God. Faith alone raises us up. Hence faith
must be put into practice, in order that we may be freed from an
evil conscience.

And in His sight we shall set our hearts at rest.

The consciousness of a life well spent is the assurance that we
are keeping the faith, for it is through works that we learn that our
faith is true. And one day my conscience will bear witness before
God that I have not been an adulterer, that I have loved my brother,
and that I have come to the assistance of the poor, even though
there are many things in which we have offended even a brother.

---

[13] Cf. Cicero, *De finibus*, I, 20, 69.

20. *Because if our heart blames us.*

If you lack works, yet you should not lack faith. Even if per-
suasion is lacking, yet faith and hope are greater. If idleness of
life blames you, still you should not yet despair. For it is the sum
and substance of the Gospel that you should believe and hope.
Although we should consider ourselves unworthy, yet we should
accept the grace that is offered and the Gospel. Even if our conscience makes us fainthearted and presents God as angry, still
"God is greater than our heart." Conscience is one drop; the reconciled God is a sea of comfort. The fear of conscience, or despair,
must be overcome, even though this is difficult. It is a great and
exceedingly sweet promise that if our heart blames us, "God is
greater than our heart" and "knows everything." Why does John
not prefer to say that He has done or can do everything? When the
conscience blames, then man is distressed and says with David in
Ps. 40:12: "My iniquities have overtaken me till I cannot see";
see also Ps. 49:6. Then a sinner sobs and says: "I do not know what
I ought to do." But in opposition to this darkness of the heart it
is said: "God knows everything." One's conscience is always fear-
ful and closes its eyes, but God is deeper and higher than your
heart and examines it more intimately. He gives us a light, so that
we see that our iniquity has been taken away from us. Satan often
disturbs our conscience even when we do what is right. In case
anyone were to be troubled because he had not celebrated Mass,
the devil can confuse him and take away all Scripture passages that
used to give him courage with respect to human traditions. But
then one must close one's eyes and consider that God is wiser in
His Word and that we are not saved by such vain works. Thus the
devil can disturb a person for having departed from the monastic
life and can suppress the joy of his heart.[14] But here one must resist
him; for God, who strengthens you in the truth, is more powerful
than the devil. As Matt. 15:9 says, "In vain do they worship Me,
teaching as doctrines the precepts of men." Sometimes the devil
interprets the best things badly and the bad things well, weakens
the good things and makes much of the things that are bad. From
a little laughter he can make eternal damnation. But you must
always consider that

[14] Apparently Luther is expressing some of the second thoughts he himself had
about his defiance of the monastic vow.

God is greater than our heart.

The heart knows nothing that is right. God knows everything and teaches me better things in the Word of the Gospel.

21. *Beloved, if our hearts do not condemn us, we have confidence toward God.*

Confidence and condemnation are mutually exclusive. For if you have confidence in God's grace, your heart does not condemn you. Love cannot calm your heart, since one often loves in words and with the tongue, v. 18. But faith, which is victory over the world and hell, as 1 John 5:4 says, calms you. From this one now understands why the devil vexes us so much, opposes the Word, and strives to take the Word away. For if the Word has been taken away, faith is taken away; if faith has been taken away, calmness of the heart is taken away. If he cannot hinder the Word, he strives to hinder faith, lest we believe the Word; he confuses and muddles the Word. If he cannot hinder faith, he strives to hinder prayer and hurls a person into so many activities that he is unable to pray.

22. *Whatever we ask, we shall receive from Him.*

That is, if we have confidence. God is omnipotent. Therefore He wants us to ask for everything that is useful to us. You must have a girdle or a sack for the things you need. Satan seeks everything that is evil. Therefore we, on the other hand, must pray that everything that is evil may be warded off. God wants to pour out His goods with a full hand if only there were people who prayed and asked with confidence. Accordingly, our hearts must be inflamed with confidence. When confidence animates prayer, great violence is inflicted on the devil. We often complain of not knowing how to pray with confidence. No one can pray unless he has confidence.

God does not always give what we ask for. Nor does He do so in accordance with the time, the place, and the person we would want. But John wants to say that everything has been heard, even though one does not know what has been heard. Even when Christ asked for His life, He was heard. But the flesh does not recognize how the hearing takes place. Therefore every prayer is heard, and whatever we ask for happens, even though we do not recognize in what ways it happens. God sometimes hurls us into greater evils in order that He may put an end to the evils. And thus He has heard our prayer.

Because we keep His commandments.

These are evangelical commandments concerning faith. When these have been observed, we fear nothing. He who believes keeps His commandments.

23. *And this is His commandment, that we should believe in the name of His Son Jesus Christ and love one another, just as He has commanded us.*

Human frailty has a heart too narrow to grasp this grace, namely, that the Son of God died for us. The principal commandment is this, that we should believe in the name of His Son. The second part of this is that we should love. Accordingly, the sum and substance is belief in the name of the Son of God and love for one's brother. Therefore we should pray in the words of Ps. 119:43: "And take not the Word of truth out of my mouth."

24. *And by this we know that He abides in us.*

Here, in my opinion, John begins a new exhortation in behalf of the preservation of purity of doctrine in opposition to the spirits who corrupt it;[15] for Satan soon rises up against the Word when it has been brought forth. Nor does he rage more than he does where he sees that the truth of the doctrine has been established.

By the Spirit whom He has given us.

For he who does not despise the Word of God, to him[16] He brings the first fruits of the Spirit, which show him how he can learn that he is in God and God is in him, since he feels that he has been invited, that he judges in a different way, and that he has been affected in a different way. When we were in the papacy, we used to think that Masses and orders were pleasing to God. At

[15] The Latin *corruptores spiritus* can mean either "spirits [who are] corrupters" or "corrupters of the Spirit."
[16] The Weimar text has *illis*, but we have read *illi* instead.

that time we concluded that these things were sound and right. Through the Gospel, however, we conclude that Christ alone justifies us. Accordingly, I condemn those cowls, take pleasure solely in the righteousness of Christ, and acquire a new frame of mind, so that I say with Paul in Phil. 3:7: "Whatever gain I had, I counted as loss for the sake of Christ." That frame of mind and spirit does not come from us; it comes from the judgment of the Spirit whom the Father has given us. From the same Spirit we conclude that the sects and the orders are godless and are not pleasing to God. On the other hand, he who despises this doctrine, still wants to regard his own works as holy while he seeks his own righteousness, and does not want to be subjected to the righteousness of God—he cannot grasp the statement that only the blood of Christ cleanses us from our sins. Nor can he assent to the statement that if the blood of Christ is righteousness for us or has prepared righteousness for us, it follows that our works amount to nothing. These people do not have the testimony of the Spirit, as our believers do. To be sure, we can be tried, as Paul was tried by the messenger of Satan (2 Cor. 12:7); but the Word remains pure in us, so that we are able to discern this. In the first place, the Spirit bears testimony to our spirit within us (Rom. 8:16); then He also bears testimony before the world, so that we say in the words of Ps. 116:10: "I believed; therefore have I spoken." By this we understand that Christ is in us. It is not within the power of our perception or judgment to recognize this, much less to confess it; but we have it all from the Spirit whom God has given us.

CHAPTER FOUR

1. *Beloved, do not believe every spirit.*

N othing is more capricious than the winds. Nor is anything more changeable than the false spirits. One is aware that the wind is blowing from the east, and immediately it veers to the west. Therefore John's words are more powerful than they would be if he had said: "Do not believe every doctrine. For by reason of the spirit they dare everything, and because of madness and an overabundance of the spirit they chide us by saying that we boast of the letter and the carnal mind." Therefore John tells us to test the spirits; for these spirits come to deceive the brethren, not to teach them. But you will test them in the following way: He who wants to teach things that are new or different must have been called by God and must confirm his calling with true miracles. If he does not do this, let him depart from this place and be hanged! Therefore the emphasis[1] is on the words "test the spirits," for with these words he touches their boasting as with a needle. It is as if he were saying: "Those who boast of the Spirit will come to you. But test the spirits."

For many false prophets have gone out into the world.

John lived a long time before he saw that the world was being filled with evil teachers of this kind. Is it not deplorable that in such a short time heresies in such great number burst into the church? For many spirits came in simultaneously with the Word — false apostles, the Ebionites, the Cerinthians, the Nicolaitans, and the others who were forerunners of the Antichrist. All these went forth and had not been sent. But on the basis of what test shall we recognize the spirit of error and the spirit of truth?

[1] Cf. p. 261, note 29.

2. *By this we know the spirits of God: every spirit which confesses that Jesus Christ has come in the flesh is of God.*

Whatever they teach, compare it with these words from 1 Tim. 1:15: "Jesus came into this world to save sinners." You must understand that whatever agrees with this is of God. But you must believe that whatever does not agree with this is from the father of lies (John 8:44). First the Jews deny constantly that Christ came in the flesh, and Cerinthus kept denying that Christ existed before Mary. If He came into the flesh, it follows that He existed before the flesh. He who denies that He came into the flesh denies that He is God and man. Accordingly, he is not of God but is of the devil. Nor is the spirit of the pope of a better sort. For the pope confesses the statement that Christ came in the flesh, but he denies its fruits. But this is the same as saying that Christ did not come in the flesh. For Christ's coming in the flesh did not take place in order that He might be made man for His own sake; it took place in order that He might save us. He who teaches that Christ came in this way for His own sake destroys the fruit and the efficacy of His coming. For Christ came to destroy the works of the devil (3:8), to redeem sinners from sins. But the pope denies this. To be sure, he keeps the same words; but he denies the efficacy of His coming, that is, that our hearts should trust in Christ's righteousness alone and be justified. In his bulls the pope condemns the article that we are justified solely by the righteousness of Christ. Yet this is the effect of His incarnation. But Paul contradicts the pope clearly when he says in Rom. 3:28: "We hold that man is justified apart from the works of the Law." And our John says in 1 John 1:7: "His blood cleanses us from all sin." Therefore Peter, in 2 Peter 2:1, condemns those who "deny the Master who bought them." To be sure, they confess the Master; but they deny that He bought them. Therefore we conclude from this text that the spirit of the pope is of the devil; for he denies that Christ came in the flesh, inasmuch as he denies the power and the efficacy of Christ's coming. I, too, have seen some spirits who indeed confessed Christ by name but actually denied Him. For they said that they believed in God yet not in a mediator.[2] But I have nothing before God and cannot think of God without knowing that Christ is His Son and the Mediator

[2] From Rörer's lecture notes it is evident that Luther intended this remark as an attack on Thomas Münzer.

of the whole world. Thus one must begin with the coming of Christ, and when stating the causes of salvation one must flee for refuge to Him who comes in order that we may hear His voice when He says in Ps. 40:7: "Lo, I come." Therefore let no one think of God without the Mediator. Consider how Philip errs when he says: "Show us the Father" (John 14:8). Christ said to him: "Philip, he who sees Me has seen the Father" (cf. John 14:9). Therefore let us abide in such a way that we receive Him as the One who comes in the flesh. He seeks the lost sheep. Let us, who are the lost sheep, follow the Shepherd. The spirit of the Sacramentarians denies grossly that Christ came in the flesh when they say that Christ's "flesh profits nothing" (John 6:63),[3] likewise that the spirit must do everything, that Baptism amounts to nothing. Therefore he is not of God. If you consider the papacy, you will not see why Christ came into the flesh. Indeed, you will regard this as superfluous. When Erasmus discusses in one of his epistles why Christ came into the flesh, he makes Him a lawgiver.[4] All the monks do the same thing. But Christ came to rescue us from Satan, death, and sin, from which we could not be rescued by our own strength. Yes, He came to remove all laws, to abrogate all righteousnesses, and to establish only His own righteousness. Satan, of course, cannot bear the content of the words but tries to divest them of their power. The pope removes the kernel of Christ and leaves the words; he leaves Him the shell and takes out the kernel. For he confesses the righteousness of Christ, yet in such a way that our righteousness is not removed. And this is no confession at all. We know that there is no approach to God unless, as Paul says in Rom. 5:1, "we are justified by faith." Christ has flesh, but in it there is the full Divinity. God has offered Himself to us in Christ. Christ came into the flesh to be with us in Baptism and at the Holy Supper. Every spirit who is at pains to teach that Christ does everything through the sacraments is of God, is glad to hear about Christ, and gives thanks. For he understands that Christ is his and that He came in the flesh. Therefore this has been stated emphatically: Behold, this is the test of a spirit, whether he is of God or of the devil.

[3] Cf. *Luther the Expositor*, pp. 122–126.

[4] In 1525 Luther had attacked Erasmus' view of the Law in relation to Christ, and here he seems to be echoing that attack (cf. W, XVIII, 766-767).

3. *And every spirit that severs Jesus is not of God; and this is the Antichrist.*

It is as if he were saying: "There are many antichrists and false prophets who do away with Christ's coming into the flesh." But the only thing that galls Satan is the fact that His coming into the flesh is ours. Because Satan sees this, he sees at the same time that his whole kingdom is toppling, the papacy, Masses, etc. No one has filled the ranks of the Antichrist so craftily and so astutely as the pope has done. To be sure, Manichaeus, Marcion, and Valentinus came along with the flat statement that the flesh of Christ was a phantom;[5] and the fanatics say that the flesh of Christ profits nothing at all. But the spirit of the pope is the subtlest. He acknowledges the coming of Christ and keeps the apostolic words and sermons; but he has removed the kernel, namely, that Christ came to save sinners. Hence he has filled the world with sects, has left everything for a show, and has really done away with everything. Skill and guile are needed to pollute everything under the best guise, to say that Christ suffered for us and yet to teach at the same time that we render satisfaction. All the rest of the heretics are antichrists in part, but he who is against the whole Christ is the only true Antichrist. Thus one must close one's eyes to all teachings, and the only thought and way of justification to which one must cling is this, that it takes place through Christ. To be sure, one must do good works; but one must do them in the manner stated above. Accordingly, we have heard that the only test by which we discover and judge all spirits is our attention to the fact that Christ, the Son of God, came into the flesh. Heretics of all times inveigh against this article. Therefore the spirit who dwells in the world today strives to take this away from us, namely, that the flesh of Christ profits us. The devil in particular did this when he left Scripture under the power of the pope. Whatever he decided in his chancery, this we were compelled to believe in the church; and whatever a monk dreamed in his cowl, this had to be accepted in the church. Mellerstadt said: "Let the teachers be teachers. One should listen to what Scripture says, not to what the holy church says."[6] But Satan is afraid of this judgment of the spirit and of Scripture. In all

[5] Cf. Tertullian, *On the Flesh of Christ*, ch. 1; also, for example, Augustine, *Reply to Faustus the Manichaean*, Book XI, chs. 7–8.

[6] Dr. Martin Pollrich von Mellerstadt was the first rector of the University of Wittenberg.

respects, therefore, he nullifies Christ's coming in the flesh, expecially in those arduous temptations. If you are tempted to call upon Mary at the same time, then Christ's coming into the flesh has not come into the heart effectually but is immediately nullified. For if I believe that Christ came to redeem me from sin, what am I doing in the monasteries? Why do I call upon the saints? And this is what is said: "This is the Antichrist," namely, the Antichrist of whom you have heard. Just as Elijah preceded Christ's coming, so the Antichrist will precede Christ's glorious coming, and "the mystery of lawlessness is at work," as 2 Thess. 2:7 says. John confirms this public statement of the church, namely, that the Antichrist will rule. Although he already sees his spirit, he predicts that the true Antichrist himself will come. Indeed, he had already come with the first fruits of his spirit. But the kingdom of the pope, which is nothing else than the kingdom of unrighteousness, grew gradually until the pope exalted himself above the kingdom of Christ. Today the laws of the pope are stressed more than are the laws of Christ. No one among the priests[7] fears the laws of Christ as he fears the laws of the pope. No one has repented of adultery, envy, and murder as he repents of neglecting the canonical hours. When they now come into a kingdom here, in that place one finds the unadulterated kingdom of the Antichrist. For "he opposes and exalts himself above every so-called god," as 2 Thess. 2:4 says, that is, above every god who is mentioned or worshiped. Look at those who worship gods and at those who worship the one true God. Yet you will not see worship so great as the worship of the pope is. Obedience to the supreme pontiff is the highest form of worship, as he says in a bull: "And if it comes to such wickedness that they have neglected to obey the pontiff to the point of endangering their souls, etc."[8] Consider how he exalts himself, as if contempt for God and other offenses did not endanger souls. Therefore the apostle consoles his disciples, who could say: "Dear John, how does it happen that so many sects and spirits arise? The Antichrist himself is already present in the world and is leading the world into so many sects, since there are only a few of us but many of them." But he adds the consolation:

---

[7] The word used here for "priest" is *sacrificulus*.

[8] Luther is referring here to a stock formula: *Si in tantam malignitatem venerit, ut in periculum animarum suarum obedire Pontifici neglexerint.* . . .

4. *Little children, you are of God.*

This is how John distinguishes those who are his from the associates of the Antichrist. When you cling to this teaching, so that you believe that Christ came into the flesh, then you are of God, and you dwell in the world as in a struggle. It is sufficient that we are of God. Therefore those spirits that are not of God will do you no harm.

And have overcome them.

For you are stronger than they are. Although they are many, yet you, who are few in number, are superior. The part that is less esteemed always clings to the teaching of Christ; but a showy teaching attracts the learned, the great, and the wise. "You have overcome," which is stated here, is certainly a statement of great importance. Consequently, the listeners must be buoyed up with these words. It seems that those people are the victors and that we are the vanquished. Therefore faith is needed. For we do not overcome with might and numbers; we overcome with faith and the Word. Consider how many fanatics there are today. Heretics are always more numerous than those who are Catholic.[9] When the Arians began to arise, they seemed to be victorious everywhere. But even though the whole world seemed to have overcome us and to have hope of victory, yet the Catholics had the true doctrine and were victorious. And they are victorious today.

For He who is in you is greater than he who is in the world.

Of course, they reason as follows: "Because we are better, more numerous, and wiser—but you are not—you are not more learned or more numerous. Indeed, you are in no respects our equals." But He who is in us is greater, richer, wiser, and more powerful. To such a high level does John's wisdom rise. They surpass us by so many thousands, and all that we have seems to recede into nothing. But do not compare yourselves with them. No, compare yourselves with your Lord, and it will be wonderful to see how superior you will be. The flock of Israel was small too, a little band. Yet the king of Israel defeated King Benhadad, as

[9] Here as elsewhere, particularly in his Latin works, Luther uses the word "Catholic" in the sense of "orthodox."

1 Kings 20:30 says. Therefore do not fear, little flocks (cf. Luke 12: 32). Christ is at our side with a small number; the devil is at their side with a large number. They would easily overcome us, but they cannot overcome that Christ who is in us. On account of Him we are superior to everyone. But no one but a believer sees this. According to the judgment of the flesh, the opposite seems to be true. We know about Elisha, who said in 2 Kings 6:16: "Fear not, for those who are with us are more than those who are with them." The arm of the flesh is with them; but the arm of God Himself is with us, the Son of God, the Mighty One.

5. *They are of the world; therefore what they say is of the world, and the world listens to them.*

Why are we not listened to? The plain truth has been told and made clear to them so often, and yet they listen to the world. The devil takes special heed, lest they fix their attention sharply on Scripture and be converted. As a result, he strengthens his kingdom most. How are we going to be able to rule on earth when our Head and all the apostles were not able to rule? This is an indissoluble proof. It is certainly something to be wondered at. "They are of the world"; we are of God. Their speech is the speech of the world; our speech is the speech of the Spirit. They say nothing else than what the world suggests, and just as they speak, so they find listeners. When we speak from the Spirit of God, the majority snore. No heresy is so absurd that it has not found its listeners. What could ever have been taught that was more absurd than that they worshiped Priapus and the male genitals, that they believed that Minerva sprang from the brain of Jupiter?[10] Absurdities like these were believed among the heathen; to these things the world adhered. In short, the devil is a god of the world. Therefore whatever that spirit breathes, this the world accepts. Meanwhile, however, He who is in us is greater than he who is in the world. So deep is the knowledge of the kingdom of Christ. How people could have been convinced of such absurdities and how so many wise men of distinction among the Romans and the Greeks could have been led astray is more than our reason can grasp. But what wonder? They were of the world, not of God. Therefore they pursued

[10] The source of this information seems to be Augustine, *The City of God,* Book IV, ch. 11.

worldly things. The Peripatetics said that God slept, that He cared nothing at all about worldly or human affairs.[11] Accordingly, these words taught the greatness of the power of Satan. Therefore like met its like and found hearers of the same stripe. Why? They followed reason, which is of the world, not of the Spirit of God. It is easy to believe that bread is bread and that wine is wine. It is also easy to teach these same things. Thus it is easy to believe that Christ did not exist before Mary. All notions of this kind are very easy, and because they are according to reason, it is easy to persuade people that they are true. For the teachers themselves are of the world; that is, they are filled with the spirit of the world. Therefore they also proclaim worldly things. Therefore they also have worldly hearers. But we are not worldly. Our preaching is from God. For this reason one must preserve it.

6. *We are of God.*

Our doctrine is of God, and therefore it prevails against the gates of the world and of hell (cf. Matt. 16:18). Do not be silent about it; but proclaim it "in season and out of season," as Paul exhorts in 2 Tim. 4:2.

He who is not of God does not listen to us.

This is a dilemma. It presents two alternatives: the listeners are either of God or of the world. Those who are of God hear the words of God, as John 8:47 says; those who are not of God do not hear the Word of God. Therefore we judge them on the basis of what they teach and hear. They either teach or deny that Christ came in the flesh, and on this basis they must be recognized. But let no one be offended by the multitude. The robber on the cross saw that he had been forsaken along with Christ, but he clung to the Word with his eyes closed and was not offended by the priests, the whole world, or the cross of Christ. For then he said, in Luke 23:42: "Remember me when Thou comest into Thy kingdom." Thus we, too, should shut out everything from our hearts, believe only the Word of God that Christ came into the flesh, and renounce the world.

---

[11] Cf. p. 226, note 7.

We are of God.

Here John turns first to those who are his. He ignores those heretics to whom the world listens, and addresses the church in general, in order that it may practice love after it has come to faith. "We," he says. This word is emphatic,[12] in order that he may point out the certainty of regeneration. "Of God." This is also emphatic. Those people are of Satan. Therefore they do not love us, for love is from God. Even if we were to humble ourselves before them, we would accomplish nothing. "If a wise man has an argument with a fool, whether he rages or laughs, yet he would find no rest," says Solomon in Prov. 29:9. And Christ Himself says in Matt. 11:17:[13] "We piped to you, and you did not dance; we wailed, and you did not mourn." Next John returns to the heretics and distinguishes them by means of an infallible sign.

He who knows God listens to us; he who is not of God does not listen to us.

Listening to the true envoys of God is a clear mark of the true religion, and spurning and repudiating them is a clear sign of error. "By this," John adds, "we know the spirit of truth and the spirit of error."

7. *Beloved, let us love one another; for love is of God, and he who loves is born of God.*

This is an easy text. Let us look only at those against whom John is writing here. He had taken the first mark from the listening and from the contempt for the Word. This is very clear. For the second mark he goes to love and to hatred for one's neighbor. Sometimes this mark is covered by hypocrisy. Meanwhile it is true in itself that "everyone who loves is born of God and knows Him," and vice versa.

And knows God.

Namely, with true knowledge. For true knowledge has two opposite and diverse appearances. Both are deceptive. The first imagines that God is angry. No matter where those people have

[12] Cf. p. 261, note 29.
[13] The original has "Matt. 9."

sought God, they have not found Him. That knowledge is false. It is despair. The second is presumption, when I imagine that God is favorably disposed toward me because of my efforts and works. Therefore to know God is to believe, to fear God, and to shun sin, which God vehemently detests, yet in such a way that you do not despair. If the law has struck you, do not despair; God has had regard for you. You, on the other hand, must have regard for Him, namely, for His mercy. "God opposes the proud but gives grace to the humble," as James 4:6 and 1 Peter 5:5 say. Ps. 147:11: "The Lord takes pleasure in those who fear Him."

8. *He who does not love does not know God.*

Here you have the opposite of what marks a Christian.

For God is love.

Those who are attacked by this statement do not believe it. For in their opinion they practice love modestly. At the same time they are filled with hatred. Paul often speaks about them. Look at what he says. For to know God is to know His love at the same time. God, who has been reconciled through Christ, loves us and is nothing but love, just as before the reconciliation He was nothing but fury against us. Moreover, He wants to be known by us as a reconciled Father, not as an angry Judge. He who does not know that he has a propitious Father does not know God.

9. *In this the love of God was made manifest to us, that God sent His only-begotten Son.*

John proves that God not only loves but is love itself. It is as if he were saying: "If you knew that God is love, you would know that He sent His only-begotten Son, that He poured Himself out into us completely and handed over to us the things that are His." This is a sure saying, as Paul states in 1 Tim. 1:15: "The saying is sure and worthy of full acceptance, that Jesus Christ came into the world to save sinners." Our text has emphasis and forcefulness.[14] We are sin and death. But through Him, the Son, we live and are righteous. If all things are through Him (cf. John 1:3), it follows that they are not through us. Take hold of this in opposition to free

[14] Here both ἐπίτασις and ἔμφασις are used.

will. Through Him, Christ, are all things; through us there is nothing. This rule of the apostles excels the rules of Augustine, Benedict, and others. Indeed, it is always contrary to their rules. For if salvation and life are through Christ alone, it follows that they are not through our works and efforts, no matter of what nature those works and efforts are. But it is just as it was in the case of Cain and Abel, who are not regarded in the same way. This is not because of the good works, which both had; it is because of the person. Abel's heart and person are better than Cain's; for he believed the promise his mother had received in Gen. 3:15: "He shall bruise your head." To this he clung. But Cain busied himself with works. And what Josephus thought up about the poor fruits that Cain offered is nonsense.[15] Therefore God does not regard us, because we for our part do not regard His only-begotten Son. And the emphasis lies in the fact that John not only says that God sent "His Son," but that He sent "His only-begotten Son."

Into the world that we might live through Him.

This is an emphatic statement, since the kingdoms of the devil, by which the elect are oppressed, are in the world. Consider the inestimable love of God, and show me a religion that could proclaim a similar mystery. Therefore let us embrace Christ, who was delivered for us, and His righteousness; but let us regard our righteousnesses as dung, so that we, having died to sins, may live to God alone.

10. *In this is love, not that we loved God.*

This explains what has preceded. It is as if John were saying: "But this is love, not that we loved before." Consider, however, how diligently the apostles strive to overthrow our merits and works. Yet in the third book of the *Sentences* there is a discussion as to whether the saintly fathers merited the incarnation of Christ.[16] But it is all right. God promised without cost and gave gratis out of love whatever He conferred on the fathers and the prophets. For we are so far from having merited anything that even before

[15] Cf. Josephus, *The Antiquities of the Jews*, Book I, ch. 2.

[16] Apparently a reference to Peter Lombard, *Sententiarum libri quatuor*, Book III, Dist. 25, *Patrologia, Series Latina*, CXCII, 809-811; this passage was quoted by Luther in his *Galatians* of 1535 (*Luther's Works*, 26, p. 209).

this time we hated God. For all our efforts, especially those with which we strive to merit grace, are inadequate and amount to nothing.

But that He loved us first.

Every word condemns our efforts. Yet we do not see this; we disregard it. Then both moral works and works of congruity [17] are trumpery. For my works are not on a par with those of Christ. Nor do they have the same power. Christ alone is our propitiation. Yet they say that we must render satisfaction for venial sins, not for those that are mortal. But let them have their trumpery, and let us leave this glory to Christ alone.

And sent His Son to be the expiation for our sins.

The whole world desires to be reconciled to God. Consequently, some have devised one manner of expiation, and others have devised another manner. But to us the Son has been given by God to be our expiation. He who does not believe this will despair. This, I fear, will happen to our monks, even to those who appear to be the saintliest. For we see that their sects are only sects of perdition, because they want to propitiate God by means of their vows and their sanctity. The works of Christ and Christ Himself are superior by far to our works, in which we have lived at least 40 years and have accomplished nothing. John wants this one and only article, namely, that God sent His only-begotten Son into the world and that we live through Christ alone, committed to us. This article Satan tries to take away from us. In this article the monks have erred; and if they have not repented, they have been damned, as Wycliffe has said. I am surprised that he saw this in his time. [18] The orders base salvation on ceremonies. Accordingly, they deny Christ, in whom alone there is expiation and life. Either Christ has erred, or they have erred. One must impress this well on people, because the devil looks most spitefully at this article. In us that statement of the Gospel in Luke 21:8, which declares: "Many will come in My name, saying: 'I am Christ!'" has been fulfilled. Those who base salvation on works and ceremonies

---

[17] Cf. *Luther's Works*, 34, p. 171, note 31.

[18] Luther is probably referring to the fierce attack on monasticism in Wycliffe's treatise *De potestate Papae*, written about 1379; it is also possible that he is reflecting common knowledge about Wycliffe's work rather than any specific writing.

actually worship the devil. Therefore they had enough money. For what do the papistic monks lack? When the devil wants to deceive, he disguises himself as an angel of light (2 Cor. 11:14). Thus when he proposed to deceive Martin, he appeared wearing a golden crown. Martin replied to him: "My Lord did not say that He would come in such adornment."[19] Another good brother said to an angel of the same kind: "My dear angel, see to it that you are not mistaken. For I am not worthy that an angel from heaven should be sent to me."[20] Thus Satan goes about and seeks in every way to dement and soon to devour us (cf. 1 Peter 5:8). We must fall down before Christ, our Propitiator; that is, we must worship God, namely, by confessing that we are truly sinners and by hoping for a blessing from God. Provide yourselves with armor from Scripture concerning justification, which takes place through faith. Collect, I say, a number of Scripture passages that ascribe righteousness to God. Then, if you put your reliance on these passages, you will be able to stand even after a fall, as, for example, after acts of fornication, murder, and other sins. If Christ, the Son of God, is our propitiation, it follows that the works of the monks are not. Consequently, Bernard did what was best. He repented and said: "I have lived a depraved life."[21]

11. *Beloved, if God so loved us, we also ought to love one another.*

This exhortation is from the previous passage. John always proceeds from faith to love for one's neighbor, and from here he returns to faith and demonstrates it on the basis of this fruit. Others may do what they please; we should love one another. One's neighbor is not served by these works of the monks. We derive the greatest joy from the fact that we have people to love, either a wife or children, and we thank God, who gives us people to love. The

[19] "Nor do I think I should pass over a very skillful ruse that the devil tried on Martin about this period. One day, announcing himself by a salutation, he came and stood before Martin as he was praying in his cell. He was enveloped in a bright red light. . . . He wore, too, a royal robe and was crowned with a diadem of gems and gold." Sulpicius Severus, *The Life of St. Martin of Tours*, XXIV, tr. F. R. Hoare (New York, 1954), p. 40.

[20] On Luther's attitude toward the visions and visitations of angels cf., for example, *Luther's Works*, 21, p. 36.

[21] Bernard of Clairvaux, *Sermones in cantica*, Sermon XX, *Patrologia, Series Latina*, CLXXXIII, 867; see also *Luther's Works*, 22, p. 52, note 42, and 26, p. 5, note 2.

monks desert them and have entered a monastery in order to save our souls there. Meanwhile they have neglected our neighbors, no matter who those neighbors have been. Thus in monkery they neither learn nor teach but serve only themselves. Therefore we should be grateful for having become acquainted with this light. I would rather be condemned by Pope Gregory and the rest of the teachers than by Christ Himself. Therefore let us work to keep that purity.

12. *No one has ever seen God.*

With this one statement I can overthrow all the orders. He who has not seen God cannot teach anything else. John wants to say: "There are many who boast of having seen God and of teaching the truth. But beware of this." "No one has ever seen God; the only Son, who is in the bosom of the Father, He has made Him known," as John 1:18 states. He alone and those whom He has sent, namely, the holy apostles, must be heard. Luke 10:16: "He who hears you hears Me, and he who rejects you rejects Me." This doctrine has been confirmed by miracles and signs from heaven. Therefore when they say that they have spoken by inspiration of the Holy Spirit, you must ask them to prove this with true and genuine miracles. True miracles are raising from the dead, giving sight to people who have been born blind, etc. Therefore we should tell those fathers who proclaim new rules and dogmas that they are speaking out of ignorance. Accordingly, we must see to it that we hold well to this. If the devil comes in a very showy manner, even with hidden thoughts, to deceive us, we shall confront him above all with this statement if doctrine is at issue. But why has God given the devil such great strength? In order that the power, the majesty, and the strength of the statement that no one has seen God might become apparent. Paul speaks about this in 1 Tim. 6:15, where he says: "Whom no man has ever seen or can see." Likewise in 1 Tim. 1:7, where he speaks of "teachers . . . understanding neither what they are saying nor the things about which they make assertions." And in Col. 2:18 he writes: "Let no one disqualify you . . . taking his stand on visions, puffed up without reason by his sensuous mind."

If we love one another, God abides in us.

This loving is an external work, but it gives us proof that God is in us.

And His love is perfected in us.

Yet in such a way that it can be increased, as Paul says in Col. 1:10: "Increasing in the knowledge of God." Nor did Paul think that he had taken hold of perfect love. I think, of course, that it is a healthy and untainted love, a true love, which is the opposite of hypocrisy. And the saints are untainted in their conduct. That love is the opposite of this hypocritical love which we have been practicing diligently up to the present time. John seems to be saying: "The love of Christians is genuine, not false and simulated." Augustine says that the Manichaeans had a false love,[22] which could properly be called a monastic love.

13. *By this we know that we abide in Him and He in us, because He has given us of His Spirit.*

This is the pledge and the proof that God abides in us. But the Holy Spirit is given in a twofold way. First in a concealed manner, then openly, as He was granted to Cornelius and Apollos — about whom we read in Acts 10, 18, and 19 — who searched so diligently. And in this way every one of the saints feels the first fruits of the Spirit. For they are happy. Their thoughts and words about Christ are the best, and they take pleasure in Him. They love Him. To them the Word is a joy, and this does not happen without the Holy Spirit. Therefore every Christian has the Holy Spirit, no matter how great and how little that may be. The fact that he fears death, that he feels disturbances — this he has from the flesh. But the fact that he becomes a partaker of peace and quiet — this is not born in us. To love Christ, to confess Christ, and to take pleasure in Him — this does not happen without the Holy Spirit. To confess the faith, to bear the hatred of the world, to undergo exile and death — all this is proof of the Spirit.

14. *And we have seen and do testify.*

John says this both about himself and about the rest of the apostles who saw Christ.

---

[22] Luther may be referring to Augustine, *Confessions*, Book VI, ch. 7, par. 12.

That the Father has sent His Son as the Savior of the world.

Previously, therefore, the whole world was damned. All the efforts of all men and the powers of free will amount to nothing. Consequently, Christ came to save sinners (1 Tim. 1:15).

15. *Whoever confesses.*

Preservation of the pure doctrine has been the apostle's chief concern.

That Jesus is the Son of God, God abides in him, and he in God.

John is speaking mainly against the Cerinthians and the Ebionites. But what are we going to say about our heretics and hypocrites, who have nothing more common and trite in their mouths than Jesus Christ, the Son of God? It is not enough to say this with one's mouth. No, the Spirit is required. "No one can say 'Jesus is Lord' except by the Holy Spirit," as 1 Cor. 12:3 declares. Therefore even though they say this with their mouths, yet in their hearts it is anathema. For they confess that they know God, but with their deeds they say no and, as 2 Peter 2:1 states, deny "the Master who bought them." When they say that they are Christians, they ascribe righteousness and salvation to their works, which they also sell to others. They deny the whole Christ and what Christ has achieved, namely, justification and salvation, and ascribe this to themselves. The sectarians do likewise. They deny the body and the blood of Christ, and in the matter of the Holy Supper they believe what they please. What displeases them, they reject. Accordingly, they call the Lord Jesus a curse. For He must be confessed in all deeds and words as the only Savior. He who denies Christ in one point necessarily denies Him everywhere. He who denies one article denies Christ. Therefore it is one thing to err, and it is something else to persist stubbornly and to deny. "I shall be able to err," says Augustine, "but I will not be a heretic."[23] Our sectarians simply persist in their vain opinions. Because of the flesh which we carry about we can err, but in the Spirit we must see to it that we do not persist in error when it has been recognized. Therefore the saintly fathers, who were also human beings themselves, must be read with discernment where they follow their

---

[23] This may be a reference to Augustine, *Enchiridion*, Ch. 5, par. 17.

own views. We know what we must follow. When our papists read Augustine, who ascribes everything to grace, they say that he said too much.[24] As a result, Augustine has to this day not been accepted by the Roman Church. Everywhere among the teachers one must see how much of the Spirit there is in them. It is the Spirit if they sincerely confess Christ as the only Savior, not only in part but completely and everywhere, not only with the mouth but also with the heart itself. But where they stumble, they do not have this from the Spirit of God; but this is due to the flesh.

16. *And we have come to know, and have believed, the love that God has in our behalf.*

It is impossible for a heart, provided that it really knows Christ and the love of God, not to have a friendly feeling toward Him. It is also drawn to the neighbor. For consider what a great thing it is that Christ does not spare Himself. He dies that I may live forever. He did not give a thousand talents for us; He gave His life. Through the love of God and Christ we come to the love of God the Father and of our neighbor. Although we do not see God, yet we believe and love; and to the degree that you mistrust, to that degree you do not love. Our papists and sectarians do not have faith. Therefore they do not have love. Hence they hate us and wish us ill. But we love God, whom the world does not love.

God is love.

Indeed, God is nothing else than love. For even though He is also goodness, yet all His blessings flow from love. These words are of great importance, and they are believed by few, yes, by very few. For the most part we look at God with a sad and hard heart, and we regard Him as a Judge. Therefore he who is imbued with the knowledge that God is love is happy. For even though the words are brief, yet they have an exceedingly profound meaning. For the flesh is weak and always has very dense clouds before its eyes. Our flesh cannot picture and place Christ before its eyes in any other way than as an angry Judge. Hence a monk comes with his Masses and is either presumptuous or in despair amid the great

[24] This seems to be a reference to the criticism and "reinterpretation" of Augustine in scholastic theology.

number of his works. The flesh cannot raise itself on high. God does not love because of our works; He loves because of His love. Therefore we must fight, in order that we may conquer and be able to say in the words of Ps. 118:17: "I shall not die, but I shall live."[25] So much about the testimony and the sign of the Spirit. He who has a true knowledge of God abides in Him.

God is love.

These are simple words, but they are words that require faith in the highest degree—faith against which everything that is not of the Spirit of God fights. Conscience, the devil, hell, the judgment of God, and everything resist, in order that we may not believe that God is love but may believe that God is an Executioner and a Judge. By "the world" I also understand the adversaries of the Word and the sects. Here, therefore, it is taught in brief that one must cling to faith against these assaults. Consequently, he who has a true knowledge of God abides in Christ, and God abides in him.

17. *In this is love perfected with us, that we may have confidence on the Day of Judgment.*

For that love of God is so great that we are able to have confidence on the Day of Judgment, on which the whole world will tremble. Is. 28:16: "Behold, I am laying in Zion for a foundation a Stone, a tested Stone, a precious Cornerstone, of a sure foundation." Therefore through the knowledge of this love we also have faith, so that we can pass muster at the judgment. Thus Christ also warns by means of the parable of the fig tree in Luke 21:28: "Look up, and raise your heads, because your redemption is drawing near." This is what the blood of love which was shed for us does—the blood which is more precious than all the merits and deaths of all the saints. But the fact that we do not consider this fittingly and do not treat of this blood in a manner that is sufficiently fitting, this is due to our very education, by which we have been brought up in various ways ever since our childhood to observe human traditions and inventions. The devil knows this weakness of the flesh, namely, that we do not fittingly value the blood of Christ. Therefore if consciousness of a great sin weighs

---

[25] Cf. *Luther's Works,* 14, p. 45.

you down, comfort yourself with this blood of love. Surely the whole world does not grasp the tiniest syllable of the statement that God is love. No human religion can hold its own in the face of the judgment, but it is solely in the blood of Christ that we have confidence on the Day of Judgment.

Because as He is, so are we in this world.

This is directed against the fanatics, who say: "Christ is a spirit." Moreover, they mean a spirit that does not have flesh and blood. But John refutes them. For just as we are in the world, so He, too, was in the world. In this life we are surrounded by all evils. So was He. But we have Christ, who frees us from all these evils. And this life is an embodiment of all evils. But the flesh does not permit us to pay close attention to them. For we see this man rushing into murder, that man rushing into adultery, someone else stealing, etc. If we weighed this carefully, we would also weigh the preciousness of the blood of Christ carefully—the blood because of which we are not struck with terror by the judgment of God and do not fear the wrath of God and death. They make Christ a spirit without blood and flesh in order that they may belittle the worth of His blood for us. But the flesh and blood of Christ still profit us. For Christ is with us in the spirit; that is, He has a spiritual body. For His flesh is no longer physical. He no longer has those physical passions. He does not eat. He does not sleep. No, He is spiritual, as Paul says in 1 Cor. 15:44: "It is sown a physical body, it is raised a spiritual body." We who live have mortal and corruptible passions. Christ does not have a body of this kind. Nor shall we have one. But we shall have a spiritual body, that is, a body that is incorruptible, that does not need food and clothing. This is our confidence.

18. *There is no fear in love, but perfect love casts out fear.*

John makes a distinction among Christians. Some have trembling and fear. They lack love. Others have fear but not trembling. In these love is made perfect. For John is speaking about the fear which is called trembling and which makes man unfit to believe. Everyone should test his faith. If he believes in Christ, he has love. The more firmly he believes, the less trembling there is. The more weakly he believes, the more he trembles. But some apostles,

even Paul, were afraid. "Fighting without and fear within," as
2 Cor. 7:5 says. Every saint feared death. Paul, on the other hand,
rejoiced in tribulations.

Christians have two times: the time of war and the time of peace.
In the time of war a Christian is affected in a way that is far different from the way he feels in the time of peace. By the time of
peace I mean the time when he is not tried in his faith, when there
is peace between God and his conscience. About this Paul says
in Rom. 5:1: "We have peace with God." It is the time of war when
a trial of our faith comes upon us. Then it is difficult to rejoice in
tribulations, just as Christ did not rejoice either. For the devil
sometimes assails our confidence and takes peace away. This
happened in the case of Job and in the case of Paul. Therefore
Paul says that there is fear within and fighting without. It is about
this time of war that John is speaking here, for everything that is
feared is hated. He who is afraid of God is afraid of Him as a Judge.
Indeed, he even hates God, because he would not want Him to
judge, would not want Him to condemn. But here John is speaking
about false and true Christians. Hypocrites lack both confidence
and love. True Christians have love, but they have this from their
confidence. For I do not flee from what I love. Therefore if I love
God, I do not flee from Him but go to Him as to a Father. Accordingly, just as in war these feelings are mixed, so trembling fights
with love, unbelief with faith. Indeed, sometimes it seems that unbelief is victorious. But God supports this weakness, as He did in
Christ, who was completely victorious even in the midst of trial.
"My God, My God!" He cries (Matt. 27:46). How great this confidence was! "Not as I will, but as Thou wilt," He says in Matt.
26:39. Therefore He puts His confidence in the will of God.

Perfect love.

To be sure, love also has fear. But that love is not healthy;
it is not pure or perfect. Perfect love, on the other hand, casts out
fear. For perfect or pure love springs from the confidence that
constantly takes hold of God.

For fear has to do with punishment.

Trembling is the sum total of the punishments of hell. Ps.
31:22: "I said in my alarm," that is, in my trembling. Here David

means rapid trembling, for he was in despair; that is, he was quaking. There is trembling haste when one fears that death and hell are impending. Yet those people should not be rejected. The war of trembling troubles even the saintliest persons. Others call this trial the spirit of blasphemy or the suspension of grace.[26] Here John is speaking about negligent Christians, who do not care about love, fear death and judgment, and do not trouble themselves about persisting in faith. Where there is faith, it is impossible for peace and joy not to be there too. Joy in tribulation necessarily results from faith. Therefore those who do not have the true faith when they are seized forsake their wives, renounce their faith, or return to the monasteries.

19. *Therefore let us love God.*

In short, let us love God; let us place love of God before our hearts. If we believe that Christ is the Son of God, who was delivered for us, our hearts are inflamed to love Him.

20. *For he who does not love his brother, whom he sees, how can he love God, whom he does not see?*

Note[27] that the apostles considered it necessary that this matter be inculcated, since many boast of love.

He who does not love his brother.

John calls everyone who is worthy of love a brother. This is a beautiful reason. For a Christian loves his neighbor as a brother. He makes no distinction between the persons or the things. He gives no thought to whether his brother is ready to serve or not, whether he is wise or not wise. The world loves in a different way. "The crowd judges friendships by their usefulness."[28] No one wants to associate with those who are deaf, weak, unlearned, and ungrateful. Christ loved all without making a distinction—even His enemies. Therefore we, too, should love as brothers even those who are not worthy of love.

---

[26] Cf. *Luther's Works*, 3, p. 7, note 6, and the reference given there.

[27] The Weimar text has Videt, but we have read Vide instead.

[28] Cf. p. 279, note 13.

21. *And this commandment we have from God, that he who loves God should love his brother also.*

John is teaching about faith and love because he sees that these two articles are impeded most by Satan. Therefore he inculcates most what must always be inculcated and repeats so often what he had said before. It is in accord with John's manner of writing to repeat twice and three times what is salutary, namely, that we should believe and love sincerely.

CHAPTER FIVE

1. *Everyone who believes.*

You see that the apostle always goes back to faith and love. For under the compulsion of necessity he saw that some Christians would be lukewarm and that others would return to vain doctrines. If faith and love are preserved, Satan has been conquered; if they have been removed, Satan conquers.

That Jesus is the Christ is born of God.

Because the heretics are of such different kinds, John meets them in such different ways. This passage is directed primarily against the Jews, who are still waiting for the coming of Christ and deny that Christ has come. The Montanists, too, as well as others, denied that we have received the Holy Spirit or indeed only the first fruits of the Spirit; but they said that they had received His fullness. Thus those who boast of the fullness of the Spirit always teach worse things than those concerning whom they deny that they have received the fullness of the Spirit. Thus the Montanists as well as the papists assert repeatedly that they have received the fullness of the Spirit. Hence they apply the words of John 16:12, "I have yet many things to say to you," to themselves.[1] But here the Savior is directing the attention of His disciples to the full outpouring of the Holy Spirit, and this took place at the feast of Pentecost. Our Sacramentarians are people of that kind. They teach that the bread is bread, and it is evident that they consider this a wiser statement than what the anointing taught the apostles, namely, that the body is under the bread and that the blood of Christ is under the wine. They also boast of knowing the mysteries and hidden things, namely, what the tabernacle of Moses is and what

---

[1] Cf. Tertullian, *On the Veiling of Virgins*, ch. 1; *On Monogamy*, ch. 2.

the priestly robe of Aaron is.[2] They say that these things were not fulfilled or revealed in the apostles. It is their opinion that the Holy Spirit was revealed in part but not yet in His fullness, but that these things were revealed to them and that their Spirit is far superior to the Spirit of the Wittenbergers. But we reply that our salvation does not rest on these things, whether one knows them or does not know them. Concerning the things that have been revealed, however, and where the sum and substance of Christianity is, they know nothing, and to this their books bear witness. They are unable to discuss the necessary topics pertaining to faith and love. Therefore Christ says and bears witness in clear words that everything necessary for salvation has been made known to us. For this is how He addresses those who are His in John 15:27: "The Spirit will bear witness to Me." And in John 16:13: "He will guide you into all the truth." Likewise in John 15:15: "All that I have heard from My Father I have made known to you." And in Acts 20: 20, 27 Paul says: "You know that I did not shrink from declaring to you anything that was profitable, and teaching you in public and from house to house. I did not shrink from declaring to you the whole counsel of God." With this very statement Paul teaches at the same time that all Scripture has been fulfilled. What they lacked at that time, this our people who say that all Scripture has not been revealed also lack today. Carlstadt is one of their kind. He says that it has not yet been revealed what the priestly robe is. Thus he speaks nonsense and does not know the sum and substance of Christianity concerning faith and love. One must observe the devil with his spirits. It is relaxation for him to possess a person in blindness. He, who is a sinner from the beginning, does a work either of lying or of murder. With the one he takes away faith; with the other he takes away love. Meanwhile where he is resisted in behalf of the truth, there he does not rest. But where he finds an empty house that is not fortified with the protection of the Word of God, he does not rest until he has conquered. Then he rests again.

And everyone who loves Him who begot loves also the One begotten of Him.

[2] From Rörer's lecture notes it appears that it was Carlstadt who "boasted" in this way.

John is speaking about Christ with other words, yet with words that say the same thing. He is doing so for the purpose of attacking those who say: "We, like the Arians, are seeking the glory of God alone." For it is impossible for you to love the Father if you do not also love the Son, whom He begot from eternity. He who denies that the Son is God does not have even the Father, as 1 John 2:23 says. Thus the Jews do not honor the Father either, for they deny Christ and do not honor Him. Thus today, too, the fanatics say: "We are seeking the glory of God; you are liars." What does seeking the glory of God mean? They reply that Christ is sitting at the right hand of the Father and that for this reason He is not in the bread. But this amounts to establishing the glory of God in accordance with human judgment. Is this not also the glory of God that Christ hung on the cross and submitted to death for us, as Rom. 5:8 says? And is the glory of God not made clear by the fact that He begot a Son of the same majesty and glory — a Son who, as we read in Matt. 28:20, is with us always, to the close of the age?

2. *By this we know that we love the children of God, when we love God and obey His commandments.*

Here John makes a distinction between the heretics and the Christians. The former do not love God, because they do not acknowledge Christ and do not keep His commandments, because they do not believe in Him. For to John to keep God's commandments is to believe. Moreover, he means the commandments of the Gospel, which are not burdensome. But the Christians love God and keep all these commandments. This he says to confound those who — falsely, of course — arrogate this birth to themselves, and also to strengthen our hearts and buoy up our confidence. If this is my feeling, if I curse no one, hate no one, yes, sympathize with those who are troubled and afflicted, there we have the testimony of our conscience that we are children of God.

3. *For this is the love.*

That is, the love with which God loves us.

That we keep His commandments.

That is, if we believe in Christ Jesus and love our neighbor.

He who feels this can console himself and has a good testimony. If you love Christ, you will have confidence in nothing but the merits of Christ. But the devil strives to wrest this from you. To be sure, I can certainly feel whether I am merciful or angry; but when a trial presents itself, this confidence wavers. Confidence in Christ, however, is the only thing that cannot be snatched away. He is a Rock, and he who stands on this Rock will not be confounded.

And His commandments are not burdensome.

This passage has been the cause of much strife at the universities.[3] For it has been argued whether Moses gave a more burdensome Law. But so far as the Law is concerned, there is one and the same severity on both sides. Moses gave the Law; but Christ explained it, vindicated it, and fulfilled it by His obedience. The severity of the Law was so great that it drove Christ to the cross. Here, however, John is speaking about the New Testament and is referring to the commandments of the Gospel, which are not burdensome. For this reason Christ says in Matt. 11:28, 30: "Come to Me, all who labor and are heavy-laden, and I will give you rest. . . . For My yoke is easy, and My burden is light." Why light? Because you receive Christ, that is, the Lamb who takes away the sins of the world (John 1:29), in faith. To have Christ is to have the Lamb who takes away our sins and pours out the Holy Spirit in order that He may give us rest and console us. Therefore let us look to Christ; let us believe in Him. Everything is contained in this word "believe." To believe is to cling to Christ with all one's heart, and not to doubt. This our fanatical spirits do not do. Therefore they do not have faith. Indeed, in our time there are some men — and they are not men of the least importance — who are beginning to doubt that Jesus is the Christ.[4] Thus the hypocritical Turks have also lost Christ because of their various thoughts. They have honored Him as the greatest prophet next to Mohammed. They have a faith put together from that of the Ebionites and the Arians. They keep the Old and the New Testament in part. They retain the luxury and the prophecies of Mohammed and all his prophets, whom they have in great number. But this faith is the work of the devil. Therefore we

---

[3] Cf. Luther's discussion, a few years later, whether the legislation of Moses was more or less severe than that of Christ (*Luther's Works*, 21, pp. 106-107).

[4] Cf. *Luther's Works*, 26, p. 312, note 101, and the cross reference given there.

must see to it with the greatest zeal that we do not lose Christ, in whom we have everything at one and the same time, "in whom are hid all the treasures of wisdom and knoweldge," as Col. 2:3 says. And it goes on to say: "In Him the whole fullness of deity dwells bodily" (Col. 2:9). Everyone who loves the Son also loves the Father. What one does for the Father one also does for the Son. For they are one. But the heretics say that they are seeking above all the glory of God, and they always use this as a pretext by saying that they love God, whom they fear in spite of this because they deny Christ, who reconciled God to us. For he who does not believe the Son in one point certainly dishonors the Father and the Son in this point and everywhere. Manichaeus, too, said that he was seeking the glory of God by declaring that it was unbecoming to God to suffer on the cross. Nor did he accept the commandment concerning love.[5] But the same man was one of those who deny that the Son of God came in the flesh and who hate the brethren. I simply believe nothing else than that Jesus is the Christ, and I do not hate my brother but bestow sincere love on him. Therefore I have in myself the sign that I love God. But in opposition to this confidence the devil exerts himself to the utmost and grudges nothing so much as this gift in us. But one must not argue with him. No, one must simply say to him: "Begone!" as Christ did in Matt. 4:10. And one must overcome him with Scripture, not with reason. You must run to the name of the Lord, which is "a strong tower," as Prov. 18:10 calls it. Münzer was not satisfied with this; he wanted to hear a living voice speaking to him from heaven. But in this way he spit out Christ, because He taught everything. And he was ignorant of that curse which Paul pronounced against new revelations in Gal. 1:8. "All Scripture is inspired by God and profitable for teaching," says 2 Tim. 3:16. And Rom. 15:4 states: "Whatever was written . . . was written for our instruction, that by steadfastness and by the encouragement of the Scriptures we might have hope."

4. *Whatever is born of God overcomes the world.*

Here the battle against doctrine is described. For the doctrine of God is not without persecutions, as is the doctrine of men. We have seen this more clearly than light in the case of the supreme

[5] Cf. p. 298, note 22.

pontiff, at the universities, and in our religious. For even though
they have sometimes been at war either with the Turk or among
themselves, yet this happened because of temporal goods. But
within a thousand years they have never suffered anything on
account of their doctrine. We are engaged in a battle, not with one
prince or emperor but with the whole world. Everywhere the devil
has spiritual weapons with which he attacks the ministers of the
Word on the right and on the left. For this reason we now have so
many adversaries — not only the fanatics but the princes, the popes,
and the kings of the whole world with all their adherents. Who
will overcome all these adversaries? He, says John, who is born
of God. This must happen through faith in Christ, which is the
victory. For what could this fragile vessel accomplish against
Satan, the god of the world (2 Cor. 4:4)? But God is greater. He
always triumphs in us through Christ (cf. 2 Cor. 2:14). Therefore
all glory of victory must be ascribed to God Himself, not by any
means to us. We are far too insignificant for this. Here, however,
the Word of God is required — the Word which promises and extends grace to the believers, so that when they have been hurled
into so many great trials and are weighed down under such great
and crafty spirits, they nevertheless fight their way out and triumph.
But to be born of God is to believe in Jesus Christ. He who believes
in Christ is now a warrior. "He overcomes," says John, not "he
has overcome." For we are still engaged in the battle itself and
are about to be victorious. Therefore we are also admonished by
Christ every day. "Be strong in the Lord," He says, "and do battle
with the old serpent." It is the old serpent who introduces lies,
heresies, and all the evils we see today too. This he has done from
the beginning. God has placed us in the midst of wolves, in the
kingdom of the devil. As weapons He has given us His Word and
Spirit, and He tells us to do battle and to conduct ourselves as bold
warriors under Him Himself as our Prince while He Himself looks
on and is also victorious.

And this is the victory that overcomes the world, our faith.

These are our principal weapons, not the wearing of this or
that kind of garb, the abstention from foods, frequent fastings, and
doing harm to the body, even though Jerome and Erasmus advise
this as the main thing. They disregard faith, which is the source

of victory. How successful this victory of his turned out to be for
Jerome, this his own life demonstrates, when after fasting for two
or four days he was almost out of his mind and thought that he was
taking part in a dance of Roman maidens.[6] But experience itself
teaches us that defilements occur most of all after fastings and that
sheer madness results after abstentions that have lasted too long.
Here, however, we are not advocating or commending excessive
eating and drinking, as though we were teaching the opposite of
temperance and fasting; but with the apostle John I am saying
that here not temperance but faith is the victory over every evil
and the whole world. Yet only he who is sober can meditate on the
Word of God fruitfully. He who eats and drinks to excess is fit
neither for faith nor for overcoming. Therefore the temptations are
manifold. This man cannot believe in the immortality of the soul.
Another cannot believe that Jesus is the Son of God. Someone else
cannot believe that there is a God who wants to be propitious.
This is the temptation with which the devil tempted Christ when
he said in Matt. 4:6: "If you are the Son of God, throw yourself
down." At that time Christ was tempted most not to believe that
God would be at His side in that affliction. Accordingly, the greatest
temptations are mistrust or despair. And things of this kind should
be called sufferings, not temptations. "Throw yourself down,"
said the devil. "Show what a merciful God you have! He could
send you an angel at once. But He will not do so. Indeed, He
should look at you!" Thus Satan mocks Christ in the worst way.
But Christ has the Word. Otherwise He would be overcome. What
does He say? "You shall not tempt the Lord your God" (Matt. 4:7).
And when He had fought with this armor, the devil left Him. Above
all, however, it is necessary for a Christian to believe in the mercy
and goodness of God through Christ. Then he should know that
in this way he is defended and made safe. Many have destroyed
themselves with abstinence and at the same time have lost life and
limb. Even we ourselves have experienced this.[7] But one must
give the body the things that are necessary, not the things that
are superfluous; and one must do battle constantly, but with faith
and the Word. This is the way one must do battle with the devil.
No rule of the monks teaches faith, but other remedies with which

6 See p. 40 , note 27.

7 This is evidently a personal reminiscence of Luther's own experience in the
monastery.

to resist the devil are given. In Augustine one finds too little faith, in Jerome none at all. No one among the ancient teachers is sincere to the extent that he teaches the pure faith. They frequently commend the virtues and good works; too seldom do they commend faith. I, too, once believed that the first four chapters of the Epistle to the Romans are not useful for teaching, that only the chapters that follow, which urge the virtues, are efficacious. But by the grace of God I was enlightened, so that from Paul's first chapters I learned about the righteousness of Christ, which makes us Christians, and from the later chapters I learned to know what the marks and ornaments of a Christian are.

5. *Who is there that overcomes the world?*

You must understand the world to mean the devil, the flesh, and everything that is evil.

If not he who believes that Jesus is the Son of God?

Faith overcomes – not efforts, not your life, not flight from association with women. It happens most of all that those who flee from association with women[8] and take refuge in a desert suffer the greatest temptations. Therefore it would have been better for them to live with women and to enter into an honorable marriage.

6. *This is He who came.*

This passage seems to be somewhat obscure. But it is certain that John employs this text for the purpose of making clear in what way Christ came to us in order that we might be able to believe in Him. But he had said (v. 4) that our faith is victory over the world. Moreover, faith is belief in Christ. Here, however, John goes on to tell from what source and by what means one has this faith. In like manner, Paul says in Rom. 10:13: "Everyone who calls upon the name of the Lord will be saved." Then he proceeds step by step. "How are they to believe?" he asks (v. 14). Finally he stops at the Word, from which this faith originates. This is directed against our fanatics, who regard the spoken Word as insignificant. We, says John, do not come in order to be the first to go to Him. If He Him-

---

[8] The Weimar text has *multorum*, but on the basis of the context we have read *mulierum* instead.

[W, XX, 777–779]

self had not come to us first, we would never come to Him. A lost sheep does not seek the shepherd, for a sinner and nature shrink from this way. The flesh seeks the things that are its own. "I was ready to be found by those who did not seek Me," as Is. 65:2 and Rom. 10:20 say, in order that no one might glory in his own efforts but might learn to know that it is the mercy of God. "This is He who came," namely, to us. But how?

By water and blood.

This they commonly explain in various ways. Most interpreters turn their attention to the two sacraments, because when Christ's side was opened, water and blood flowed out.[9] Although this explanation does not displease me, yet I simply take this statement to mean Baptism, provided that it is applied in the right way, so that the very sprinkling of the blood of Christ comes to us. For the blood is considered in two ways. First it is shed[10] physically, then spiritually, as Peter says in 1 Peter 1:2, for the called saints in the sprinkling of the blood of Christ. This is the application of the blood of Christ; this is the value of the shedding. For He comes to me through the Word and is received through the Word and faith. And thus the blood that was sprinkled physically cleanses and washes me spiritually. Thus this meaning can stand, namely, so that Christ's blood is rightly distributed and applied. For Christ does not come through water alone; He comes through water joined with the blood, that is, through Baptism, which is colored with the blood. Otherwise the blood is of no use, unless you believe that this blood was shed for you. For John came by water alone when he was baptizing into the Christ who was to come. Yet he also came by blood, for the water of Baptism is sanctified through the blood of Christ. Therefore it is not plain water; it is water stained with blood because of this blood of Christ which is given to us through the Word, which brings with it the blood of Christ And here we are said to be baptized through the blood of Christ, and thus we are cleansed from sins. For the water alone does not cleanse us from sins. By this text all human powers and efforts are condemned. The Antichrist comes with his efforts, but the blood of Christ does not profit him at all. The Jew comes with his ceremonies; but the

---

[9] Cf. *Luther's Works*, 8, p. 258, note 48, on this interpretation of John 19:34.
[10] The Weimar text has *offenditur*, but we have read *effunditur* instead.

blood of Christ does not profit him either. But those who follow
Christ come by water and blood, that is, through Baptism; and
thus they enter into the kingdom of Christ. Therefore the new
spirits, who ridicule Baptism and invent new ways, are completely
in error. They call it a dog's bath.[11] This is not surprising. They
have only water, but we have blood in addition to the water.

And it is the Spirit who bears witness that Christ is the truth.

Here again the texts vary, and it is possible that through an error
the word "Christ" was put into the old translation instead of
"Spirit."[12] To be sure, Christ comes through the blood and the
water; but one thing must still be added, namely, that no matter
how much the Gospel is preached, no one accepts it unless the
Spirit is present. Therefore John says: "It is the Spirit who bears
witness in our hearts that the Spirit is the truth." The water is
there, and the blood is there. This distribution to us never ceases.
So long as the Gospel is preserved, this distribution lasts; but it
is not accepted unless the Spirit is present. This proclamation
alone, and no other, is the vehicle of the Spirit. Indeed, it is the
Word of grace and salvation, as is stated in Acts 10:44: "The Holy
Spirit fell on all who heard the Word."[12]

That the Spirit is the truth.

In John the Word is called the Spirit by metonymy, because the
Word is from the Holy Spirit, as John 6:63 says. For it is not a common letter and a human word, but it is filled with the Spirit. The
fanatics say: "The letter does not profit; external things accomplish nothing." John is speaking against these and calls the Word
"the Spirit." Therefore when the Word, which has redeemed us
through Baptism and the blood, is proclaimed purely, then, when
this Word concerning the blood and the water has been heard, the
Spirit bears witness that this Word is from the Spirit of truth and
is the truth itself. Then, when the Spirit has been received, the
heart is certain and has confidence.

[11] On the statement of an Anabaptist that infant baptism was a "dog's bath"
cf. *Luther's Works*, 40, pp. 258-260.

[12] Here Luther reflects the most reliable textual evidence of his (and our)
time, suggested also by the translation in the Revised Standard Version: "And the
Spirit is the witness, because the Spirit is the truth."

7. *For there are three that bear witness in heaven.*

The Greek books do not have these words, but this verse seems to have been inserted by the Catholics because of the Arians,[13] yet not aptly; for wherever John speaks about the witnesses, he speaks about those on earth, not about those in heaven.

8. *There are three that bear witness on earth: the Spirit, the water, and the blood. And these three are one.*

According to the Greek text, the three witnesses "are one." In German one would say: "And these three belong together" *(und die drey dinge gehören zu sammen).* The water and the blood —and much less the Spirit—are not actually one thing, but they "are one," they belong together *(sie gehören zusammen).* Thus Paul says in 1 Cor. 3:8: "He who plants and he who waters are equal." They do this together. Thus the water cannot be proclaimed without the blood. Nor is the blood of Christ given without the water of Baptism. Besides, the blood and the water do not come to us except at the instance of the Holy Spirit, who is in the Word. Therefore those three cannot be separated, but the three do one thing. Now observe how miserably those miserable spirits mutilate this text. John makes these three one; they separate them. In Baptism there is the blood and the Spirit. If you are baptized with water, the blood of Christ is sprinkled through the Word. If you are baptized in the blood, you are washed at the same time with the Holy Spirit through the Word. Therefore these three must be accepted as one testimony. For these three constantly accompany one another, and through the Word a daily immersion and a perpetual Baptism takes place, a perpetual shedding of the blood of Christ and of the Holy Spirit, a continual cleansing from sins. For although we have been immersed only once, yet Baptism endures every day, until we have been wholly washed and are presented to God as a glorious church, as Paul says in Eph. 5:25-27: "Christ loved the church and gave Himself up for her, that He might sanctify her, having cleansed her by the washing of water with the Word, that the church might be presented before Him in

---

[13] The so-called Johannine Comma has been omitted from the first edition of Erasmus' Greek New Testament; its appearance in subsequent editions accounts for its translation into the standard versions, including Luther's own.

splendor." Thus we have been cleansed through the blood, the water, and the Word of the Spirit; and thus we are saved.

In the last lecture [14] we heard about the manner in which faith or the Spirit of our victory comes to us, namely, through the testimony, that is, the Gospel, or the Word. He who seeks to be made righteous as the result of something else deceives himself. The spoken Word is proclaimed after the apostles have been sent. They did nothing in the world, yes, bore witness of nothing, except through the Word. Thus today the Spirit bears witness in no other way than through the word of the apostles. Accordingly, John proceeds in his way and exhorts us to have faith and to cling firmly to this word as to the testimony to which everything else comes together.

9. *If we receive the testimony of men, the testimony of God is greater.*

John is arguing from the less to the greater. [15] Since I have transmitted to you the way to acquire faith, you must now take care to observe this way. For there is nothing that Satan attacks more than he attacks this testimony. To this he directs all his armament, to keep us from preserving this testimony. We accept the testimony of men; that is, we believe men who testify, as is stated in the Law, in Deut. 17:6, "On the evidence of two or three witnesses there is truth." But what are all the testimonies of men in comparison with the testimonies of God? We not only accept the testimony of men, but we are ready to accept the testimony even of heretics; we believe the detractors, etc. Why do we not rather accept the divine testimony? It is our wretchedness that we believe the testimonies of men. There is a similar argument in Gal. 3:15, where we read: "No one annuls even a man's will . . . once it has been ratified."

For this is the testimony of God, which is greater.

John is speaking about the testimony which we are announcing to you.

[14] This material seems to have been delivered on November 5; the "last lecture" seems to have been given on October 30.

[15] Luther is referring to the familiar logical idea of the argument *a minori ad maius.*

That He has borne witness concerning His Son.

It is the whole function of our preaching to establish this testimony concerning the Son of God in the hearts of men. But Satan employs all his delusions for the purpose of denying that Christ is that Son of God. Thus the fanatics deny Christ because they deny His words. Accordingly, John stresses only this testimony, in order that we may believe that Christ is the Son of God. If I believe this, I now believe that God is truthful in His Word and does not lie.

10. *He who believes in the Son of God has the testimony in himself.*

Here John makes clear what accepting the testimony is, namely, believing. For he who accepts the testimony of God believes in the Son of God; he who rejects it does not believe and does not have in himself the testimony concerning the Son.

But he who does not believe the Son makes Him a liar.

The apostle seems to be employing many useless words. But they are necessary. He states how dangerous it is not to accept the Son. For he who does not do so makes the Father a liar, which is horrible. The fanatics make God the Father a liar, at least in order that they themselves may be truthful. You see how they teach. Of course, they urge us for show to abandon everything and profess only the Spirit, and to abandon the elements of the world (cf. Gal. 4:9) and cling to piety. They delude people with these deceptive words. Besides, those words "This is My body" are not elements of the world. To make God a liar is to deprive Him of His divinity; but when His divinity has been taken away, this is tantamount to making Him the devil. To make oneself the truthful one is tantamount to making oneself God. These are horrible things. They terrify him who is not certain that he is teaching things that are divine, especially in this doctrine of faith. In the matter of works it is not so dangerous to stumble. For if the foundation remains solid, you will be able to rise again. But not to believe in the Son is fraught with great danger, for it amounts to calling the Father a liar to His face. To deny God's truth is to deny His divinity. Not to believe in the Son is the same as not believing the testimony of the Father concerning the Son, as the Arians and Cerinthus did. "Take and eat" are exceedingly simple words, and here Christ is speaking without using any figure at all. Yet they do not believe this word. Therefore they deny the Son; for when I say: "What you are saying is not true," I am saying at the same time: "It is not true that you are God." Thus every heretic dashes against this stone of offense. For if they say: "Those words are wrong according to the letter," then I say: "Therefore the devil has spoken them." O wretched people! Our Lord lets you fall! May He guard our path, lest we, too, fall in this point! When we hold to the foundation and the testimony, then we shall easily rise again from all evil deeds. Those who sin gravely in other respects will acknowledge this someday and find a remedy. But where one has no knowledge of the error and the sin, there no remedy is at hand. This is the soul's greatest danger. Beware of it!

11. *And this is the testimony, that God has given us eternal life;
and this life is in His Son.*

This passage of exhortation has to do with the advantage, just as the previous passage has to do with the danger and the harm. If you accept this testimony, you will have eternal life. It is not pretense or hypocrisy. No, it is a serious matter. It is not a testimony that boasts of its own splendor. No, it is a testimony that gives eternal life to him who believes the testimony of the Father concerning the Son. Therefore we guard this testimony. For it is of the utmost importance that the divinity of Christ be preserved, then that we have eternal life. Every false teacher does away with the divinity, does a devilish thing, and puts the devil in God's place. For every false teacher is the cause of idolatry and ever-lasting condemnation. For a false teacher does away with God and every man so far as he himself is concerned, not by doing away with God according to His nature but by taking Him out of the hearts of men. Therefore Peter says of these people in 2 Peter 2: 1, 10 that they are bold and not afraid to introduce blaspheming sects. How, then, has He given eternal life? This life He has given in His Son.

12. *He who has the Son has life; he who does not have the Son of
God does not have life.*

Therefore if you want to have eternal life, it is necessary for you to have the Son. If you want to have the Son, it is necessary for you to have the testimony of the Father concerning the Son. And thus our entire life consists in clinging to the testimony of the Father concerning the Son. But if the truth is in the Son, and if the Son is our life, it is necessary for Him to be true God. But just as the fanatics now devise glosses, so the Arians — in a certain epistle which has the appearance of being completely Catholic — once attributed everything to the Son of God but denied that He is God in His essence. Read Hilary in his books on the Trinity.[16] He who receives life from another must have his essence from him from whom he has received life. No one who does not believe in a man is condemned; but he who does not believe in the Son of God will be condemned, and he who does believe in the Son of God will be saved. Therefore He in whom we believe must be true God. God should not be sought or known except through the testimony; for to be unwilling to be content with the manner in which God wants to be found by us but to seek and prescribe one's own manner is to find the devil, not God. We must take care to preserve this testimony, just as the apostle does here; for we know the danger and the profit.

13. *These things I am writing to you that you may know that you have eternal life.*

This, says John, pertains to all our doctrines and exhortations, in order that our conscience may be persuaded that we have a sure way to know eternal life. For our heart is too narrow. Consequently, it cannot understand these blessings of God unless it is continually admonished and exercised. For, as 1 Cor. 2:9 says, "no eye has seen, nor ear heard, nor the heart of man conceived, what God has prepared for those who love Him." We barely grasp these earthly and transitory things. How much less the heavenly things! Therefore the Spirit has been given to us in order that we may know what great things have been presented to us by God. But nothing contributes so much to the understanding of these things as assiduous practice and the cross. For contrary to the manifest understanding of all men I must believe and be certain that I must live forever, even though I see in the meanwhile that I am being consumed by

---

[16] Cf. Hilary, *On the Trinity*, Book IV, pars. 12–13.

worms. Indeed, I must believe and be sure that I not only shall have but do have eternal life. For "he who believes in Me has eternal life," as John 3:16 says. But because this is a difficult mystery, we must treat of it constantly in order that we may retain it and grow in faith. It is not like geometry, which suffices once it has been grasped; but these things must be learned assiduously, and it is through tribulations that we must be exercised in learning them. Thus in Rom. 15:4 it is Paul's wish "that by steadfastness and by the encouragement of the Scriptures we might have hope." In us we have fear, trembling, and darkness. Yet in such great darkness we must believe that we have life. Therefore John wants us to know and no longer to doubt or tremble but to have the certain knowledge that we live and grow in faith. Then, lest someone deceive us, John says once more that he is writing against the fanatics. To them the letter is something dead on the paper. But John says: "I am writing to you"; for Scripture must serve the purpose of bringing it about that his epistle is a means and a vehicle by which one comes to faith and eternal life. For in the last chapter of his Gospel, John speaks as follows: "These are written that you may believe" (John 20:31). Accordingly, we should know that God's testimony does not come to us except through the spoken Word or through Scripture. "All Scripture is inspired by God and profitable," as 2 Tim. 3:16 says; and (v. 15) "from childhood you have been acquainted with the Sacred Writings which are able to instruct you through faith." Likewise in 1 Tim. 4:13: "Attend to reading." Why do they themselves produce and write books if the letter avails and profits nothing? Why do they want to instruct others for us with their writings? If they say that the Spirit comes before the Scriptures and that they have the Spirit first and then write, this is nothing. For in this way Scripture is useful for nothing else than a display. Listen to Christ, who says in John 17:20: "I do not pray for these only but also for those who are to believe in Me through their Word." Certainly through the spoken or written Word, not through the internal Word. Above all, therefore, one must listen to and read the Word, which is the vehicle of the Holy Spirit. When the Word is read, the Holy Spirit is present; and thus it is impossible either to listen to or to read Scripture without profit.

You who believe in the name of the Son of God.

Not in our name but in the name of the Son of God. Many be-

lieve in the name of Benedict or Francis; few believe in the name
of Christ. I am referring to those who trust in works alone, not in
the merits of Christ.

14. *And this is the confidence that we have toward God, that if we*
    ask anything according to His will, He hears us.

This is an exhortation for Christians, who have been taught how
they should believe and love, that they have this godliness from
the Word that has been proclaimed, and that there is no other way
to live than in faith and love. Now John anticipates a question:
"What if I should have a frigid heart and feel that I lack this faith?"
"This is the remedy," says John. "Pray, ask; and He will hear you."
Thus James says in chapter 1:5: "If any of you lacks wisdom, let
him ask God, who gives to all men generously and without re-
proaching, and it will be given him." Therefore the main thing is
that you devote yourself to prayers. Thus Paul says in Phil. 4:6:
"Have no anxiety about anything, but in everything by prayer and
supplication with thanksgiving let your requests be made known
to God." Likewise Augustine: "Lord, give what Thou com-
mandest."[17] We, too, should say: "Lord, grant that we may believe." Therefore this is an exhortation to prayer, and John describes it in an excellent manner. First he arouses to confidence,
which is the soul of prayer. Next he prescribes the way you should
pray, namely, that you should ask for what is expedient according
to the will of God. The confidence that you will be heard should be
present. For as James 1:7, 6 says, "a double-minded man is unstable
in all his ways. Therefore let him ask in faith, with no doubting."
Consequently, he who desires to pray properly should not pray the
canonical hours but should say brief prayers, as David and Jeremiah
did, yet in such a way that he is persuaded that he will be heard.
"Before they call, I will answer," Is. 65:24 says. Then we should
accept His promises and pray according to His will. If I feel that
I am being afflicted and that I am being tempted by lust, and if
I know His will, I pray that I may be free from lust or everything of this kind. When we are sure that we are praying according
to His will, we may have the confidence and be certain that He
hears us.

---

[17] These words of Augustine figured prominently in the Pelagian controversy;
cf. Augustine, *On the Spirit and the Letter*, ch. 22.

15. *And if we know that He hears us in whatever we ask, we know that we have obtained the requests we have made of Him.*

If because of this confidence you are persuaded that you are heard, He will also give you what you have asked for. When Solomon prayed, as is told in 1 Kings 3:5-11, God said: "Ask what I shall give you." But Solomon said: "Give Thy servant an understanding heart." This prayer pleased God. Therefore He said: "I will give you what you have asked for." Because Solomon had asked according to the will of God, he was heard. But it is not seemly to fix the manner and the time. To Abraham the Seed had been promised, and a son from his body, as Gen. 13:16, 15:5, and 18:10 show. This fulfillment was put off for almost 20 years. Abraham waited patiently. Sarah also thought: "Perhaps not from me but from another woman." Therefore we should determine for God neither the time nor the manner of hearing and granting our prayers. We should only wait patiently and diligently. And this suffices for a Christian, because a Christian is content to know that he pleases God. And he is persuaded that his prayer is heard, that it is not neglected, but that it is accepted. And this is confidence according to His will, as John said above. "Behold," he says, "they have obtained their requests." Yet this is not apparent. Indeed, sometimes the opposite seems to be true. But the outcome proves that they had faith and were in grace. When God was about to deliver the Children of Israel from the hand of the Egyptians, He led them into difficulties, so that wherever they looked, they saw death and destruction. Then reason said, as in Ex. 14:11: "Is it because there were no graves in Egypt?" They have deliverance, but they see neither the manner nor the persons. The sea opens, but this manner could not go up into their hearts. There were also countless other ways in which the divine power could have delivered them. Maybe He could have removed a mountain. Thus we, too, must say: "Lord, Thou wilt give the where and the when, and in a better way than I shall understand." The ways of deliverance are not known to us, yet meanwhile we should be sure that we shall be heard, yes, that we have been heard. St. Bernard says to his brothers: "Brothers, do not despise our prayer; for when it has gone forth from your mouths, it has been heard in heaven. And be sure either that what you have asked for will be granted us or that what has been asked for has not been beneficial."[18] This was

---

[18] This was a favorite quotation of Luther's; cf. *Luther's Works*, 24, p. 395.

certainly said correctly. Thus we, too, should not despise our prayers.

In the past it has happened to us that we did not know how to pray but knew only how to chatter and to read prayers. God pays no attention to this. For no one thinks like this: "Lord, Thou hast commanded to pray. Lord, Thou hast promised to hear prayer." Yet these two things will be necessary. Later on one comes and asks for something great for the church, for the ministers of the Word, and for the government. For prayers poured out for many great things give pleasure. Therefore I often pray like this: "Give assistance to the government, be with our brethren, recall those who go astray, strengthen and preserve those who are steadfast. This, Lord, is my prayer. I would not have the courage to pray if Thou hadst not commanded it and hadst not promised to hear, etc."

16. *He who knows that his brother is committing a sin that is not unto death shall ask, and life will be given to him who does not commit a sin unto death. There is sin unto death; I do not say that one is to pray for that.*

Here a secret objection lies hidden. I know, dear brother, that there are sinners in the church. They sin against a brother "I do not say to you seven times but seventy times seven," as Matt. 18:22 says. There are some sins that cannot be remitted. Therefore one prays for them in vain. But from this text a gloss has flowed, namely, one sin is venial, another is mortal. I understand a mortal sin to be like the sin committed by Korah, Dathan, and Abiram, about which one reads in Num. 16:15, where Moses prays against them, saying: "Lord do not respect their offerings. Thou knowest that I have never taken even an ass from them." Sins of this kind are those that are committed under the guise of godliness and do not mean to be sins, as they actually are. Sins of this kind are those of the heretics, who are hardened after one or another rebuke. Therefore the apostle gives the injunction in Titus 3:10 to avoid them. For other sins—sins that are committed either because of weakness or on some occasion—I can pray that they be remitted and not imputed. For the heretics I cannot do this when they do not acknowledge their sin. To be sure, I can pray that God may convert them before they are hardened through and through; but when they refuse to be corrected, I pray: "Lord, do not let what these people desire be righteousness or right; but reveal Thy righteousness in them." Therefore I understand heresy, which they substitute for the truth, to be a mortal sin. When they do not come to their senses after being admonished once and once again, then it is a mortal sin. Yet to these one can add those who sin stubbornly and defiantly, like Judas, who was warned enough but, because of his stubborn wickedness, could not be corrected. Saul, too, died in sin because he did not hope in the Lord. But those who sin in such a way that they want to uphold and defend an acknowledged error — in them one finds the height of obstinacy. In addition, there is the sin against the Spirit, or obstinacy in wickedness, an assault against the acknowledged truth, and impenitence to the end, of which Matt. 12:32 speaks. Another sin is not mortal, as, for example, the sin of Paul, who says in 1 Tim. 1:13 that he "had acted ignorantly in unbelief." In like manner, the sin of the crucifiers was not mortal. To them Peter says in Acts 3:17: "And now, brethren, I know that you acted in ignorance." "For if they had known, they would never have crucified the Lord of glory," as 1 Cor. 2:8 says. On the other hand, this sin, because it is defended after it has been sufficiently revealed and known, is mortal; for it resists the grace of God, the means of salvation, and the remission of sins. Where there is no acknowledgment, there is no remission. For the remission of sins is preached to those who feel sin and seek the grace of God. The others, however, are not troubled by scruples of conscience. Nor do they acknowledge and feel sin.

17. *All wrongdoing is sin. And there is sin which is not unto death.*

Wrongdoing, of course, is referred to sin against God and one's neighbor. But not all wrongdoing is a mortal sin. Satan harasses us with imagined and true sins. Where he finds a true sin, he makes it greater than it is; and he makes the wrath of God greater in order that he may thrust us away from confidence in God. If it is not a true sin, he takes a work that is good and has been done out of a pious heart and makes a great sin of it. This is the kind of master of making sin he is. Therefore John seems to be saying: "Every wrongdoer is a sinner, but some sins are not mortal." Let us not despair; let us stretch out our hands to one another and take heart.

18. *We know that anyone born of God does not sin, but the birth from God keeps him.*

This is a finishing touch and a brief recapitulation. But the substance is this: We know that anyone born of God does not sin, but that his birth from God — that is, the fact that he is born of God — or the birth of faith — which he has from God — keeps him. Therefore those things are in conflict: that he is born of God and that he sins. But it can happen that he falls now and then. Then he sins not as one born of God but as a human being. Thus Paul says in Rom. 7:25: "I serve the Law of God with my mind, but with my flesh I serve the law of sin." A Christian is divided into two parts. At times a person is overtaken when that birth is not sustained on the basis of the Word of God and the flesh prevails, so that he does what he would not do in other circumstances. At times the Spirit overcomes unbelief and the emotions, and thus he does not sin.

And the evil one will not touch him.

The evil one is either Satan or the world. But why will he not touch him? That is, why does he not do what the evil one would want him to do? Because so long as he remains standing in the birth, he can be tempted but cannot be overcome. And soon he rises again. Satan touches him by tempting him, but he does not touch him by overcoming him. Therefore let us be zealous to remain in the faith and in the birth from God. In this way we are fortified, so that we cannot sin.

19. . . . *the whole world is in the power of the devil.*

This is its own proper title: the world is a realm of wrongdoing, and the devil is lord over it. Those who do not believe are citizens of the world, submit to its rule, and, together with the world, are in the power of the evil one. But those who believe tear themselves away from the world and the realm of wickedness and are gathered into the realm of faith and salvation. Therefore a Christian should trust no one; but everyone should act as though he were dealing with one who is evil, with a foe and an enemy — should act as though he were dealing with one who is ungrateful, and should expect persecution and the height of ingratitude in return for deeds of kindness. For what do they pay for our troubles? Nothing else than their desire that we be thrust into hell and be afflicted with evils of every kind. For the greatest deeds of kindness they return the greatest deeds of wickedness. Accordingly, this passage pertains to patience.

20. *And we know that the Son of God has come and has given us understanding.*

Understanding, discernment, that is, the Holy Spirit. This is beautifully stated. For when I have this understanding, that is, this discernment, that Christ came, I now have the discernment of the Holy Spirit. Then we can boast of having the Holy Spirit, because He is never torn away from His Word. And then we learn to know the true God.

That we may be in His true Son.

For there are many who believe that Christ is the Son of God but not the true Son. Therefore John adds that we are in the true Son of God, and indeed in His own Son, the Son begotten from eternity.

He [namely, *the Son*] *is the true God and eternal life.*

Now this is the sum and substance. This is a compendium of salvation, because of which the church triumphs and exults, namely, that the man is true God and that in this God and man we all have eternal life. The Arians concede that Christ is God but not the true God; and although they sometimes called Him "true," they denied that He is consubstantial with the Father, and thus they acknowledged neither the Father nor the Son. Nor did they have eternal life; for "this is eternal life, that they know Thee, the only true God, and Jesus Christ, whom Thou hast sent," as John 17:3 says.

21. *Little children, keep yourselves from idols.*

I believe that this was added for the sake of those who were weak. For because at that time they were being urged by imprisonment and torture to deny the true God, they had to be encouraged not only not to adore idols but to keep themselves from them and not to defile themselves by worshiping them in any way.

Index

By WALTER A. HANSEN

INDEX TO SCRIPTURE PASSAGES